THE NIETZSCHE-WAGNER
CORRESPONDENCE

THE NIETZSCHE-WAGNER
CORRESPONDENCE

EDITED BY
ELIZABETH FOERSTER-NIETZSCHE

TRANSLATED BY
CAROLINE V. KERR

INTRODUCTION BY
H. L. MENCKEN

LIVERIGHT

NEW YORK

SBN 87140-510-5 Clothbound
SBN 87140-023-5 Paperbound
Library of Congress Catalog Card Number 22-2499

Printed in the United States of America

CONTENTS

viii CONTENTS

FOREWORD

Richard Strauss once said, so I am told, that he considered the years in which the friendship between Richard Wagner and Friedrich Nietzsche was at its zenith, one of the most impressive and significant cultural moments of the nineteenth century. Many others must have thought the same, as I have frequently been asked to assemble all the available documents bearing upon this relationship, and thus present more clearly the ties uniting my brother to Richard Wagner, and all the nuances of this friendship—that was impossible in my hitherto published accounts of my brother's life, in which emphasis was laid upon other important matters.

A few weeks prior to his mental collapse in 1888, my brother himself wrote: "Here where I am speaking of the vivifying influences of my life, a word is necessary to express my gratitude for that which above all other things, refreshed me most profoundly and most genuinely.. This was, unquestionably my intercourse with Richard Wagner. All the rest of my human relationships I treat quite lightly, but at no price would I be willing to blot from my life the Tribschen days—those days of mutual confidence, of cheerfulness, of sublime flashes—the *deep* moments. . . ."

It seems to me, therefore, that there could be no more appropriate anniversary offering for the seventieth birthday of my beloved brother than a detailed account of his relations to Wagner, at the time of their closest friendship, written in the spirit and from the viewpoint of those years.

I have collected all the material best suited to this purpose; among this are my brother's letters to Wagner, here published for the first time, as well as hitherto unpublished Wagner letters. This book contains much that is entirely new—in fact, everything that could contribute to a true estimate of this friendship, as far as such material is still extant, and was made accessible to me. I must mention here the regrettable fact that a large number of my brother's letters to Wagner were destroyed in Bayreuth about five years ago from some reason utterly inexplicable to me. Without exception, they expressed only the deepest reverence and respect for Wagner and Frau Cosima, and as it was my privilege to read many of them before they were sent off, I can testify that among them were cultural documents of the highest significance. These are said to have been the very ones destroyed, and only a few letters showing my brother's innate modesty and courtesy were placed at my disposal. It has been possible, however, to reproduce the larger part of the missing correspondence from the rough drafts found in my brother's note-books.

This little book closes with the cessation of the correspondence between Wagner and my brother. All later observations and sentiments, written after the break in their friendship, must be looked for in other places. In this birthday book I wish to set in vibration only the tenderest chords of the closest friendship, which even though they be written in a melancholy minor, at least reveal no harsh dissonances on either side.   ELIZABETH FOERSTER-NIETZSCHE.

Weimar, October 15, 1914.

INTRODUCTION

The Nietzsche-Wagner quarrel, for long the subject of vague rumors and dark whispers, is made so clear by this correspondence that little remains to be said about it. The underlying cause of it was simple and unescapable: Nietzsche grew so vastly during the years that the two men were together that it was quite impossible for him to go on as a mere satellite, even of a Wagner. It is to the credit of Wagner's discernment that he saw almost instantly the great ability of the younger man; it is to the shame thereof that his valuation of it stopped far short of the reality. What he beheld before him was a young professor of extraordinary parts, eagerly responsive to his revolutionary (and often anything but transparent) ideas, full of a chivalric but ferocious bellicosity, and extremely effective as a propagandist. What he actually *had* in front of him was a European figure of the first calibre—perhaps the most salient and original personality seen in the groves of learning since Goethe. It is always hard for an old man to fathom the true importance of a young one. He is blinded by the conventional superiority that goes with his mere age; he is losing his old resilience to ideas; perhaps he is also a bit jealous, as a fading charmer is of a flapper. In Wagner all these impediments to understanding Nietzsche were helped by his personal weaknesses: his theatrical egomania, almost suggesting that of an actor; his lack of the hard training necessary to a comprehension of Nietzsche's veriest fundamentals; above all, his jumpy dread of rivals, challengers, enemies. The thing he needed, in those early Tribschen days, was not advice but enthusiasm; among all his supporters he searched uneasily for the predestined fanatic. This fanatic seemed to appear in Nietzsche. He was converted absolutely; he put away all doubts and whereases as almost unmanly; he was willing to sacrifice everything, including even his own career as a philogist, to the cause. But in the end, as we all know, it was not Wagner who reaped the rewards of that sacrifice: it was Nietzsche himself, and the world of ideas. Wagner asked for too much, and got, in the end, nothing. He had seduced the young professor from the straight and narrow path, but he was quite unable to follow the fugitive into the high mountain ways that presently invited him. Wagner's limitations were no less marked than his abilities. I believe that his music dramas are, by long odds, the most stupendous works of art ever contrived by man—that it took more downright genius to imagine them and fashion them than it took to build the Parthenon, or to write "Faust" or "Hamlet," or to paint the Sistine frescoes, or even to write the Ninth Symphony. But whoever enters the opera-house gets a smell of patchouli into his hair, and a dab of grease-paint on his nose. He may remain a genius, but he is a genius who is also a bit of a mountebank—a genius who thinks of his audience as well as of his work, and is not forgetful of box-office statements. Actors make bad philosophers—and a man who writes operas, however gorgeous, becomes thereby partly an actor.

Introduction

It is astonishing that Nietzsche did not notice the mounte-
bankish touch in Wagner from the start; certainly it was
obvious enough to most of the other Wagnerians of the time,
including even King Ludwig. Frau Förster-Nietzsche hints
that he actually discerned it, but put away all thought of it
for the good of the cause. But it is much more likely that
the colossal gaudiness of Wagner simply blinded him—that
he was completely bowled over by the man's terrific splendors
as an artist. To a young German of Nietzsche's traditions
and education, music is quite as important a matter as base-
ball is to a young American, and he knows it just as thoroughly. Thus he brought to his study of Wagner's music,
not only a ready response to its overwhelming sensuousness,
its profound beauty as mere sound, but also an intelligent
comprehension of the technical difficulties that had been sur-
mounted in the making of it—in brief, an educated delight.
This delight, in the first days, simply bewitched him; he
could see only the magician, and quite forgot the man. But
it was not long before that man began to intrude in a very
disconcerting way, and so, bit by bit, Nietzsche became res-
tive, and in the end he rose in open revolt. I believe that it is
quite probable, as Frau Förster-Nietzsche says, that it was
Wagner's snuffling gabble about Christianity that finished
him. Put the thing on the best ground possible: say that
Wagner was genuinely self-deluded, that his going to mass
was honest, that the romantic mystery of the faith had at
last found a weak spot in his armor and penetrated to his
heart. In any case, the apostasy was incomprehensible to
Nietzsche. He could no more imagine an intelligent man

succumbing to all that ancient rubbish than he could imagine an honest man subscribing to it for worldly gain. The convert was as abhorrent to his tight and uncompromising mind as the hypocrite. In Wagner, I daresay, he saw parts of both. The one outraged him and the other disgusted him. After those walks at Sorrento there was nothing for him to do save make his bow, click his heels together, and say good-bye.

Wagner's failure to apprehend the full significance of Nietzsche is equally easy to understand. As I have said, his mere age was an impediment, and his great fame was another. Though his largest triumphs were still ahead of him, he was already a European, and even a world figure—and such a man is seldom able to detach himself from his own eminence sufficiently to see clearly the eminence of another, particularly of another who is young and still obscure. It flattered him to have a university professor, however young, enlisted for his cause and faithfully attached to his person, but he lacked the special information, and, above all, the attitude of mind, necessary to comprehend that this professor was one of a decidedly unusual sort—that his rebellion against orthodox classical philology was but the first dawn of a rebellion enormously more daring and important. Both Wagner and Cosima could understand "The Birth of Tragedy" well enough, for if some of its Greek history was difficult, there was an abundant clarity in the somewhat lyrical arguments for the Wagner music-drama. They could understand, too, the polemical pamphlets that followed, for they were, at bottom, nothing save overblown newspaper editorials—articles such as any contumacious young professor might send to a learned review. But "The Dawn of Day" was something new and strange to them, for it was, in fact, something quite new under the sun. They could no more grasp it than any other opera-composer and his wife could have grasped it. It seemed to them to be chaotic, obscure, fantastic, pointless, deliberately offensive—and most of these things, in truth, it was. They had no time to study it as it deserved, and Nietzsche himself, who might have explained, was already showing an impertinent independence, a lamentable falling-off of his old filial fidelity. So they threw the book behind the stove, and turned to the new apostles brought out by the first season at Bayreuth—a brigade that must have depressed Wagner severely at times, but that nevertheless showed no sign of alarming the house with ideas of its own. Among equals there can be no disciples. Wagner resigned Nietzsche as flighty and incomprehensible, and Nietzsche resigned Wagner as half a charlatan.

I doubt that either man had much permanent influence on the other. Nietzsche was fond of hinting, in after years, that Wagner borrowed many ideas from him, but I have been unable to find any trace of them in the Wagner pronunciamentos. Wagner's ideas were actually his own, and most of them were quite simple, and needed no help from Nietzsche for their clarification and statement. All that Nietzsche gave him, in the Tribschen days, was a certain learned support; it pleased him, but he would have been just as well off without it. Nietzsche's efforts to bring the Wagner notions into harmony with his own theories as to the origin of the

Greek drama were never very convincing, even to the Wagnerites; later on he himself saw their folly. These efforts marked the period of his most complete illusion. The Wagner he then saw before him was an impossible compound of artist and scholar; he lived to find out that the artist is far more likely to be wedded to a mountebank; before he died he even descended, in "Also sprach Zarathustra," to monkeyshines himself. Nor can I find any sign of Wagner's influence in the main work of Nietzsche—that is, in "The Dawn of Day" and the books following. He kept up a secret and wistful affection for his old friend to the end; on his death he said, "Den habe ich sehr geliebt." But when he plunged into the great exhortations and expostulations of his maturity, when he turned up the reluctant sod of his high and lonely valleys, then Wagner was far below and behind him, and could be no more imagined guiding him than Rossini could be imagined guiding Wagner. They spoke different languages, and inhabited different worlds. Wagner's fundamental philosophy was colored by the German Liberalism of his time; he was daring, but always within the limits of accepted concepts. Nietzsche was a pure revolutionary, a magnificent disdainer of both the past and the present— as he himself was fond of saying, an anti-Christ. What he had to say may not have been always sound, but it was certainly always thoroughly original. Despite his veneration for Schopenhauer, he was his own man from the start. His ideas came into the world with a note of challenge and defiance. They attacked the very foundations of modern civilization. To all men they were startling and disquieting; to most men they were appalling. But the years deal kindly with them. More and more they tend to prevail, or, at all events, to get themselves heard. Only blockheads today know nothing of them, and only fools are unshaken by them.

H. L. MENCKEN.

THE NIETZSCHE-WAGNER
CORRESPONDENCE

THE NIETZSCHE-WAGNER CORRESPONDENCE

CHAPTER I.

FIRST MEETING.

MY brother writes in *"Ecce Homo"*: "From the moment a piano edition of *'Tristan and Isolde'* appeared (my compliments, Herr von Bülow!) I became a confirmed Wagnerite."

I must modify this statement, however, as my brother's admiration for Richard Wagner began at a somewhat earlier date, in fact, as early as the autumn of 1860, at which time he and two other sixteen-year-old boys by the names of Wilhelm Pindar and Gustav Krug, founded a little society and christened it with the high-sounding name of "Germania," despite the fact that it consisted of only three members.

The purpose of this society, as set forth in the constitution, was to acquire a wider knowledge of the arts and sciences, and one of the first steps taken was to subscribe for the "Zeitschrift für Musik"—the only musical journal at that time in Germany which had actively espoused the cause of Richard Wagner and his works. By pooling their modest pocket money, the three enthusiastic Wagnerites were also able to purchase the piano arrangement of *"Tristan and Isolde."* This was in the winter of 1862, and no sooner was the coveted treasure in their possession than the members found themselves embroiled in a discussion provoked by a paper written by Wilhelm Pindar on the theme: "Music, the Daughter of Poetry." Among other things he said: "Any effort to effect a close union of the various arts cannot be regarded as a fantastic attempt, for even though it be denied the genius of one individual to achieve this result, it is, nevertheless, a possibility, provided the one artist is in close sympathy with the intentions of the other, and displays consideration and sensitivity in uniting the two related arts. But a genuinely harmonious union of hitherto independent elements can never be entirely successful, and therefore, the artwork of the future will ever remain an unrealized ideal."

This standpoint was vigorously opposed by the two remaining members, but unfortunately, my brother's views on the subject have not been preserved. Gustav Krug, however, expressed himself at some length in the chronicles of the society, and it is safe to assume that he voiced my brother's theories.

Krug wrote: "I ask why should such an ideal be unattainable? Has not Wagner, in his *'Tristan and Isolde'* and *'Nibelung,'* demonstrated his ability to put this theory into practice? Now that the close union of music and poetry has been so splendidly achieved in these works, should it not also be possible for the singer to become a genuine actor? Have we not the Schroeder-Devrient and Johanna Wagner to bring forward in proof of the capacity of the genuinely great singer to possess the parallel qualities of a really great actress? And is not the same thing true of the stage machinery and the mise-en-scène? On this point, Brendel observes quite rightly: 'In the earlier operas only the music was taken seriously, and all else was, more or less, an artistic lie. Hitherto, opera has displayed the paradox of claiming to represent the union of all the arts, but in reality, of refusing to do justice to the essential characteristics of these arts. The art-work of the future will be the solution of this paradox. The time has come for all the arts to be taken with equal seriousness, and for a union, in this sense, to be attempted.' "

It was at our house that the three friends met to study the music of *"Tristan and Isolde,"* as Wagner's art met with lively opposition at the homes of Pindar and Krug. And I must confess, that at first the music did sound frightful as played by Fritz and Gustav; they apparently did not understand how to make the melody stand out from the rich harmonic background, and our good mother, unwilling as she was to interfere with my brother's enjoyment, frankly admitted that she took no pleasure in this "frightful noise," as she called it. Even I could not get up any enthusiasm about it at first, but the boys persisted in their efforts until they succeeded so well in bringing out the effect of the hunting horns at the opening of the second act, that I fell completely under the spell of the music. "Everyone *must* be enraptured by it!" declared my brother, but my mother, who thought it judicious to throw an occasional wet blanket upon his ardor, answered: "Not at all! There is no *must* in the matter, and on all sides I hear that this music is repudiated by the most eminent musical authorities. For example, Wagner's music is completely tabooed at the home of Frau Frege, the meeting

3

place of a group of Leipsig musicians. A strange artist, not knowing of this antagonism, began to play something of Wagner's one evening, whereupon Frau Frege fainted dead away and had to be carried from the room, and the remainder of the company was also most unpleasantly affected."

I should not like to create the impression that my brother allowed himself to be carried away by an unreasoning enthusiasm. Such was not the case at all, as is indicated in a letter written to his friend, Baron von Gersdorff, on October 11, 1868: "I have played but little as I have no piano here in Kosen, but I brought along the piano score of Wagner's '*Walküre*,' in regard to which my feelings are so confused that I dare not venture an opinion on the subject. The greatest beauties and virtues are offset by equally great shortcomings and positive ugliness, at times. And according to Riese and Buchbinder $+ a + (- a) = 0$. The newspapers state that the same composer is at work on a Hohenstaufen opera, and receives an occasional visit from the king whom he calls in the dedication of the work: 'the noble protector of my life.' It would do no harm, by the way, for the 'king to go with Wagner' ('to go,' in the boldest sense of the term) but naturally with a respectable life annuity."

And again, my brother would give free vent to his enthusiasm and write thus to his friend, Erwin Rohde: "This evening I attended the opening concert of the Euterpe society and refreshed my soul by listening to the *Vorspiel* of '*Tristan and Isolde*' and that of the '*Meistersinger*.' For the life of me, I cannot preserve an attitude of cool criticism in listening to this music; every nerve of my being is set

tingling and it has been a long time since I have experienced
a feeling of such sustained enjoyment as I did while listering
to the latter overture." . . . Some weeks later, in attempting to console Rohde for some disagreeable personal experience, my brother pointed out the case of Richard Wagner,
emphasizing that trait in his character, which compelled
my brother's admiration as long as he lived. "Think of
Wagner and Schopenhauer and of the undaunted energy
with which they preserved their faith in themselves, and this
amid the 'halloo of the entire cultured world!' "

At last the moment arrived when my brother was to make
the personal acquaintance of the long-revered genius, an
event humorously described in the following letter to Rohde
written November 9, 1868: ". . . When I got home I found
a note stuck in my door reading: 'If you wish to meet
Richard Wagner, come to the Theatre Café at a quarter
to four. Windisch.' . . . Naturally I rushed off to the
appointed place where I found our good friend and learned
further details. It seems that Wagner had arrived in
Leipzig on a visit to relatives, but was preserving the
strictest incognito; the press had not been allowed to get
wind of the matter and the servants of the Brockhaus
family were as silent as graves in livery. Wagner's sister,
Frau Brockhaus, had naturally taken great pride in introducing her genius to her most intimate friend, Frau
Ritchelin (the lucky creature!) Wagner played the
Meisterlied for the Ritchelin, and the good woman told
him that she was already familiar with the music—*mea
opera;* astonishment and delight on the part of Wagner.
Signifies his royal wish to make my humble acquaintance.
I was to have been invited for Friday evening; Windisch,

however, explained that it would be impossible for me to get away from my work; whereupon, Saturday was suggested as the day of the meeting. At the appointed hour, Windisch and I hurried off to the Brockhaus home where we found the Professor and his family assembled, but no Richard, he having unceremoniously sallied forth with an enormous hat on his big cranium. But, at all events, I made the acquaintance of this interesting family, and received an invitation to come again on Sunday evening.

"I seemed to be living in a dream during the time that intervened, and you must admit that the events leading up to this meeting, together with the well-known inaccessibility of this unique personality, savored strongly of the romantic. Under the impression that the soirée was to be a ceremonious affair, I resolved to don gala attire and was overjoyed at the thought that my tailor had already promised to have my new suit of evening clothes ready by Sunday. The weather was abominable, rain alternating with snow, and I had no inclination to venture out, and was therefore, highly pleased when Roscher dropped in to see me during the course of the afternoon . . . it began to grow dark, but the tailor did not put in his appearance. When Roscher left, I went along, looked in at my tailor's and found his slaves busily sewing on my suit; it was to be delivered in three-quarters of an hour. . . .

"With my mind set at ease, I went on my way, met up with Kintschky, read the *Kladderadatsch* and beamed with joy when I came across a notice stating that Richard Wagner was at present in Switzerland, but that a beautiful house was being built for him in Munich, while all the time I knew that I was to meet him that very evening, and that

6

the day before he had received a letter from the little king addressed: 'To the great German tone-poet, Richard Wagner.'

"No tailor in evidence when I got back to my room, so I seated myself with the greatest composure to read the dissertation on Eudocia: from time to time, I was disturbed by the shrill ringing of a bell that seemed to come from a great distance. Finally, it was borne in upon me that someone was ringing at the primitive old iron gate; this was locked as well as the front door, and I was obliged to scream across the garden to the man to come in through the side entrance, but it was impossible to make myself heard for the splashing of the rain. The excitement communicated itself to the entire house, and finally, the doors were opened to admit a queer-looking little man carrying a parcel. It was then half-past six and the highest time that I should be about my toilet as I had some distance to go. Right enough, it was a man with my suit: I tried on the coat and found it an admirable fit.

"Suspicious turn in affairs! The man presents the bill; I accept it politely. He expects it to be paid on the spot; I express great surprise and explain that I can have no dealings with one of the workmen but only with the tailor to whom I gave the order. The man becomes more insistent; the time grows shorter and shorter. I lay hold of the garments and attempt to put them on; the man seizes them and prevents me from carrying out my intention. Display of force on my side; display of force on his side. Tableau! I continue the struggle as I am determined to wear the new trousers at all hazards.

"Finally, I resort to a show of injured dignity, solemn

7

threats, curses upon the head of the tailor and his accomplices, upon whom I vow everlasting vengeance. In the meantime, the man disappears, triumphantly taking my suit with him. End of 2nd Act! Shirt-clad, I sit on the sofa, scrutinizing an old black coat and trying to decide whether or not it is good enough for Richard.

". . . Outside, the rain descending in torrents . . . A quarter to eight; at half-past, I had arranged to meet Windisch at the Theatre Café. I rush forth wildly into the dark and stormy night, in a mood of exhilaration despite the old coat. After all, fortune had been kind to me; there was even something uncanny and extraordinary about the scene with the tailor's apprentice.

"We arrive at the hospitable Brockhaus home: no one there but the immediate family, Richard, and the two of us. Introduced to Richard and say a few deferential words. He inquires very minutely how I come to be so familiar with his works, inveighs roundly against the production of his operas, with the exception of the famous Munich performances. He ridicules the conductors, who good-humoredly call out to their men: 'Now, gentlemen, just a trifle more passionate!'—'Meine Gutsen, noch ein bisschen leidenschafterlicher!'—W. is fond of using the Saxon dialect.

"Now let me tell you briefly what happened on this eventful evening; it was enjoyment of so unique a character that I have not yet been able to get back into the grooves of everyday life, but am fit for nothing but to talk to you, dear friend, and tell you 'wundersame Mär.' Before and after dinner Wagner played all the important episodes from the '*Meistersinger*,' imitating the different voices. He is an astoundingly vivacious and high-spirited man, speaks very rapidly, is extremely witty, and is very animated when in the company of intimate friends.

"During the course of the evening we had a long conversation about Schopenhauer, and you can imagine my unbounded joy at hearing him say, with indescribable enthusiasm, how much he owed to Schopenhauer and to hear him called the only philosopher who had recognized the real nature of music. Then he inquired what attitude the professors now took towards Schopenhauer, and laughed heartily over the Philosopher's Congress in Prague, referring to them as 'philosophic porters.' Later in the evening, he read us parts of his autobiography upon which he is now at work, among other things, a delicious scene from his student days in Leipzig, of which I cannot yet think without bursting into laughter. By the way, he is very clever and witty with his pen. As we were leaving, he pressed my hand and cordially invited me to come and see him so that we might continue our conversation upon music and philosophy. He also commissioned me to familiarize his sister and her family with his music, which I solemnly pledged myself to do. . . . You shall hear more when I am able to look back upon this evening more objectively, and from a greater perspective. . . ."

CHAPTER II.

(Spring of 1869.)

SOME months after this meeting, my brother was called to the University of Basle as professor of classical philology, his appointment being due to a number of striking scientific treatises published in the *Rheinisches Museum* and to the personal recommendation of Prof. Ritschl of Leipzig. During the Whitsuntide holidays of the same year he went over to Lake Lucerne with the intention of visiting the various points of historic interest in which this region abounds. Finding himself in the immediate vicinity of Villa Tribschen he debated with himself as to the propriety of accepting Wagner's invitation and paying a call at the villa.

In a vacillating frame of mind, he set out along the lake shore road leading to the romantic old country house almost hidden from view in the enchanting landscape which lay spread out at the foot of Mount Pilatus. Upon arriving at his destination, he hesitated outside the garden hedge for some time listening to an excruciating discord repeated again and again. Later he learned that this was from the third act of *"Siegfried"* at the point where the hero exclaims: "Verwundet hat mich, der mich erweckt."

Finally he was observed by a servant who came out to say

10

that Herr Wagner was in the habit of working until two o'clock and could not be disturbed before that hour. Upon hearing this, my brother left his card and was some distance from the gate when the servant came hurrying back to inquire whether the "Herr Professor" was the same "Herr Nietzsche" whom Wagner had met in Leipzig. No sooner had this fact been established than my brother was invited to remain for dinner, but this he was unable to do as he had arranged to meet his friends at Tell's Chapel further down the lake.

The visit was, therefore, postponed until Monday, when he went over to Tribschen early in the morning and spent the first of those enchanting days with Richard Wagner and Frau Cosima which were to form veritable oases in the desert of his solitary life. I must explain here that some time elapsed before my brother began to feel at home in Basle. He was tremendously impressed by the solidarity of this firmly established little commonwealth, and by the extreme cordiality manifested by his colleagues, all of whom were men much older than himself. He also had a high regard for the serious-minded and reserved burghers, but his was not the temperament to make friends easily, and the same has always been said of the good folk of Basle.

He was, therefore, made indescribably happy by the unexpected cordiality displayed towards him by Wagner and Frau Cosima von Bülow from whom the first advances came in a note written on May 20, 1869:

"As you were kind enough to promise us that you would repeat your visit to Tribschen, I am now writing to ask you to come over next Saturday, May 22. It is Herr

Wagner's birthday and I feel that I should be giving him genuine pleasure by inviting you to an informal family dinner and also to spend the night, provided you are willing to put up with very modest sleeping accommodations. Kindly send me a few lines so that we may know if we are to expect you. Cordial greetings from

"Yours sincerely,
"Cosima von Bülow."

Unfortunately my brother's university duties prevented him from accepting this invitation, and he was obliged to content himself with writing the following letter:

Friedrich Nietzsche to Richard Wagner.

"Most honored sir:

"It has long been my intention to express unreservedly the debt of gratitude I owe you. As a matter of fact, the highest and most inspiring moments of my life are closely associated with your name, and I know of only one other man, and that man your twin brother of intellect, Arthur Schopenhauer, whom I regard with the same veneration—yea, even more, as *religione quadam.*

"I take especial pleasure in making this confession to you on this auspicious day and even do so with a feeling of pride. For if it be the fate of genius to belong to the 'select few' for the time being at least—these 'few' have every reason to feel highly honored by virtue of the fact that it has been vouchsafed them to see the light and bask in its warmth, while the larger public stands shivering in the cold outside. Moreover, this ability to take delight in genius is not a thing that falls lightly in the lap of these

12

few, but is rather to be regarded as the result of a valiant fight against powerful prejudice and antagonism. Having fought this fight successfully, they come to feel that right of conquest has given them quite an especial claim upon this particular genius.

"I make bold to count myself among these 'select few,' since realizing how incapable the world at large is of comprehending your personality, or of feeling the deeply ethical current by which your life, your writings, and your music are permeated—in short, of sensing an atmosphere of that serious and more spiritual outlook upon life of which we poor Germans have been robbed overnight, as it were, by every conceivable sort of political misery, philosophical nonsense, and aggressive Judaism.

"It is to you and Schopenhauer that I owe my ability of holding fast to the vital seriousness of the Germanic race and to the deepened contemplation of our enigmatical and perplexing existence.

"How many purely scientific problems have been elucidated for me by dwelling on your own singularly lonely and unique personality! All this I should have liked to have said to you face to face, just as I should have preferred not to have been obliged to *write* all that I have just written.

"How gladly would I have been with you in your lake and mountain solitude had not the chains of my professional duties bound me to my Basle dog-kennel.

"In closing I beg you to remember me to Baroness von Bülow, and remain

"Your most faithful and reverential disciple and admirer,

"DR. FR. NIETZSCHE,

"Prof. in Basle."

13

The Nietzsche-Wagner Correspondence

Early in June, my brother wrote to Erwin Rohde:

". . . I am very happy in my friendship with Richard Wagner and spent Whitmonday at his delightful country home with him and the intelligent Frau von Bülow (the daughter of Liszt). The latter also invited me to come over and surprise Wagner on his birthday but I was obliged to make a virtue of necessity and say 'No.'

"Wagner is really everything that one could expect; he has an extravagantly rich and noble nature, energetic character, fascinating personality and strong will power. But I must call a halt, or I shall find myself singing a paean of praise."

Richard Wagner to Friedrich Nietzsche.

"Lucerne, June 3, 1869.

"Most valued friend:

"Accept my most heartfelt thanks—even though somewhat belated—for your beautiful and significant letter. Had I wished to have you pay me a visit before receiving this letter, I now urgently repeat the sincere and spontaneous invitation extended to you when we parted in front of the '*Rössli*.'

"Do come—you need only send me a line in advance. For instance, come Saturday afternoon, remain over Sunday and return early Monday morning. Every day laborer can dispose of his time to this extent, and it should be all the more possible for a professor to do so. . . .

"Now show yourself as you really are! As yet, my experiences with my German countrymen have not been altogether pleasurable. Therefore, come and rescue my faith in

14

that which I, together with Goethe and a few others—call German liberty.

> "Cordial greetings from
> "Yours sincerely,
> "RICHARD WAGNER."

My brother hastened to accept this invitation and during the last night of his visit, Wagner's son, Siegfried, was born—a fact Nietzsche did not learn until later in the day as he was obliged to leave the house at an early morning hour. That the birth of Wagner's son should have coincided with my brother's first visit to Tribschen was regarded by both as an auspicious omen for the newly-formed friendship.

In a letter dated June 16, my brother wrote to Rohde: ". . . A short time ago I indiscreetly read Wagner a beautiful passage from one of your letters and he was so deeply moved that he begged me to let him have a copy of it. Please do me a great favor and write him a long letter. You are no longer a stranger to him. His address is, *'Richard Wagner, Tribschen near Lucerne.'* . . . I was again his guest for two days and felt myself wonderfully refreshed by this visit.

"Wagner embodies all the qualities one could possibly desire. The world has not the faintest conception of his greatness as a man and of his exceptional nature. I learned a great deal from my intercourse with him and it is like taking a practical course in Schopenhauerian philosophy. This sense of nearness to Wagner is an inexpressible source of consolation to me. . . ."

15

CHAPTER III.

Friedrich Nietzsche to Erwin Rohde, Aug. 17, 1869:

BUT now let me tell you something about my Jupiter, in other words, about Richard Wagner, in whose society I am occasionally permitted to take a good long breath, and thereby refresh myself to a degree that would be incomprehensible to my entire corps of colleagues. As yet, no honors have been conferred upon this remarkable man, and he has only just received his first mark of distinction, an honorary membership in the Berlin Academy of Arts.

"His life has been a rich, fruitful and agitated one, absolutely unique and unprecedented when compared to that of average mortals. There he stands, firmly rooted by his own efforts, with his thoughts directed above and beyond everything ephemeral and unseasonable. A short time ago he gave me a manuscript of his to read entitled: 'State and Religion.' This essay is intended as a memorial to the young king of Bavaria, and is of such nobility of thought and Schopenhauerian seriousness that I could only wish I were a king to be admonished in like manner. By the way, I recently copied certain passages from your letters and sent

16

them to Frau von Bülow as she had repeatedly expressed the wish to have them.

"A son to be christened '*Siegfried*' was born during one of my recent visits to Tribschen, and when I was last there, Wagner had just finished his music drama '*Siegfried*' and was glowing in the full consciousness of his powers.

"You say you do not wish to write to him? And that you think he must be satiated with the homage of the enraptured laity? But I did not mean that you were to write to him in his capacity as musician, but as a like-minded serious man. He receives few enough demonstrations from people of that sort and each time he is as pleased as if he had made an important discovery. Moreover, you are no longer a stranger to him."

It was Wagner's wish that my brother should spend the greater part of his summer vacation in Tribschen, but this he was unable to do. Upon learning of this decision, Wagner made the half-playful, half-vexed comment: "The Professor makes himself scarce!" This did not prevent the family at Tribschen from following my brother's movements with friendly interest, as may be seen from a letter of Frau Cosima's written late in June, 1869.

". . . We suffered with you in your wretched Pilatus adventure. While indulging in a bourgeois game of ten-pins in Stanz on Sunday evening, we persuaded ourselves that you were going to have fine weather for the ascent, but when we awoke on Monday morning, we were genuinely frightened about you. This feeling was shared by young and old alike, and 'What will Professor Nietzsche do?' ran like wild-fire through the entire house, from the kitchen to the nursery. Isolde came to me and said: 'But Uncle Rich-

ard's man is up there.' All this was on Monday, and w
the sun broke through the clouds on Tuesday, we conclu
that you must have remained on the summit all night.
When noon came and you still had not put in an appearance, it occurred to us that you had been punished for having treated Tribschen so badly, in having been either not
willing or not *able* to postpone your excursion for a day.
But be that as it may—whether punishment or fate—the
whole thing was, and remains, abominable of you."

My brother was immediately taken back into favor,
despite the fact that he had made himself "scarce" and
had deserted Tribschen for the sake of the Pilatus adventure. Frau Cosima wrote:

"Now I am writing to ask if you feel inclined to spend
the coming Saturday and Sunday with us? Bad weather
is assuredly less of a hardship here than on the top of
Pilatus, and I do not need to tell you how welcome you
always are. Herr Wagner adds his assurances to mine
and sends you cordial greetings. Last week he actually
had a letter from Prof. Brockhaus in which he announces
their departure and the possibility of a visit to us."

Naturally my brother could not refuse this second invitation, and he was again summoned to Tribschen when Prof.
Brockhaus (whose wife was a sister of Wagner) arrived.

Richard Wagner to Friedrich Nietzsche.

Telegram, August 3, 1869.
"The Brockhauses dine with us tomorrow (Saturday)
at two o'clock. Your presence requested, whereby complete
freedom promised for you for Sunday afternoon.
"WAGNER."

18

The Summer of 1869

Frau Cosima neglected no opportunity of showing her delight at having my brother at Tribschen, where his arrival was always a signal for general household rejoicing. Frau Cosima wrote that even the servants participated in this demonstration:

"Come to us soon again. You know that Jacob is only too glad to wait upon you and I hope no assurances are needed from the master and myself."

It is not surprising that my brother should have spent all his leisure moments at Tribschen and to this he refers in a letter to Rohde written September 3, 1869: ". . . Like yourself, I, too, have my Italy, but I can only take refuge there on Saturdays and Sundays. I have been over three or four times of late, and a letter flies over the same route nearly every week. Dearest friend, it is impossible to tell you all that I learn and see, hear and comprehend during these visits. Schopenhauer and Goethe, Aeschylus and Pindar still live—I give you my word for it."

My brother not only received but gave inspiration, by carrying his own world with him to Tribschen. Among other things, he sent Wagner a copy of his inaugural address on the *"Personality of Homer,"* of which Frau Cosima made the following acknowledgement:

". . . This evening between Beethoven, Goethe and Schiller, we read your address with deep interest and I now say to you that you will not only find the great Aeschylus at Tribschen but also *your* Homer. You will find him very much alive and persistently productive. Herr Wagner sends you his best thanks and says that he is in close sympathy with all your views on aesthetic questions as well as with the subject matter of your address. He congratulates you

19

on your presentation of a problem which to his mind, is the beginning—perhaps the end, of all wisdom, and yet is the one most frequently overlooked. If I may add a few words of minor importance, it would only be to say that your sympathy with Goethe's conflict, and the manner in which you treat Schiller's antipathy to the entire question, have given me the greatest pleasure and seem to me to be moments of the deepest significance.

"Furthermore—not to lose sight of the purely formal side of the question—you seem to have been extremely felicitous in achieving the transition from a general problem to a specific question. You have done this with consummate art, and thereby succeeded in compressing one of the most difficult subjects into the circumscribed limitations of an address, and to have done this with astonishing clarity and a remarkably sure touch.

"I fancy that your listeners must have followed you at times, with a halting comprehension and that the expression 'in our hands we have a symbol,' must have created genuine consternation. Do you not intend to publish this little work? Even though it was meant only for Tribschen, there is surely other fruitful soil in which it would take root."

To all outward appearances life in Tribschen moved on serenely, and peacefully, but there were a number of things to keep Wagner and Frau Cosima in a painful state of agitation. One of these was the projected performance of the "*Rheingold*" in Munich in direct opposition to Wagner's wishes. The king could not comprehend Wagner's reasons for objecting and this made the matter all the more painful. Wagner wrote to Cornelius: "The king loves my music,

20

but attaches no importance to the way in which it is given."
Referring to the web of intrigues woven about this performance, he again wrote to Cornelius: "No one can have the slightest conception of all that we have been called upon to suffer and endure."

During this period, my brother was a source of genuine comfort to Wagner and Frau Cosima, or as the former touchingly expressed it: "He was ever like a messenger from a higher and purer world." Wagner did not take the matter so seriously as long as he believed that the production of the opera would be in the hands of the faithful friends whom he had been instrumental in bringing to Munich. The artists who were to sing the parts of *Wotan, Loge* and *Alberich* came to Tribschen where Wagner not only initiated them into the music but also gave them practical suggestions as to their acting. To be sure, these rehearsals were not very inspiring, but every one was comforted by the thought that the burden of the performance would be borne by the orchestra cf one hundred and seven men under the direction of Hans Richter. Wagner resigned himself to his fate and even tried to find comfort in the thought that the public, having neither the inclination nor the ability for a full understanding of the matter, would thereby be given, at least, a faint idea of his great work. But Wagner had not reckoned with the intrigues and machinations of his avowed and secret enemies in Munich. If I remember rightly, the fight centered around the person of Hans Richter who was not acceptable as the conductor of the work. This resulted in the postponement of the *Rheingold* performance, *ad calendum graecas* and every one at Tribschen breathed more freely for a time. But as Frau

Cosima truthfully said: "It is written in the stars that nothing in Wagner's life is to be allowed to suffer only a partial shipwreck. Everything must go to pieces precipitately and overwhelmingly."

Wagner made a secret visit to Munich to talk the matter over with the king's secretary, who, however, assured him that if he continued to place obstacles in the way of the performance and did not agree to dispense with the services of Hans Richter, the consequences could be of the most humiliating character. Thereupon, Wagner allowed matters to take their course and deeply moved by the outcome, Frau Cosima wrote: "I could endure all these indignities with composure did not the master's health suffer so inexpressibly under the strain. And this suffering is not the result of the humiliating conditions to which he has been compelled to submit, but because he sees therein the irrevocable failure of all the most beautiful hopes of his life. You will understand me; I know nothing of a 'break,' but alas! of a fatal rupture, made all the more serious by the fact that one side seems not to have the slightest comprehension of this, and it is therefore all the more keenly felt by the other side. . . . He must now go to work again on his '*Siegfried.*' I rely upon the quiet and solitude of our life here in Tribschen to restore his shattered nerves. If only the matter could be entirely dropped!"

My brother displayed the deepest sympathy in all these conflicts and annoyances, and was taken into the closest confidence on all questions of an intimate nature. When Wagner passed through Basle on his way to and from Munich he sought counsel of my brother and he was also summoned to Tribschen to hear Richter's account of all

22

the incredible happenings and intrigues that had set Munich by the ears. After the performance had finally taken place, Frau Cosima wrote to him: "You have probably heard much more about the '*Rheingold*' than we have. The unanimous verdict of the press seems to be that the performance was magnificent but that the work itself was unendurable. You can imagine that our hearts are heavy and that a melancholy mood has taken possession of us. But God be praised, the heavens here give forth warmth and sunshine and that is some consolation! I am enclosing some lines written by the master the day he received news of a performance so humiliating for him.

> "Spielt nur ihr Nebelzwerge mit dem Ringe,
> Wohl dien' er euch zu eurer Torheit Sold;
> Doch habet acht: euch wird der Reif zur Schlinge;
> Ihr kennt den Fluch: seht ob er Schächern hold.
> Der Fluch, er will, dass nie das Werk gelinge.
> An dem, der furchtlos wahrt des Rheines Gold.
> Doch euer ängstlich Spiel aus Leim und Kappe
> Bedeckt gar bald des Niblung Kappe."

CHAPTER IV.

WAGNER, Frau Cosima and my brother were drawn very closely together during all the hours and days spent in this remote spot, and the feeling of intimacy was heightened by the sharing of many heavy cares and burdens. It was during this autumn that Frau Cosima wrote ". . . We regard you as one of the family and this is saying a great deal in view of the material and moral seclusion of our little court."

It was due to this seclusion that manifold commissions were intrusted to my brother by both Wagner and Frau Cosima. For example, certain of Wagner's letters had been published without his knowledge and consent and my brother was asked to see that a statement to this effect appeared in all the leading newspapers. Then he was also requested to conduct a search for a missing portrait of one of Wagner's uncles in Leipzig, a task in which my brother enlisted my services as well as those of Doris Brockhaus, a niece of Wagner's. Frau Cosima makes acknowledgement in one of her letters: "Please thank your sister for her efforts in regard to the portrait and still more for this proof of her kindly feeling towards me. In a life filled with trials and suffering, one learns to value such demonstrations of friendship. Notwithstanding the discouraging

24

attitude taken by the Brockhaus family, I am still hopeful of obtaining possession of the portrait." After quoting this passage, my brother adds: "So you see that concrete results are expected from you. As far as I am concerned you can accomplish this behind the back of the Brockhaus family." I acted upon this suggestion and was soon able to report the discovery of the portrait.

As Christmas drew near, my brother was deluged with commissions of all sorts and practically all of the Tribschen presents were bought by him in Basle. Not only was he called upon to select Dürer engravings, antiques and books, but he also had the novel task of buying dolls and toys of all sorts, even a doll's theatre being on his list. With each fresh request, Frau Cosima expressed her deep mortification for annoying my brother with such trival matters. She said that the master was very indignant with her, and that she only gained her own consent to trespass upon his good-nature by endeavoring to forget that he was a dignified professor and philologian, and remembering only that he was a young man of twenty-five. Her lists were prepared in such a way as to facilitate his task in every possible way, but Fritz took a very serious view of his mission and not only were the books, engravings and the like, subjected to a close scrutiny, but he was extremely difficult to please when it came to the selection of the toys. For instance, he found the king belonging to the ensemble of the doll's theatre not sufficiently royal in appearance, and the devil not as black as he should be painted. He also developed an unexpected degree of fastidiousness in regard to the robe worn by the Christmas angel, finally scorning the one offered by the Basle shops and ordering one from Paris.

But commissions of far greater importance than the inspection and purchase of Christmas presents were intrusted to my brother by Wagner himself, who was engaged in writing his autobiography. This was to be privately printed and a few copies distributed among his intimate friends. The following letter will show the magnitude of the task devolving upon my brother.

Richard Wagner to Friedrich Nietzsche.

"Most excellent friend:

"I am giving you the most extraordinary proof of my confidence, by sending with this letter a large package of valuable manuscript, namely, the opening chapters of the dictated copy of my autobiography. This is done with a twofold intention; first of all, I wish you to read this part of the manuscript so that we can take up the reading at this point when you come to Tribschen, for what, I hope, will be a long visit. In the second place, I wish very much that you may be able to have about sixteen pages printed before Christmas as I wish to present it to our revered friend. I shall be guided entirely by your judgment in the matter. The chief thing is that the manuscript shall be given to the printers exactly as it is. I have already gone through it, after a fashion, in getting it ready for our friend (Frau von Bülow) to make a copy for the king, but all further polishing-off must wait until the proof-sheets are ready, as it will then be easier for me to indicate any desired changes. On the other hand, I reserve the right of inserting dates or even paragraphic notes in the proof-sheets. Marginal notes, such as dates or dates of dictation, are naturally to be omitted. Roman print, everything 'noble,' as they say in Berlin. That is to be taken for granted.

"Five copies to be printed on the best vellum paper; 10 additional ones on a good quality of writing paper. More than that will not be necessary at present. You will see that the printer receives only so much of the manuscript as is needed at one time.

"What do you think of the beginning?

"Shall we not see you again *before* Christmas?

"It is snowing today and the effect is very good. On the whole, I am not good for much; catarrhal and abdominal pains frequently interrupt my Nornes at their weaving. And then again, I feel very well and am unalterable in my resolve to live to a high old age. This would mean terrifying printer's bills for me.

"Most cordial greetings,
"Yours,

"Tribschen, Dec. 3, 1869.   R. W."

My brother had received the most pressing invitation to spend the Christmas holidays at Tribschen. Cosima also telegraphed:

"Expect you Friday afternoon. Marionettes heavenly. Greetings and thanks.

"Cosima."

In the meantime my brother had selected all sorts of appropriate presents, his gift for Wagner being an enlarged copy of a Schopenhauer photograph, lent to him for the purpose by a friend of the philosopher. This piece of work was executed by Gustav Schultz, a well-known painter and photographer of Naumburg, and the carved frame, displaying Wagner's coat of arms, was also the work of a Naumburg wood-carver. My brother was delighted with the way in which I had executed these commissions to which he attached the greatest importance. He also collected an astonishing array of presents for the children who were devoted to "Herr Nü—tzsche." This amused me very much as, up to this time, my brother had not concerned himself greatly about the wishes of little girls. The hospitable old country house was transformed into a beautiful fairy tale in which the blissful children and their parents moved about as if in a dream—the latter not without a tinge of melancholy in their pleasure. In the exchange of presents, Frau Cosima received from my brother a beautiful privately printed copy of his inaugural address already mentioned, the title of which had been changed from "*Homer's Personality*" to "*Homer and Classical Philology.*"

Two rooms were set aside for my brother's use, the little salon being christened the "*Thinking Room*" in his honor. He was at liberty to withdraw whenever he chose and occupy himself with his literary work, but, as a matter of fact, neither Wagner nor Frau Cosima had the faintest idea of the demands they made upon my brother's time, both in the way of commissions and in the realization of their hospitable intent.

Aside from this, Wagner turned over to my brother all the onerous work connected with the printing of his autobiography owing to the difficulty he had in making himself understood by the Italian, Bonfantini. It must not be forgotten that my brother was already taxed to the utmost

by the new and exacting duties of his university position
to say nothing of his private work, and had he not had the
faculty of accomplishing everything with marvelous ease,
it would have been impossible for him to have met all these
demands upon his time and strength. The only criticism
he permitted himself in this connection, was that Wagner
and Frau Cosima had not the slightest conception of the
heavy work he was carrying at that time. But so great
was his admiration for the master and Frau Cosima that
he bore all these burdens in a spirit of joyful self-sacrifice,
and not content with this proof of his friendship, voluntarily offered his service for further tasks.

CHAPTER V.

THE new year opened with increased work for my brother, as he had promised to deliver two special lectures on the "*Greek Music Drama*" and "*Socrates and Tragedy.*" By reason of this, his letter of thanks to Tribschen was delayed and this called forth a reproof from Wagner.

Richard Wagner to Friedrich Nietzsche.

"My dear friend:

"Your silence surprises me, but I hope that this feeling will soon be dispelled.

"For today, parenthetically, a request.

"From the family letters sent me as a Christmas gift, I see that there is a chronological error in my biography. In case the first sheets have not been struck off, I beg of you to correct the chronological data throughout the manuscript, as well as certain typographical mistakes which still cling but will be easily found by going through the proof again.

"Please do not be vexed with me about this!

"As the one left behind, I should have preferred to have kept silent until you—the one who went away—had been heard from. But now that the family chronology has taken the matter in hand, I will further inform you that everything

30

at Tribschen is at sixes and sevens. Coughs, colds, catarrh —or however it is spelled—have prostrated all of us. At last my work on the Nornes has been resumed, and the king has let himself be heard from in his customary erratic manner. It is *possible* that '*Rheingold*' and '*Walküre*' will be given in Munich this year, but it is scarcely *probable* that this will be done in accordance with my wishes. So much for this matter.

"My investiture from the Berlin Academy has arrived and I have instructed Jacob to admit no one who does not inquire for the '*Foreign Member in Ordinary, R. W.*' This is my newest title!

"But now not another word, for I am beginning to have my suspicions about you.

"Yours,

"Tribschen, Jan. 14, 1870.   R. W."

As may be imagined my brother answered this letter immediately and it seems as if Wagner began to have faint misgivings as to the demands that were being made upon my brother's time. Frau Cosima, on the other hand, seems not to have grasped the situation, if one may judge by the following letter:

". . . I have never been angry with you, but I am now going to make a beginning in that direction. I have been genuinely concerned about you and feared that you might be ill, but I am not going to scold you and thus spoil my satisfaction at hearing the contrary, as I am too well pleased at having my perpetual distrust of fate disproved in this manner. The master has told me how much work you have on hand."

Wagner also wrote in a sympathetic and conciliated strain:

"Dearest friend:

"There are certain persons who invariably lay themselves open to suspicion! But that will soon right itself. For today, I wish you an easy deliverance of all your labors and herewith send you the two latest numbers of my essay *'On Conducting'* to help in assuaging your pains.

"The crest turned out very well and we have every reason to be grateful to you for the careful attention you gave the matter. However, I still have the same misgivings in regard to the *vulture*, which unquestionably will be taken for an eagle at the first glance. This may be easily explained by referring to any reliable work on natural history and establishing the fact that there is a so-called 'monk-vulture' closely resembling an eagle. It is of the greatest importance, on account of the associations, that the 'vulture' be instantly recognizable, and for this reason we beg that you secure the best available picture of such a beast and instruct the engraver to hang the characteristic ruff of the vulture around the neck of our bird. I realize the difficulties connected with such a change in the design, but hope that it may be found possible of execution.

"I quite agree with you in the choice of the paper to be used for *all* the copies of which only

TWELVE

are to be struck off. I find that this will be sufficient for my present needs, as aside from my anxiety in regard to the preservation of my manuscript, I am only concerned about safe-guarding it from abuse. Under these conditions, these twelve copies should possess genuine historic value.

"We have nothing but catarrh and grippe here. Wretched weather and air like that in a hermetically sealed peasant's hut. My work moves along slowly and laboriously.

"I am still having difficulties with my young monarch; I anticipate no good results from the matter and fear that great vexation of spirit is again in store for me. The Academy has sent—but you already know that? Therefore, the essay '*On Conducting*' is not to be dedicated to the Academy.

"Furthermore, I hope for the speedy and satisfactory adjustment of many trying domestic relations, so that even the 'world' will not be obliged to shake its head over us much longer.

"In the meantime, Plato has again been called to the rescue. Yesterday we finished reading Theatos, and in February we mean to have a good look at Socrates and Euripides to which I look forward with delight. Therefore, be of good cheer like a real Prussian cavalryman!

"Cordial greetings,

"Yours,

R. W."

"Tribschen, Jan. 16, 1870.

Wagner's family crest, upon the suggestion of my brother, was to appear as a title vignette for the autobiography (but without the vulture's ruff).

Much to my mystification, my brother requested me to look out for a good picture of a vulture, although I could not understand why it should be so vital a matter to have an absolutely correct picture of this bird appear on the crest. Later my brother told me that Wagner always regarded his alleged stepfather, Ludwig Geyer,* as his real father. I feel no hesitancy in repeating this remark, as this question is now freely discussed and my brother himself alludes to this in his book *"The Case of Wagner."* As for that matter, the stepfather seems to have been a gifted and admirable man in more ways than one. He painted, wrote (his *"Murder of the Children of Bethlehem"* is a most diverting comedy) and was said to have been extremely musical. Recent research has established the fact that Geyer's father was an organist in Eisleben.

Wagner also sent the next lot of proof-sheets to my brother for a final correction before they were returned to the Italian Bonfantini, to whose name Wagner was in the habit of hanging an extra syllable or two. Gradually, Wagner seemed to feel that he was imposing too much work upon my brother, and he commenced sending his instructions directly to the printer.

Richard Wagner to Friedrich Nietzsche.

"Friend! Do I not burden you too much with these proof-sheets? I am sending the accompanying copy through your hands rather than directly to Herr Bonfantini, because I attach great importance to certain corrections (or alterations) and do not yet feel myself sufficiently familiar with the methods of these Italian printers and compositors. But these matters will soon be straightened out, I hope.

* "Geier"—German word for "vulture."

Experiences during the Winter of 1870

"Your lectures to the *'mothers'* * made me shudder. But you can console yourself by the thought of one who has had dealings with the 'fathers' all his life, and whom he has been ridiculing in all sorts of futile ways, of late. Write soon to

"Yours sincerely,

"R. W."

"My work is going fairly well."
"Jan. 27, 1870."

These two lectures on *"The Greek Music Drama"* and *"Socrates and Tragedy,"* which my brother had written he was to deliver before the "mothers," soon found their way to Tribschen where they created something of a sensation. Here for the first time, my brother developed with greater precision of detail his ideas on the overthrow of the Dionysian tragedy through the spirit of Socrates and Euripides. Wagner wrote at length of the impressions he had received upon reading these two treatises.

Richard Wagner to Friedrich Nietzsche.

"Dearest Herr Friedrich:

"Last evening I read aloud your treatise to our friend. After finishing it, I had the greatest difficulty in quieting her, as she found that you had treated the awe-inspiring names of the great Athenians in a surprisingly modern manner. I was obliged to remind her that the entire character of public address and the present-day elegant manner

---

* "Mothers—goddesses of life" used by Goethe in *"Faust,"* Act I, Part II.

of book-writing had influenced the traditional style hitherto used in the discussion of the great antique ideals, and that thereby, this had been lowered to the *niveau* of the methods employed in disposing of transitory modern phenomena. (Mommsen's *"Cicero"* as feuilletonist occurred to me as I was speaking.) This idea was quickly grasped and accepted as an explanation of the weakness of our age. For my own part, I was terrified by the boldness with which you launched so new an idea, and the concise and categorical manner in which you imparted this idea to a public which has but little inclination for culture. I warn you that you will have to reckon upon a complete misunderstanding from this quarter.

"Even those who are initiated in *my* ideas will undoubtedly be frightened upon finding your ideas coming into conflict with their established belief in Socrates and even Aeschylus. But as for me—I call out to you: *It is true!* You have hit upon the right idea, and the real issue is so sharply characterized that I can only await with a feeling of admiration your further efforts to convert persons of ordinary dogmatic convictions. At the same time I am deeply concerned about you and from the bottom of my heart, I hope that you will not injure your career. Therefore, I should like to advise you 'not to touch upon such incredible views in dissertations written with the intention of producing an immediate effect, but to concentrate your efforts for a larger and more comprehensive work on this subject, if, as I believe, you are thoroughly convinced of the correctness of these ideas.

"When that time comes, you will undoubtedly find the

36

right words for the divine errors of Socrates and Plato, both of whom were creative natures of such overwhelming power, that even in turning away from them, we are compelled to worship them.

"O friend! Where shall one find adequate words of praise in looking back from *our* world upon these incomparably harmonious natures? And on the other hand, what high hopes and aspirations we may cherish for ourselves, if we realize fully and clearly that we *can* and *must* achieve something that was denied them.

"Above all things, I hope that I have left you in no doubt as to my *own* opinion of your Socrates and the others, in what I have just written you about your work.

"Yours,

R. W."

"Tribschen, Feb. 4, 1870.

Frau Cosima was much more agitated than Wagner and, under the influence of her immediate impressions, wrote as follows:

" '. . . Everything significant is disquieting.' These words of Goethe came to my mind in listening to your dissertation, dear Herr Professor. No doubt the master has told you how excited I became and that he was obliged to spin out the theme with me the entire evening. For although your fundamental views impressed me sympathetically, even familiarly at first, I cannot deny that the boldness and originality with which you developed the idea was simply overwhelming, and certain passages, such as the decline of Greek tragedy beginning with Socrates,—or even with Aeschylus—and then what you have written about the form of Plato's *'Conversations,'* were so startlingly new

37

that the master was obliged to convince me that you were in the right.

"I was not so much excited by what you said and your manner of saying it, as by the succinct form in which you were obliged to present the deepest and most far-reaching problems. This demands of your listeners that they become active collaborators, and thereby an exciting situation is created.

"After having gone through almost every sentence with the master, and finding upon closer scrutiny, that everything proved the correctness of your views—I read the work through again yesterday and let it quietly take effect. The impression I received after this second reading was a very deep and beautiful one. Had your assurance fairly frightened me at first, I now found it uncommonly satisfying, as I recognized in it the pregnance of a powerful impression. These remote geniuses whom I had always approached with reverential awe, and to whose voices I had listened as to those of prophets and high priests, suddenly became individualized and the mighty portent of Greek art passed before me in its lofty tragedy."

My brother's answer to these two agitated and agitating letters must have been exceptionally beautiful, as Wagner's answer is very touching. How deplorable it is that the world is denied a knowledge of this missing letter, which is said to have been destroyed at Wahnfried!

Richard Wagner to Friedrich Nietzsche.

"Dear Friend!

"It is a wonderful comfort to be able to interchange letters of this kind! I have no one with whom I can dis-

cuss things so seriously as with you—the *only one* ex-
cepted. God knows what I should do without you two!
When, after a period of deep dejection, I come back to my
work, I am often thrown into a mood of sheer good humor,
simply because I cannot comprehend it and am, therefore,
obliged to laugh about it. At such times, the reason for
all this comes to me like a flash, but to attempt to analyze
this feeling and endeavor to express it in terms of 'Socratic
wisdom' would require an unlimited amount of time and the
elimination of all other claims upon me. Division of labor
is a good thing. You, for example, could assume a large
part, in fact the half of my objectives, and (perhaps!)
thereby be fulfilling your *own* destiny. Only think what a
poor showing I have made as a philologist, and what a
fortunate thing it is that you are on about the same terms
with music. Had you decided to become a musician, you
would have been, more or less, that which I should have
become had I persistently clung to philology. As matters
now stand, philology exerts a great influence over me, in fact,
as an adjunct of prime importance, it even directs me in
my capacity as a musician. On the other hand, you remain
a philologist and allow your life to be directed by music.
What I am now saying is meant very seriously. In fact,
it was you, yourself, who gave me the idea of the unworthy
circle in which a philologist by profession is doomed to
revolve at the present time, and you have assuredly learned
from me something of all the mathematical rubbish among
which an absolute musician (even under the most favorable
circumstances) is obliged to fritter away his time. Now
you have an opportunity of proving the utility of philology,
by helping me to bring about the grand 'renaissance' in

which Plato will embrace Homer, and Homer, imbued with Plato's spirit, will become, more than ever before, the truly supreme Homer.

"These are just random thoughts which occur to me, but never so hopefully as since I have taken so strong a liking to you, and never so clearly—and (as you see) never so clamoring for expression—as since you read us your 'Centaurs.' *   Therefore, do not doubt the impression created upon me by your work. A very serious and profound wish has been awakened in me, the nature of which will also be clear to you, for should you not cherish the same wish, you will never be able to carry it into fulfillment.

"But we must talk this all over. Therefore—I think—in short, you must come to Tribschen next Saturday. Your sleeping room, the 'Gallerie,' is ready and 'Der Rauchfang ist Dir auch gewiss' †—in other words: auf Wiedersehen!

"With all my heart,
                              "Yours,
                                        "R. W."

Not only Wagner, but also Frau Cosima, advised my brother to develop this dissertation on Socrates and the Greek Tragedy into a larger and more comprehensive work. My brother smiled at this suggestion, as a wealth of aesthetic problems and their solution had been fermenting in his mind for years, and he had only taken advantage

* The expression "Centaurs" refers to a remark of Nietzsche's to the effect that "science, art and philosophy have grown so closely together in my works that I shall most likely give birth to a 'Centaur' one of these days."
† "The chimney is also at your disposal." Goethe's *"Faust,"* Part I. Opening scene between Faust and Mephistopheles.

of the two public lectures to work out a very small part of the material ultimately designed for a big work on the Greeks. It is very characteristic of Wagner, that despite his intimate relations with my brother, he could have made the mistake of believing that these two abbreviated lectures were only apercus, so to speak, and that he should not have recognized the fact that they were fragmentary parts of collective experiences which could only have been assembled by years of close study and profound thought. Other persons fell into the same error, owing to the fact that my brother, notwithstanding his fluency in daily intercourse, rarely ever gave expression to his great new ideas and plans, but preferred to let them ripen quietly into maturity, before speaking of them. Whether my brother acted upon Wagner's suggestions and revealed to him something of his innermost plans, or whether he considered it too premature to discuss the matter even with his intimate friends,—we have no means of knowing, as his reply to Wagner's letter is unfortunately missing.

The originality and boldness of expression in the Greek dissertation had not only created surprise and delight in Tribschen, but it also seems to have had a gratifying effect upon the depressed spirits of the family. Frau Cosima wrote:

". . . Your treatise and our pre-occupation with it has marked a turning point in the mental atmosphere. We were both so depressed that we had about abandoned our evening readings, but the pilgrimage we took with you back to the most beautiful period of the world's civilization, has had so salutary an effect upon our spirits, that on the following morning the master sent his *Siegfried* down the Rhine,

41

heralding his approach with a spirited theme accompanied by the boldest and most extravagant violin figurations, and upon hearing this, the *Rhine Maidens* responded with a most joyous and vigorous outburst of their favorite motive."

(Overture to the *"Götterdämmerung"* after the parting of *Brünhilde* and *Siegfried.*)

My brother often referred, in later years, to the inspiring effect his new theories upon the essential character of the Greek drama had upon Wagner and Frau Cosima. It was but natural that two persons of such high intelligence should immediately perceive that some powerful new message was being heralded here. In fact, my brother was the first to afford us a glimpse into the profoundest depths of the Greek soul, by his apprehension of the true significance of the Dionysian, as an opposing force to the Appollonian, tragedy.

The "dejection of spirit" of which Frau Cosima wrote was due, primarily, to the projected performance of the *"Walküre"* in Munich, upon which the young king insisted in apparent miscomprehension of Wagner's objections to the plan. Wagner owed King Ludwig an enormous debt of gratitude, as it was due to his royal generosity that Wagner, for the first time in his life, was relieved from finarcial worries and enabled to devote himself wholly to his lifework. He, therefore, felt compelled to yield to the king's wishes in regard to the Munich production of the *"Walküre,"* although he was dismayed at the attitude of the Intendant of the Court Theatre, who showed not the slightest inclination to conform to Wagner's wishes in the matter. In writing to Karl Klindworth, Wagner said: "This then is the price I have paid for such a degree of household quiet as will enable me to complete the composition of my life-work!" But the whole matter was extremely painful to Wagner and he used strong language in characterizing the events. How deeply he took the matter to heart may be seen from the circumstance that he was highly offended with all his friends and admirers (among whom was Franz Liszt with his customary train of followers) who attended the Munich production.

Nor was Wagner much better pleased with the "*Meister-singer*" performances in Vienna and Berlin, although the one in Berlin was of a much higher order of excellence than the one in the Austrian capital, owing to the fact that there were so many influential "patrons" in the former city, who did everything in their power to make the work a success. For example, Baroness von Schleinitz, whose husband was a member of the Prussian cabinet, declared that she "would live and die for the Meistersinger performance."

In Vienna, strong disapproval was manifested after the Beckmesser "*Serenade,*" as Wagner's enemies had started the report that it was intended as a parody on an old song from the Hebraic ritual. Notwithstanding the undeniable success of the work in Vienna, the press of the city was unfavorable, on the whole, and when one of the leading critics commenced his review with the words that "altogether too much praise had been expended upon the work," and that, therefore, he would "endeavor to speak the truth about the matter," the family at Tribschen asked the astonished question: "Where, pray?"

Despite glaring inadequacies in the staging of the work, the Berlin production was really a triumphant success and was promptly reported as such by Baroness von Schleinitz and Baron von Gersdorff, my brother's best friend. The A. A. Z. also reported that the "*Meistersinger*" had scored a decided success. A letter from Tribschen called my brother's attention to the interesting statements in this review to the effect that: (1) the blonde Germans had been derided in the work; (2) that it had been established that the work had been written in a spirit of pure vanity and as an *oratio pro domo* against music critics, but that, nevertheless, it must be pronounced a masterpiece.

There were a number of other things to annoy Wagner during this winter, among them being the announcement of the engagement of his niece, Doris Brockhaus, to a man by the name of Richard Wagner. This led to no end of unpleasant complications as it was generally assumed that Wagner had become engaged to his own niece, as a result of which he was deluged with well-meant congratulations and my brother with no end of inquiries. A short time thereafter, the papers reported the sudden death of Richard Wagner (the fiancé) which caused a repetition of the confusion and vexation of the Tribschen family.

During his entire life Wagner was the object of much speculation on the part of the public and gossip was ever busy with his name. My brother took this very much to heart and made every effort to prevent these irritating pin-pricks from reaching Wagner. Frau Cosima, also, was touching in her efforts to shield Wagner from everything of an unpleasant nature, and to create a cheerful atmosphere by which he would be inspired to continue his work on the "*Nibelung Ring*" and the big autobiography.

She was unconsciously helped in this task by the five children, Daniela, Blandine, Isolde, Eva and Siegfried, all of whom were charming little creatures whose roguish pranks afforded Wagner boundless delight. My brother was also very fond of the children and was regaled with a new assortment of children's stories each time he went to Tribschen. Little Eva, in particular, was fond of making up all sorts of stories about the "good Herr Nützsche." Sometimes she called him the "Good Herr Fressor"—a name which always brought forth a reproof from Isolde who insisted that it was "Professor, not Fressor; he is not going to eat anyone!" (The point of this little story is entirely lost in English as the emphasis lies on the word "fressen"— "to eat"—which is only used when applied to animals.)

Eva also took the greatest interest in my brother's physical well-being and was very much concerned that there was "never any meat on the good Herr Nü—tzsche's plate."

Both Wagner and Frau Cosima made strenuous efforts to convert my brother from the vegetarian diet to which he was addicted, and, in time, he did abandon this, whether out of love of Wagner, or of little Eva, I cannot say.

CHAPTER VI.

(April-June, 1870.)

EARLY in April, 1870, my brother was made Professor in Ordinary of Classical Philology by his faculty and the Swiss government, an appointment which made a great stir in academic circles, by reason of the fact that he had not yet reached the age of twenty-five. There had already been some talk of a call to a German university, and one of my brother's Leipzig friends made the prediction that "Nietzsche will be a Privy-Councillor by the time he is thirty"—this being considered the highest honor that could be conferred upon a professor at that time, and the be-all and end-all of academic ambitions.

No one dreamed of my brother's dissatisfaction with his professional duties, but a short time thereafter, he admitted as much to me *sub rosa*. That spring, my mother and I paid him a visit and together we made a trip to Lake Geneva, where we had an ideal sojourn at Pension Ketterer in Clarens-au-Basset.

The Tribschen friends took the greatest interest in my brother's new honors and also in the trip to Lake Geneva. In fact Wagner felt greatly relieved at the turn in affairs,

46

as my brother had suffered so keenly from all the painful and humiliating experiences to which Wagner had been subjected during the winter, that he had already intimated his readiness to give up his professorship and place himself entirely at Wagner's service. Wagner was seriously opposed to this, as however much he might wish to have Nietzsche devote himself to him and his cause, he, nevertheless, realized the tremendous prestige to be derived from having this done by a university professor. We were always greatly amused at the importance Wagner attached to my brother's position and title.

This will explain the satisfaction Wagner felt at having my brother return to Basle apparently reconciled to his position, and alert to continue his philological studies. He intimates as much at the close of the following letter, otherwise occupied with his affairs at the printers':

Richard Wagner to Friedrich Nietzsche.

"Valued friend!

" . . . I am glad to hear that you have been cheered by your sojourn on the shores of Lake Geneva. The same places which you mention in your letter are indelibly associated with various periods of my own life. At Hotel Byron in Villeneuve, I passed through one of the most extraordinary catastrophes of my whole life. In Montreux, I made an amazing discovery in regard to a young friend, and four and a half years ago, I sought a winter asylum in Vevey, where I took long walks with the Grand-duke of Baden and discussed German politics and other matters with him.

"I now perceive that philology 'weird and gray' has again taken possession of you, and that even diverting excursions into the realm of 'style' will be difficult for you. Therefore, let me be also silent on trivial things connected with my own work. By doing this I may possibly be able to deflect your mind from the confusing impressions that surged in upon you from a sphere, in which another *can*, or *must* feel himself called upon to give himself up, heart and soul, to the contemplation of this world of ideas.

"I am working slowly but 'surely' on my music dramas and take great comfort in the thought that when I wrote my *"Meistersinger,"* I came in contact with the opera and the theatre for the last time.

"Cordial greetings to you from
"Yours,

"Tribschen, May 10, 1870.   Richard Wagner."

I should like to add here that Wagner was somewhat astonished to find my brother in so cheerful a frame of mind upon his return from Switzerland, and again alluded to this on two subsequent occasions when my brother had quickly rebounded from a pessimistic mood. Somewhat apologetically my brother replied: "It is due to my sister's companionship, as there is something very exhilarating about her that reconciles one to the world." Erwin Rohde's name for me was always: *"Fräulein Euphrosyne."*

For the second time, my brother's duties made it impossible for him to take part in Wagner's birthday festivities, but he sent twelve flowering rose bushes to Tribschen, reserving his chief gift, a copy of Dürer's *"Melancholie"* until it could be delivered in person, as he felt that an engraving of so depressing a character was not altogether a suitable birthday present. Again he took recourse to his pen and

48

wrote the master a letter in which allusions were made to a recent conversation between them, and with this he sent a new photograph of himself.

Friedrich Nietzsche to Richard Wagner.

"Pater Seraphice:

"As it was impossible for me to participate in your birthday festivities last year, so again an unfavorable constellation prevents me from being with you. It is with a very bad grace that I take the pen so unwillingly forced into my hand, whereas I had hoped I might be able to make a Mayday pilgrimage to Tribschen.

"Permit me to make my wishes today an expression of my most intimate personal feelings. Let others bring you congratulations in the name of divine art, in the name of their high hopes, in the name of their own individual wishes, but for me the most subjective of all wishes suffices. May you remain what you have been to me during the past year, my mystagogue in the esoteric doctrines of life and art. Even though the gray mists of philology should seem to separate us from time to time, my thoughts in reality shall ever be with you. If it be true, as you once wrote me (to my great pride!) that my life is directed by music, then you, and no other, are the director of that music, and you, yourself, have said that even a mediocre composition can create a good impression if well conducted. It is in this sense that I offer you the rarest of all wishes—may everything remain as it is, may the moment abide, for ah! it is so beautiful! All I ask of the coming year is that I may not prove unworthy of your priceless sympathy and your unfailing encouragement. Accept this wish as one of the myriads of other wishes with which you enter upon a new year of your life!

"ONE OF THE 'BLISSFUL YOUTHS.' " *

The birthday festivities at Tribschen were uncommonly beautiful this year. Frau Cosima had transformed the entire house into a flower garden and the four little girls —dressed alike in white, with wreaths of roses in their hair—were stationed at different places to represent living flowers. Frau Cosima with Siegfried on her lap, occupied the center of this tableau. At eight o'clock in the morning, the strains of the "Huldigungs March" came from the garden where was stationed a military band of forty-five pieces from the barracks in Lucerne. Frau Cosima, herself, had given them instructions in regard to the tempi and at first Wagner was so overcome that he was unable to utter a word, and Frau Cosima almost regretted having planned the poetic and romantic program. Daniela, the eldest of the four Bülow daughters, had conceived the pretty idea of liberating her five dearly beloved birds in honor of Uncle Richard's birthday. This formed one of the most charming episodes of the day. After reciting a poem written for the occasion, Daniela opened the cage and four of the birds flew joyfully into the air. But the fifth, unaccustomed to freedom, at first refused to leave the cage and had to be taken out and placed on a bush in the garden. Later in the day, it must have fallen from its perch and been devoured by the dog. The children were not allowed

---

* "Pater Seraphice," "Mystagogue," and the "Blissful Youths" are all expressions used by Goethe in the Finale of his *"Faust."*

to learn anything of this little tragedy, but the fate of their feathered friend made a very mournful impression upon Wagner and Frau Cosima, the latter remarking that my brother might just as well have sent the Dürer "*Melancholie*" after all. But despite these clouds, the day was one long to be remembered, though with mingled feelings of sadness and joy, as is all that is precious in life.

Richard Wagner to Friedrich Nietzsche.

"My valued friend:

"You will already have learned from a dear hand, how welcome the '*Blissful Youth*' was to '*Pater Seraphice.*' I know that you need no further assurance of this. You will also have heard of the blissful hours, which will live in my memory so long as I am capable of emotion. Therefore, I shall not tell you of all the "blessings" but rather speak of matters that require attention in quite another phase of life. This time, it is in regard to a letter from Bonfantini, written in Italian, to which I was obliged to reply in French, telling him that I would inform you of the agreement I have made with him in regard to the future correction of the proof-sheets of my autobiography. The man seems not to be getting on with the work at all, and is no doubt highly delighted at being able to shift the responsibility for his own dilatory methods to other shoulders. This he does by attributing it to the difficulty he has in communicating with a scholar so deeply engrossed as you are at times. I can understand this perfectly, but I am also mindful of the fact that I cannot continue to burden you in this way. I mentioned something of this kind to you in my last letter and I again earnestly beg you to consider yourself relieved of the burden of this responsibility. But whenever you happen to be passing the office of our Italian, you would greatly oblige me by looking in and inspecting the work of my manuscript. . . . It is a curious circumstance that in the course of publishing this essentially Germanic autobiography, I should be called upon to translate an *Italian* letter!

"You need never think, my dearest friend, that you will ever be denied an insight into these pages for, as you know, it is you whom I have in mind as the custodian of these memoirs when I am dead and gone. Everything is going well here. Tomorrow, I expect to finish the sketches for the first act of *"Siegfried"* (*"Götterdämmerung,"*—I meant to say!) Day after tomorrow, we celebrate my son's first birthday and at the same time, the anniversary of your first visit to us. May the stars look down benignly upon this twofold celebration! At the time it seemed to me as if you had brought good luck to my son. Since then, a year full of difficulties and yet one rich in joys has passed over our heads, and now it almost seems as if the constellation which watched over my birth— I mean, Taurus!—is to be taken into the reckoning. All things come to him who waits! I dare to hope that within a few months, the high-hearted mother of my son will become my wife.

"Farewell, and be of good cheer, by that I mean not according to modern, but ancient Greek ideas!

"With heartfelt greetings,

"Yours faithfully,

"Tribschen, June 4, 1870.   RICHARD WAGNER."

Wagner's Birthday

As has already been seen from passages in my brother's letters to Erwin Rohde, he was unremitting in his efforts to bring his dearest friends in closer touch with Wagner, and was never happier than when he was successful. Thus he writes to Gersdorff: ". . . . That you and I are agreed in our feelings for Richard Wagner, is the best of proof for me that there is a close bond of union between us. For this is not an easy matter, and great courage is required if one is not to be led astray by the hue and cry of the world. Moreover, one must be prepared to meet occasional honest and intelligent persons in the opposing party. Schopenhauer must help us to rise above this conflict, theoretically, just as Wagner, the artist, can give us practical aid. Two things I endeavor to keep ever before me. In the first place, that the incredible seriousness and the truly Germanic profundity of Wagner's views of art and life, gushing forth from every tone of his music—is just as abhorrent to the majority at present, as is Schopenhauer's asceticism and negation of will. In the second place, Wagner's ideal art in which he shows a close affinity to Schiller, is especially detested by our 'Jews'—and you know what a far-reaching element this is—and these high-hearted conflicts from which is to emerge the 'day of the noble souls'—in other words, the chivalrous element—are repugnant to the plebeian political clamor of our day. Furthermore, I often find in persons of the most exceptional character a tendency to *indolence*, as if no individual effort or thorough-going study was demanded of them with a view to a better understanding of such an artist and such art-works.

"What a joy it was to me then to learn that you had made a serious study of *'Opera and Drama'*! I at once reported

53

this to Wagner. My friends are no longer strangers to him and if after the first '*Meistersinger*' performance you wish to write a letter to R. W., I can assure you that it will be warmly welcomed. In the meantime, I will see to it that they are fully informed in regard to the author of the letter. It is also understood that when you come to pay me a visit, I am to take you over to Tribschen.

"My life has been infinitely enriched by my intimate intercourse with such a genius. All the highest and most beautiful experiences of my life are associated with the names of Schopenhauer and Wagner, and I am both proud and happy to know that these views are shared by my nearest and dearest friend. Have you read '*Art and Politics*'? I should also like to call your attention to a little essay by R. W. called '*On Conducting*,' which may best be compared to the '*Professor's Philosophy*' of Schopenhauer."

Baron von Gersdorff and Erwin Rohde were my brother's most intimate friends and in inviting them to Tribschen, Wagner said: ". . . Your brother is one of us, and his friends are our friends." The first to be introduced at Tribschen was Erwin Rohde who stopped off in Basle on his way back from Italy in the spring of 1870. My mother and I were also there at the time and the four of us took a little trip to the Bernese Oberland, and upon our return Dr. Rohde was presented to Wagner and Frau Cosima. He made the best possible impression upon Wagner who said to me later: "Your brother and his friends are a wonderful new type of men, such as I had hitherto deemed impossible." In recalling this memorable visit, both Rohde and my brother never failed to speak of the "profound moments lived through in Tribschen."

During this visit, the sensation created by my brother's new views upon the Greek soul was often the topic of conversation, and he learned that the *"Greek Music Drama"*—the first of these two lectures—had only been read in part in Tribschen.

Upon learning this, my brother carefully copied out the two lectures and presented them to Frau Cosima. She was delighted, expressing her gratitude in the most extravagant terms and referring to the fact that Wagner had reproached her for having drawn such premature conclusions under the stress of the moment, and before she had had time to grasp fully the ideas Nietzsche meant to convey. She wrote: ". . . . How touched I am by the dedication of the two lectures you were kind enough to send me. Accept my warmest thanks for having vouchsafed me this great pleasure. I have now re-read the lecture on the music drama and can only repeat that I regard it as an invaluable vestibule to your Socrates structure. I could have spared myself the most unnecessary agitation at the time of the first reading had I known by what a warm pulsing description of the Greek art works it had been preceded. Your broad-boughed tree is now rooted in the most glorious past, in the home-land of beauty, and proudly rears its head into the most beautiful dreams of the future. Many details which capitivated and stimulated me even during your reading are now indelibly stamped upon my mind. For instance, your comprehension of creation and evolution, of the *'Fanget an!'* in art as well as in nature, and particularly, your views on the high consecration of the drama. Your thoroughly trenchant characterization of the chorus as a separate organism—an idea quite new to me—seems to me to

55

furnish the only correct interpretation of the Greek drama. Moreover, the bold and striking analogy you draw between the religious dance of the chorus and the Beethoven *Andantes*, and between the English tragedy (you mean, of course, the Shakespearean) and the *Allegros*, has again demonstrated to me your deeply musical nature, and I think it not improbable that this striking musical instinct, has given you the key to the innermost secrets of the Greek tragedy, to suffering instead of action—just as if a person had been led through the Indian religion to the Schopenhauerian philosophy. . . . With unqualified delight, I have placed the green Socrates side by side with the violet Homer, and both shall be cherished and nourished to the best of my ability until one of them, at least, shall be crowned in Bayreuth by the fulfillment of his hopes. . . .

"You will write your book in Bayreuth and we will strive to do it honor. And even though I am only building castles in the air, I will nevertheless, cherish them as has never been done with any worldly good, that by so doing, their frail outlines may furnish a protecting roof for the growth of the magnificent plant, ever endangered by unfavorable weather and changes of temperature.

"When once the '*Nibelung*' is completed, the beautiful images will have performed their duty, let existing conditions be what they may. As a matter of fact, I should not know how to counterbalance the humiliation of the recent '*Walküre*' performance, were I not sustained by the thought of Bayreuth.

"It is extremely gratifying to hear, especially in the beautiful way you express it—that you and your friend enjoyed your visit to Tribschen. These days will also live in our memory. The master was very much pleased with your friend, and both of us were deeply impressed by his manly seriousness, his sympathetic attitude, his unmistakable feeling of friendliness for us which illuminated, at times, his somewhat austere features. Should he be called to the university of Freiburg, you must bring him often to Tribschen as 'zweieinig geht der Mensch zu best,' to quote our authority.

"You left a melancholy souvenir of your last visit in the *'Melancholie'* of Dürer; this has been the theme of many of our conversations and we are agreed that Dürer must be regarded as the keystone of the Middle Ages, by reason of the fact that he permits 'the enigmatic, infinite symbolism of the Christian Church' as it were, to speak its last word. Not suspecting, or wilfully ignoring mere beauty of form and outline, he only reveals to us the sublime. Bach also belongs in this category, and both seem to me to be, not a beginning, but an end. . . ."

When Hans Richter was expected in Tribschen, Wagner sent word to my brother that there was to be a regular musical feast, but that no special invitation would be sent him for fear of interfering with his university duties. Upon receiving this message, my brother sighed deeply as he knew that it would be impossible for him to avail himself of this treat, presumably, the *"Götterdämmerung"* music.

CHAPTER VII.

L ATE in June my mother returned to her home in
Germany, but at my brother's urgent request, it was
decided that I should remain in Basle. Letters and
all sorts of greetings were exchanged between Basle and
Tribschen, but my brother had sprained his ankle rather
seriously and was therefore unable to accept any invitations.
The execution of the Tribschen commissions devolved upon
me, and it was I who answered Wagner's humorous appeal:

"Fresh Holland herrings longed for in Tribschen. Would
not Marie Walther be willing to come to the rescue, if she
knew that thereby she would be saving the art-work of the
future? Conductor Richter now installed at Tribschen.
And the Professor?

"WAGNER."

Here again was a veiled plea for my brother's society
and as he still felt quite wretched and unfit for active work,
we took advantage of the so-called "Bündeli Tag," a national
holiday, to make a little pilgrimage to Lake Lucerne.

In Lucerne we parted, my brother going to Tribschen
and I to pay a promised visit to the mother of one of my
brother's Basle colleagues, who owned a villa on the lake
shore just across from Tribschen.

Our field glasses were often turned upon the little peninsula and one day someone came running in to say that a rowboat had just put off from the opposite bank, in which sat my brother and another man. I had gradually become sensible of the fact that the union of Wagner and Baroness von Bülow was not as innocent, as I, in my youth and ignorance, had always assumed it to be. The fact that Frau Cosima was constantly surrounded by her four little girls (the entire "Bülowiana", as Wagner jokingly called them!) lent an innocent aspect to the relationship and furthermore great stress was laid upon the sojourn in Switzerland as one necessitated by considerations of health.

As my brother was evidently coming to fetch me and I had lost confidence in my own judgment, I appealed to my hostess to decide the matter for me. The reply of the aristocratic old lady was: "It is perfectly proper for you to go any place your brother sees fit to take you," an answer which indicated my brother's standing in these exclusive patrician circles. My heart was beating high as I sat in the boat Hans Richter was rowing back across the lake. I was received most cordially at the landing by Wagner and Frau Cosima, but just at first, I was somewhat confused at finding Wagner such a pigmy compared to Frau Cosima. I must admit that I was also unpleasantly impressed by the interior decorations of the old-fashioned country house, which consisted of rose-colored hangings and amorettes in lavish profusion, evidently designed by some Parisian *meubleur*.

But I found Wagner and Baroness von Bülow delightful and the children fascinating, especially the little Siegfried of whose advent I had been kept in ignorance. I feel sure that a great weight fell from my brother's heart when this visit passed off so pleasantly, and without my having caused him any embarrassment by asking awkward questions. Even though this visit opened my eyes to the true relations existing between Wagner and Baroness von Bülow, nothing diminished my admiration for them. Cosima's action in deserting Hans von Bülow seemed to me the most supreme sacrifice she could have made for the genius of Richard Wagner and his life-work. She must have sensed my sentiments, as she wrote to my brother: "I am overjoyed to have made your sister's acquaintance and to know that brother and sister entertain the same feelings towards me. Please share in my cordial and most heartfelt greetings and interpret them as an expression of my most genuine appreciation."

Shortly after this visit, my brother and I went to the Axenstein and then on to the Maderan Valley. In the meantime the war cloud had burst, creating indescribable confusion in Switzerland by the calling to the colors of innumerable Germans and French who had come to Switzerland for a peaceful summer outing. Basle could not furnish night-quarters for all the men who were hurrying back to their respective countries. The waiting room at the station was crowded to overflowing and those who could not endure the stifling air considered themselves fortunate to be able to hire a cab for the night. (Everything just as it was at the beginning of the present war!)

My brother was very much depressed at not being eligible for active service, but before accepting the call to the Basle university he had been compelled to expatriate himself. He sought consolation in intensive literary labors in this remote Alpine valley and wrote a dissertation on the *"Dionysian Viewpoint."* I remember quite distinctly that while he was

reading this aloud to me one day, we were interrupted by
several charges from an old cannon. The guests came
rushing from all sides to know what was the matter and
learned from our landlord (a physician who had studied in
Germany) that "the Germans had had a glorious victory!"

It was not long before the official communiqués penetrated
to our mountain solitude and the names of *"Wörth"* and
"Weissenberg" were on every tongue. But there was also
news of "heavy losses" and my brother turned as white as
a sheet. For a long time he walked up and down on the
terrace with Mosengel, a Hamburg painter, and finally approached me with a solemn mien. I felt what was coming
and tears sprang to my eyes: "Lisbeth, what would you do
if you were a man?"—"Why, I should go to war, of course;
it would make no difference about me—but you, Fritz!"—
and I broke off into an uncontrollable fit of weeping. After
quieting me, he explained that he felt it to be his duty to
try and enlist for active service. Should the Swiss government not agree to this, he would then offer his services as a
field nurse. We left at once for Basle, my brother having
already sent in a written request to the Swiss Board of
Education through Herr Vischer, one of the councilmen.
Only a rough draft of this request has been preserved: "In
view of the unexpected situation in which Germany now
finds herself, you will not be surprised to learn of my decision to place my services at the disposal of the fatherland.
It is for this purpose that I address myself to you with the
request that you use your influence with the Board of
Education in securing a leave of absence for me for the
remaining weeks of the summer semester. My health is now

so greatly improved that I feel myself unqualifiedly strong enough to serve either in the ranks, or as a field nurse.

"Nowhere will my determination to throw the infinitesimal mite of my personal effort into the sacrificial box of the fatherland meet with readier sympathy and understanding than from a Swiss Board of Education.

"Deeply conscious as I am of my Basle obligations, I feel that I could be held to these duties only by the most painful coercion, in the face of the powerful appeal Germany is making to *every single one of her sons to perform his duty as a German,* and that from now on my work, under these conditions, would have only a negligible value. And I should like to see a Swiss burgher who would feel himself bound by any such considerations if confronted by similar conditions." (The last sentence is crossed out.)

This request was granted, but only under the condition that my brother volunteer as a field nurse, thus frustrating his own wish to enter the active service. On August 12 we started for home. Mosengel joined us in Lindau and the two proceeded to Erlangen where they were to take a course in nursing.

On the way back to Basle my brother paid a flying visit to Tribschen, only remaining long enough to read his friends the above mentioned dissertation on the *"Dionysian Viewpoint."* His intention of participating in the war was only mentioned tentatively, as my brother knew full well that he would meet with vigorous opposition from Wagner and Frau Cosima, who argued that "this was not 1813, when young scholars like himself were called upon to organize a Lützow corps."

When they learned later that he had secured the permission of the Swiss government to serve his fatherland in the capacity of a field nurse, they became somewhat reconciled to the idea. Both of them felt, and not without justice, that the hideous reality of war would have a most injurious effect upon my tender-hearted brother, but agreed that "the sight of active suffering might be more endurable for him than the passive conception of this suffering."

My brother was one of the few philosophers who not only understood the necessity of war but justified it. He always laid great stress upon its purifying, ennobling and elevating influence and it was at this time that he found the magnificent words descriptive of war:

"Terrible is the sound of his silver bow, and, though he (the war-god) draws near like the night, he is, in reality, Apollo, the god of consecration and purification."

While my brother was on his way to the theatre of war, a family festival was being celebrated in Tribschen. The marriage of Wagner to Frau Cosima von Bülow took place in Lucerne on the twenty-fifth of August, the only witnesses being the old family friends, Malvida von Meysenburg and Count and Countess Bassenheim, who had made their home in Lucerne for many years. Malvida later related that Wagner was in transports of joy at the thought that his domestic relations had at last been brought into conformity with the civil laws. His only regret was that my brother could not have been one of the witnesses at the wedding as he "knew of no one who would so rejoice over the matter." Wagner also confided to Malvida that his "beloved Nietzsche," who came from a family which could look back on generations of virtuous living, had "suffered unspeakably" over the irregular relations of Wagner's household.

(And this was quite true, for as late as 1877, my brother, in speaking to me of one of his women friends, said: "All illegitimate relations are repugnant to me, because they necessitate so great a degree of subterfuge.")

Wagner further said that the reason Nietzsche had "overcome his scruples in regard to associating with a family of such reprehensible morals, was because he regarded him (Wagner) and Frau Cosima as persons of extraordinary qualities which placed them far above the average, and consequently beyond the jurisdiction of all regulated domestic relations."

On this point, Wagner was absolutely correct in his judgment of my brother, as throughout his writings he has given repeated expression to the thought that extraordinary persons are at liberty to adjust their personal relations according to their own standards, and that this was particularly true of artists. He writes on this subject: "Our artists lead a freer, more unconventional and honest life and the most striking example we have, I mean Richard Wagner, proves to us that genius need not fear to take an inimically hostile attitude towards existing social forms and laws, if by so doing he is endeavoring to disclose the still higher truth and law dwelling in him."

Again and again my brother emphasized the thought that the rights and privileges claimed by a man should be in relation to the obligations he thereby assumed and the tasks he felt himself equal to perform. Uncommon works and deeds were thus to furnish justification for those uncommon persons who placed themselves outside the pale of the moral code. But my brother regarded it as a terrible responsibility for a man to assume, and protested that he should never lose sight of the fact that the hour and the day would surely come when the works and the life of these immortals would be strictly weighed in the balance. Fortunate would then be those, who by virtue of the real greatness of their work and conduct, would be able to banish from the memory of the world everything that was unsavory and paltry! Furthermore, my brother always manifested the strongest sympathy for men of strong will power even though they were not geniuses. For such men he had no virtuous advice, but rather spoke to them in the words of Richard Dehmel's beautiful poem: *"First seize—then suffer!"*

It would be unjust to my brother did I not add here that, despite his tolerance, he found it unnecessary for persons of the highest order of talent and strength to disregard social laws and traditions. On the contrary, he believed that such laws and traditions threw the strongest protection around peculiarly conditioned natures, liberating them from the petty struggles and annoyances of everyday life, and enabling them to rise higher in the realm of the spirit.

He, himself, furnishes the most striking example of his own theory, a fact recognized by Wagner, who out of consideration for my brother's well-known sentiments and moral scruples, took great pains to conceal from him much that was reprehensible in his own life during the years prior to their friendship. It has always been my firm conviction that it was considerations of this nature which influenced Wagner in relieving my brother from the arduous task of reading the proof-sheets of his autobiography, as he knew that much therein revealed would be offensive to Nietzsche's fastidious tastes. At other times, my brother's chastity seemed to irritate Wagner, and he would suddenly break forth into the coarsest and most objectionable expressions concerning himself and Frau Cosima.

But on the whole, he was keenly sensitive to my brother's thinly-disguised disgust, and when he had gone too far in one of these outbursts, would proceed to indulge in recriminations against himself and his incurable tendency of making vulgar jokes. No one could be more lovable than Wagner when he made the effort, and as he made a point of showing his best qualities to my brother, the latter had only an idealized picture of Wagner's life and character.

While the nuptial festivities were being celebrated in Tribschen, my brother completed his course of training at the Society of the Field-Diaconate in Erlangen and was sent to the front as a confidential messenger and leader of a sanitary unit. Large sums of money were intrusted to him and so many messages of an intimate personal nature, that he often had to make his way from ambulance to ambulance, and from hospital to hospital, under a rain of bullets, stopping as occasion demanded to receive the last words of dying men. No one knows what a strain this was upon my brother's sympathies, but it is a curious fact that despite the strong mental agitation resulting from the painful impressions received on the battle-field, his mind remained normally active. He tells us that "under the very walls of Metz," he found himself "brooding over the enigmatic problems" contained in the first of the two above-mentioned lectures. These were later developed into the larger work: *"The Birth of Tragedy,"* and it was in the same surroundings that he received the first impressions for his chief work: *"Will to Power."*

He told me that once after a day of heart-breaking ex-

66

periences, he saw several regiments of our marvellous German cavalry rush by to almost certain death on the field of battle. Superb in their vigor and courage, these men conveyed the impression of a race that is born to conquer, to rule, or— to die. It was then that he was made to feel deeply for the first time, that the strongest and highest will to live does not reach its fullest expression in a miserable struggle for existence, but in the will to conflict, the will to power and superiority. This feeling, no doubt, was experienced by thousands and thousands of other Germans at that time, but the eye of a philosopher sees things in a different light and his perceptive faculties are so sharpened by a certain chain of events that he derives from them quite a different set of conclusions than do the rank and file.

With these thoughts in his mind, how different must he have felt towards Schopenhauer's much-glorified feeling of sympathy, when compared with this magnificent spectacle of *will to life, will to conflict* and *will to power*. Here he came face to face with conditions in which men feel the strongest impulses and dictates of their own conscience to be identical with their highest ideals; he found this spirit aroused not only in those engaged in carrying out these designs, but, above all, in the commanders-in-chief themselves. He now became convinced that a great military leader has the right to sacrifice his fellow men, if, by so doing, he can achieve the highest aims—in fact, he conceived this to be the positive duty of generals, no less than of the intellectual leaders of humanity, and of all great inventors in the successful prosecution of their plans.

An account of his experiences on the battlefield and the disastrous effect upon his health, was sent by my brother to Tribschen in reply to the letter containing news of events there.

Friedrich Nietzsche to Richard Wagner.

"Dear and revered master:

And so your house has been firmly established in the midst of the storm. Although far from home, I have often thought of this and never without calling down heart-felt blessings upon you both. I was overjoyed to learn from your dear wife, for whom I cherish the deepest affection, that the possibility of celebrating this event came quite suddenly, at least, much earlier than you had any reason to expect when I saw you last.

"You know what a powerful and irresistible current tore me away from you and prevented me from being an eye-witness of this solemn and long-hoped-for consummation of your wishes. For the time being, my activity has unfortunately been interrupted by illness. My manifold duties and commissions took me as far as Metz where Mosengel, my highly esteemed friend, and I were able to discharge our task successfully. In Ars sur Moselle we were placed in charge of an ambulance of wounded men who were being sent back to Germany. This close contact with severely wounded men for three days and nights marked the climax of my activities. Only wretched cattle cars were available for the transport and in one of these were six sufferers of whom I had sole charge. All of them had pulverized bones, some had as many as four wounds, and my diagnosis established two cases of diphtheria. In looking back upon this experience, it seems nothing short of a miracle that I was able to eat and sleep in this pestilential atmosphere. But I had scarcely delivered my transport in Karlsruhe, than alarming symptoms of a complete breakdown made themselves noticeable, and it was only by a supreme effort that I was able to get as far as Erlangen and make a report to my organization. That accomplished, I went to bed and am still not able to be up. A very competent physician pronounced my trouble to be dysentery and diphtheria, and as vigorous measures were taken for getting these two contagious diseases under control, I am already on the way to recovery. So you can see that I am making the simultaneous acquaintance of two of the most dread hospital diseases, the effect of which has been so weakening, that I shall be obliged to give up all thought of resuming my relief work for the time being. After a brief four weeks' period of activity for the general good, I am again thrown back upon myself—in a wretched plight to boot!

"I do not like to say a word about the German victories; these are like the handwriting on the wall, which should be intelligible to *all* nations.

"I am forbidden to write more today; my next letter will be to your wife at whose feet I lay my most heartfelt good wishes. Good luck, also to the newly christened son! Good luck to the entire Tribschen household!

"Yours faithfully,

"FRIEDRICH NIETZSCHE."

From the close of this letter, it will be seen that christening ceremonies had also taken place in Tribschen. Siegfried, who was already fifteen months old, was given the official name of Helferich Siegfried Richard. The only witnesses were Dr. and Mrs. Willis, old friends of Wagner's from the Zurich days. In describing this event, Wagner humorously wrote: "Siegfried, called 'Fidi,' did not behave very well." It seems that he babbled to himself all during the pastor's exhortation and at the great moment when "The Holy Ghost was about to descend upon him," began to whimper distressingly. But Frau Cosima ignored those trifles and wrote in an exalted strain to the effect that "at all events, he is now a Christian and even though he did not give our good pastor much pleasure, it is to be hoped that he will remain true to the Saviour to the end of his life."

Whenever Cosima indulged in pathos of this sort, Wagner usually applied a counteractant in the shape of some sarcastic, atheistic remark, which never failed to give offense to my brother. For however free and unprejudiced he was in his own views upon religion, my brother possessed too much tact willfully to hurt others. As a matter of fact, his own extremely liberal views were not generally known at that time.

In later years, he was very bitter about Wagner's sudden coversion to a somewhat aggressive Christianity as he suspected this of having been done for unworthy and self-interested motives. But I distinctly remember a remark he made to me in this connection to the effect that "a somewhat romantic Christianity would make Wagner happier and bring him more into harmony with his true nature," and in a private document written three years later, he declared that "Wagner is a modern and is, therefore, not able to encourage and fortify himself by his belief in God. In fact, he does not believe in the guiding hand of a good spirit, but believes only in himself. No one can be wholly honest with himself if he believes only in himself."

As soon as my brother was able to travel he was moved in easy stages from Erlangen to Naumburg, but he never fully recovered from the intense strain his nervous system had undergone and from the disastrous effects strong medicines had wrought upon his hitherto splendid digestive organs. Our dear mother often said that she only marvelled that he had not died from the medicines if not from the diseases. Influenced by his strong sense of duty and by love for his scientific work, he placed too much confidence in his naturally robust constitution and made the mistake of returning to Basle at the beginning of November, although he was by no means in a condition to resume his university work.

While all this was happening, Wagner had finished his essay on *"Beethoven,"* the manuscript of which he sent to my brother with heartfelt greetings and received in reply the following letter:

Friedrich Nietzsche to Richard Wagner.

"Most revered master!

"In the first onrush of the opening semester, made particularly strenuous this year by reason of my long absence, nothing more stimulating could have happened to me than to receive a copy of your *'Beethoven.'* How much it has meant to me to become acquainted with your philosophy of music—which is as much as to say, with *the* philosophy of music—I could prove to you by an article I wrote last summer on the *'Dionysian Point of View.'*

71

"Indeed it was by the aid of this study that I am enabled to grasp your arguments fully and to enjoy them profoundly, however far removed is your range of thought, however surprising and amazing is everything you have to say, especially the explication of Beethoven's real achievement. And yet I fear that the æstheticians of our day will regard you as a somnabulist whom it would not only be unadvisable, but positively dangerous, to follow, were such a thing possible. Even the majority of the *cognoscenti* (students) of the Schopenhauerian philosophy will find difficulty in translating into concrete concepts the profound harmony between your ideas and those of your great master.

"For this reason I regard your essay as 'published and yet not published,' as Aristotle said of his esoteric writings. I like to dwell upon the thought that it is chiefly those to whom the message of *Tristan* has been revealed, who will be able to follow Wagner, the philosopher, and I, therefore, consider the capacity for a genuine appreciation of your work as a priceless distinction bestowed only upon the select few (here a large part of the letter has been torn off).

"Your grateful and faithful,

"Basle, Nov. 10.   "FRIEDRICH NIETZSCHE.
"Luther Day."

This letter affords one of the most touching proofs of my brother's unfailing tact and courtesy towards Wagner. Instead of reminding him that while making a visit in Tribschen on his way back from the mountains, he had read aloud his lecture on the *"Dionysian Viewpoint,"*—he pretends to have quite forgotten this incident, in order that Wagner might not be embarrassed by the suggestion that he

72

had appropriated some of the ideas contained in my brother's unpublished work and made use of them in his own essay on *"Beethoven."*

It is barely possible that under the stress of the war my brother may have really forgotten having acquainted Wagner with the contents of his new treatise, but it is scarcely believable that this would have slipped his mind a second time when he was writing the above letter. The circumstance that a large part of the letter is missing, would seem to support the theory that my brother had made some allusion to the matter.

There was a time, when misinformed Wagner admirers intimated that Nietzsche owed some of his outstanding ideas to Wagner, but any unprejudiced reader of Wagner's literary work of this period must have noticed that this was not at all the case, and that on the contrary, Nietzsche's influence upon Wagner was unmistakable from the very beginning of their friendship. When Wagner, for example, in his essay: *"On the Destiny of Opera,"* speaks of the compromise between the Apollonian and Dionysian art in the Greek tragedy, it is easy to see that this thought was borrowed from my brother. And to be perfectly just to Wagner, he never attempted to deny this.

As early as the spring of 1870, when my brother and Erwin Rohde were paying a visit in Tribschen, this theme of the Apollonian and Dionysian influence was frequently discussed, and it is to this that Rohde alludes in a letter dated May 28, 1870: ". . . . I have read with keen interest Wagner's essay, *'On the Destiny of the Opera,'* and at times, I fancied I could detect your voice, dear friend, *coming from the*

73

prompter's box, particularly when Greek drama was under discussion."

As my brother has been with us in Naumburg until late in November, he accepted the pressing invitation to spend the Christmas holidays in Tribschen, and wrote us from there: ". . . I am as well off here as it is possible to be, and we have had delightful Christmas days. Frau Wagner's birthday festivities on the twenty-fifth of December were perfect and deserving of a detailed description. The *'Tribschen Idyll,'* as Wagner's wondrously beautiful symphonic movement is called, is one of the most exquisite works in all musical literature. The musicians were just as enthusiastic as we were about it."

Wagner had planned this composition as a birthday surprise for his wife. Surreptitious rehearsals were held in Lucerne with a small but excellent orchestra and my brother was the only one admitted into the secret.

Wagner telegraphed him: "If you would care to hear the last rehearsal meet me at the Hotel du Lac at three o'clock, but announce your arrival (in Tribschen) ostentatiously for five."

The musicians arrived at Tribschen early in the morning of the twenty-fifth and were stationed on the staircase leading to the upper storey, so that Cosima might be awakened by strains as enchanting as if they came from the music of the spheres. Her particular name for this composition was the *"Blissful Morning Dream Melody."*

"Es war ein schöner Morgentraum
Woran zu denken wag' ich kaum."

It was christened the "*Staircase Music*" by the children as the position of the musicians appealed to their imaginations, and this was the title used by all the intimates of the house. To the musical world, it is known under the name of the "*Siegfried Idyll.*"

CHAPTER VIII.

MY brother resumed work on his big Greek dissertation at the beginning of 1871. It was impossible for him to make use of all the material on hand and the selective process had to be rigorously applied before he could begin the task of "bringing the book together." As yet there was no relation between this work as projected and the new art of Richard Wagner.

Scarcely was he launched in this great undertaking than he was obliged to call a halt, owing to the fact that his premature resumption of his university duties had given rise to new and alarming symptoms; jaundice and intestinal inflammation had set in and he was further tormented by insomnia. The family at Tribschen was very much depressed by the news as he had been counted upon as a regular week-end visitor and it was on his account that the series of chamber music evenings (Beethoven Quartettes) to be given under the direction of Hans Richter had been set for Saturdays and Sundays. All this had now to be renounced; "Must it be?" asked my brother in the beautiful strain from Beethoven's *F Major Quartette*, and unrelenting necessity gave back the answer: "It must be!"

Prof. Liebermeister was already very much dissatisfied with my brother for having curtailed his period of convalescence and now ordered him to take a long leave of absence to be spent at some point on the Italian lakes, further prescribing that his "cheerful little sister" accompany him as travelling companion and nurse. Only delaying our departure until my brother could pay a farewell visit in Tribschen, we went directly to Lugano where we had an ideal sojourn. At the Hotel du Parc we made the acquaintance of the brother of Field Marshal von Moltke, who with his wife and daughters, was also wintering at this resort. We were constantly in the company of this delightful family, and Frau Cosima wrote that she "envied us the brother."

Patriotism ran high at Tribschen as Wagner expected that a German victory would also mean a victory for his art and he was already at work on his *Kaiser March.* The children soon picked up the melody of the folk-song used in this work and the house re-echoed to the jubilant strains of "Hail the Kaiser," much to the displeasure of Cosima's mother who was spending the winter in Tribschen. According to Wagner, the Princess d'Agoult possessed in the highest degree the beautiful French characteristic of "heroic frivolity," but notwithstanding this she was fanatically French in her sympathies.

We returned in April, somewhat sooner than we had expected, as Wagner had written us that they would start out on their big concert tour about the middle of the month and my brother was bent upon seeing them before they left. He wished very much to read them parts of his new Greek manuscript intended as a sort of Vol. I. to the complete work, which he hoped to get ready for the printers during their absence. I travelled through to Basle, leaving my brother at Tribschen where his sensitive nature was deeply wounded by perceiving that Wagner expected this work, in some way, to be a glorification of his own art. Despite my brother's enthusiasm for Wagner and his art, his scholar's conscience revolted at the thought of uniting so many diverse elements in a book that was to bear the title of *"Greek Cheerfulness."* But again, consideration for his friend won the day, and no sooner had he returned to Basle than he set about re-writing the work, that is to say, he eliminated several chapters and confined himself strictly to the discussion of Greek tragedy, as it was only in this way that any justifiable reason could be found for introducing allusions to Wagner's art.

The manuscript was ready for the printers by the twentieth of April and was sent off to Engelmann of Leipzig who had expressed a wish to publish the work.

In the meantime, Wagner and Frau Cosima had started on their tour through Germany and had visited Augsburg and Bayreuth. In the latter city they inspected the old rococo theatre, hoping to find that it could be utilized for the production of the Wagner's music dramas, and it was during this visit that the incredibly bold and daring plan of erecting a special Festival Theatre was first broached. After a visit to Berlin, where Wagner was invited to address the Academy on the theme, *"The Destiny of the Opera,"* they proceeded to Leipzig to pay a visit to Wagner's relatives, the Brockhaus family. It was not without serious misgivings that Frau Cosima set out on this trip, but she was happily spared all of the anticipated unpleasant experiences.

Upon their return, we received a pressing invitation to spend the Whitsuntide holidays at Tribschen and these days will ever be cherished among my most beautiful memories. I remember well the last evening of our stay! The moon had risen clear and full over the snow fields of Mount Titlis, while the sun's last rays still touched the peak. As the glow of the sun was gradually blended into the silvery light of the moon, the picturesque outlines of the mountains became more delicately transparent until they almost seemed spiritualized. Our conversation ceased and we relapsed into a dreamy silence. We four (five, in fact, counting Russ, an important member of the family) wandered along the so-called "Robber's Path" close to the water's edge. Frau Cosima and my brother went ahead, followed by the splendid, coal-black Newfoundland, who also seemed alive to the impressiveness of the hour, and Wagner and I brought up the rear of this little procession. Cosima was wearing a semi-negligee of rose-colored cashmere, with broad revers of real lace falling to the hem of the garment, and upon her arm hung a large flower-trimmed hat of Florentine straw. Wagner was in his habitual costume worn by the Netherlands painters, black satin knee trousers, black velvet jacket, black silk stockings and a light blue satin cravat falling over a shirt of fine linen and real lace. The familiar velvet barret was posed upon his luxuriant brown hair. Even now, after all these years, I can visualize the scene and see the light falling through the trees upon the four figures as we silently walked along looking out over the sea of glistening silver. As we listened to the soft lapping of the waves, each one of us heard the song of his own thoughts sounding out of this sweet monotonous melody as if some magic horn were sending forth a piercingly sweet echo. The goal of our wanderings was the so-called Hermitage, a pavilion built of birchbark on the highest elevation of the estate. From this vantage point, we were afforded a magnificent view of the surrounding mountain peaks, now thrown into sharp relief by the bright moonlight.

Gradually the spell of silence was lifted and Wagner, Frau Cosima and my brother began to speak of the tragedy of human life, of the Greeks, of the Germans and of their mutual plans and wishes. Never in my whole life, either before or since, have I heard such marvellous harmony in the conversation of three persons so fundamentally different. Each one had his own strong personal note, his own theme which was sharply emphasized, but withal, the whole was like some wondrously beautiful symphony. Each one of these three rare natures was at its best, each shone in its own brilliancy and yet no one of the three was overshadowed by the others. Never shall I forget these indescribable hours!

During the summer, Baron von Gersdorff, who had returned safe and sound from the war, paid my brother a visit in Basle and was taken over to Tribschen where he made the best possible impression. He was one of the "Patrons" of the Bayreuth undertaking, and, at my brother's suggestion, had already written to Wagner. Cosima wrote of him: "He made an excellent impression upon us both and we welcome him as one of the 'Patrons.' We find united in him all the best traits of the Prussian character, in the highest sense of the term, and we hope that this may be the beginning of a life-long friendship."

During that summer there were many guests in Tribschen, among them the men who were interested in the organization of the so-called *"Patronat"* and the Wagner Society, by which the Bayreuth undertaking was to be financed. Now that the domestic life of the Wagners had been brought into conformity with the world's moral code, all of the old friends and acquaintances flocked to Tribschen, as a result of which my brother felt himself relieved of some of the obligations he had felt towards his friends during the period of their comparative seclusion.

And it must be admitted that my brother welcomed this respite, as despite his great affection for Wagner, he was keenly sensible of the strong influence exerted upon him by the master.

CHAPTER IX.

CARES AND JOYS (1871).

WE spent the summer in the charming little resort of Gimmelwald near Lauterbrunn, my brother returning to Naumburg with me as his leave of absence had been extended until the end of the autumn vacation. He had been greatly concerned during the summer about the publication of his Greek work which seemed destined to cause him much disappointment and anxiety. After waiting for a long time for an answer from Engelmann, the publisher, my brother learned that the reader of the firm had been thrown into "mild shivers" by the book. Irritated by this news and impatient at the delay, he took the book out of Engelmann's hands, although it later transpired that the latter had not been unwilling to publish the work.

Erwin Rohde and Baron von Gersdorff who had come to Naumburg on a birthday visit, finally persuaded my brother to go with them over to Leipzig and try Wagner's publisher, who could certainly have no objection to the work on the ground that it dealt with such modern problems as those raised by Wagner's own art. According to my brother, the two friends fairly "dragged" him to this publisher, E. W. Fritzsch, who after some hesitation agreed to publish the

book. Wagner was greatly surprised to hear of this and
disagreeably so, as it would seem from the following letter:

Richard Wagner to Friedrich Nietzsche.

"My dear and valued friend!

"I beg of you to let me know the real reasons which influenced you in placing a work I regard so highly and from
which I expect so much, in the hands of a music publisher
like Fritzsch. My sincere friendship for you prompts me
to make this inquiry. The fact that you have broken with
Engelmann gives rise to all sorts of surmises and it is out
of genuine interest in your welfare that I ask for confidential
information on the subject. For fear that you may interpret this as due to a certain hesitancy on my part in regard
to Fritzsch, I herewith assure you that this is not the case,
and that my solicitation in the matter is to be attributed
solely to my concern about your making a highly creditable
and significant literary début.

"I beg you to place the most friendly interpretation upon
my motives and accept my heartfelt greetings!
                    "Yours
"Tribschen, Oct. 16, 1871.   RICHARD WAGNER."

After my brother had explained the situation to Wagner,
the latter wrote warm words of recommendation to Fritzsch
to which reference is made in the following letter:

Friedrich Nietzsche to Richard Wagner.

"Most revered master:

"News reached me today from our Fritzsch in Leipzig
who has kept me in a state of complete mystification by his

83

long silence. I did not know what was expected of me, and it is only now I learn that, even before receiving your words of recommendation, he had turned the manuscript over to one of his staff for critical judgment and this man, who seems to have been a sad procrastinator, did not return it until Nov. 16.

"Now I hear that the printing is to be rushed as rapidly as possible and Fritzsch makes me the most reassuring promises in regard to the book. There is one passage in his letter which you will have to˙ explain to me. He says: 'In the meantime you will have thought over the question of the financial arrangement and it is possible that Herr Wagner may have made some suggestions to you in regard to this.'

"If you were here you would find me almost buried under a pile of ponderous tomes from which I am brewing a Latin *epigraph* for my students, or surrounded by hundreds of volumes of Plato, by the aid of which I hope to initiate my hearers into the study of this philosopher. Whenever I raise my head from this mountain of books, I immediately hear something that is taking place in Bologna, or is up for discussion in the city council of Bayreuth, or the Academy calls attention to itself by sending me an essay by Franz Hueffer, the pseudo-Englishman, or a review of Fuchs' *'Preliminaries of the Art of Music,'* or my eye falls upon an astounding advertisement signed by my friend Gersdorff, etc. In short, I only need to listen with half an ear in order to remain fully informed as to your movements and all the external tokens of your existence.

"I hold my last visit to Tribschen in affectionate remembrance and realize full well how much I owe to my

84

good geniuses; not long ago, I offered up a libation with
a bottle of red wine, pronouncing the spoken words
Χαίρετε Δαίμονες. This solemn ceremony took place simul-
taneously in Basle, Kiel and Berlin and it is safe to say
that each one of us had you in mind, for what could we ask
of our good geniuses and what do we owe them, which is
not closely and intimately associated with your name!

"Yours faithfully,

"Basle, Nov. 18, 1871.   FRIEDRICH NIETZSCHE."

Having reached a satisfactory agreement with Fritzsch,
my brother felt himself at liberty to proceed more boldly
in the matter of introducing ideas relative to Wagner and
his art-works into his book on Greek tragedy.   Much new
material was added to the manuscript, and writing to Rohde
on this subject, he said: ". . . You will doubtless be greatly
surprised by the entire last part of the work which is un-
familiar to you.   I have ventured much in making these
changes and would be justified, to a tremendous degree, in
calling out to myself: *Animam salvavi*.   This gives me
courage to think of my manuscript with deep satisfaction,
and I do not allow myself to entertain any misgivings, although it has turned out as offensive as possible and I seem
already to hear the 'shrieks of indignation' that will go up
from certain quarters when it is published."

Even at this time, my brother intimated to me that certain
of his own ideas had been suppressed out of deference of
Wagner.   He also wrote to Rohde: ". . . No one can form
the faintest conception of the genesis of such a work, of the

85

trouble and torment it is to keep one's self from being corrupted by *other ideas* pressing in from all sides: of the courage required in conceiving and carrying out one's own ideas, and above all, in this particular case, of the tremendous obligations I felt towards Wagner and which, to be perfectly frank with you, caused me much inward contrition."

In justice to Wagner, it must be stated that he had only a vague idea as to the extent he and his art were to figure in my brother's book. Before going to Naumburg and Leipzig, my brother had paid a visit to Tribschen, where nothing was discussed but the unsuccessful negotiations with Engelmann, as Fritzsch had not yet entered upon the scene. My brother had consistently refrained from any further mention of his intention of amplifying or altering the manuscript out of deference to Wagner, and had charged me in particular not to divulge the secret. Wagner was, therefore, left in complete ignorance of the revisions as well be seen from his next letter:

Richard Wagner to Friedrich Nietzsche.

"Most valued friend!

"Fritzsch has not given me the slightest intimation of anything I was to impart to you, and I am inclined to believe that the passage you quote was only used as a means of shifting his own embarrassment on the subject to your shoulders. My own pecuniary relations to Fritzsch were determined, quite accidentally, by the opportune appearance of my quasi-festival essay on Beethoven, and by the tremendous sensation created by my essay on the Jews, which would naturally react favorably upon my other publications and justify expectations of an immediate and rapid sale. Much will depend upon your ideas in regard to the sale of your book. If you are confident of good results, you will be guided by my views, well-known to you, as to the relation between the size of the edition and the corresponding terms of payment in making your arrangements with Fritzsch.

"In any case it would be advisable to have a complete agreement on this point so that the relations would be determined once for all, so soon as anything had been accepted for publication and that quite regardless of the 'business' success. You will find this a much better plan than having it made to appear, each time an agreement is reached (as was the case with me!) that never before since the world was created had a book been accepted for publication.

"Good luck to epigraphs and Plato; the latter is also being studied in Tribschen. We are all fairly well and send cordial greetings.

"Yours,

"Nov. 21, '71.   RICHARD WAGNER."

Amusingly enough, my brother was also engaged in composing that autumn. He had been made very happy by the reunion with his friends in Naumburg and Leipzig, and was now endeavoring to give concrete expression to these feelings in a musical composition dedicated to the "Memory of Our Happy Autumn Vacation." This work brought him into contact with a very clever copyist, in reduced circumstances, whom he endeavored to help by recommending him to Wagner. This effort was unsuccessful as will be seen from the following letter:

Richard Wagner to Friedrich Nietzsche.

"Most valued friend!

"At present my roof shelters a Brandenburg singing teacher from Zurich, to whom I am paying a terrifying salary for copying out my difficult manuscript. Moved to compassion by your letter, I have given much thought to the matter and tried to find some way of rescuing this worthy Suabian from the lion's den, but just as soon as the most urgent copy has been sent off, I shall have no further use for such a musician until I am ready with the instrumentation. That will not be before next summer, and I am not in a position, therefore, to help the poor man other than by a small gift of money and will ask you to hand him twenty francs in my name and charge this sum to my account. My wife has written you today of our Mannheim adventure. May we not cherish the hope that you will join us? . . .

"My hopes are placed in Nietzsche if only Fritzsch serves him as he should. During the last few days, my gaze wandered from Genelli's 'Dionysius among the Muses' to your last work (that is to say, in so far as I am acquainted with it!) with a feeling of the most genuine astonishment. It was as if some oracle had revealed a message to me. It is a singular, in fact a marvellous coincidence, this thing of seeing my own life, as it were, reproduced in your thoughts as you here portray them.

"Can you not get away some Saturday before we leave,

which will be about the ninth of December? That would be
delightful. As you know, I no longer give you a definite
invitation and, therefore, you are spared all embarrassment
in case you do *not* come.

"With cordial greetings.

"Yours

"Nov. 26, '71.   R. W."

At the beginning of December, Wagner set out on another
trip through Germany to win new friends for his cause, and
also to push the preliminary work in Bayreuth. One of his
chief objectives was Mannheim, where the first of the series
of big concerts for the benefit of the Wagner Society was
to be given under his personal direction. My brother and
his two most intimate friends had planned to hold a reunion
here as a means of expressing their devotion to Wagner,
but at the last moment, my brother was the only one able
to be present.

A vivid description of those Mannheim days was given
by Karl Heckel in the course of a lecture delivered by him at
the Nietzsche Archives in Weimar in October, 1913. Among
other things he said: ". . . It was in December, 1871, only
eight days before Christmas. The clock pointed to midnight
and the city lay wrapped in sleep. The only signs of life
were in and around the railway station, where friends called
out cheery greetings to each other, enviously watched by
groups of curious bystanders. The train from the east was
eagerly awaited and as it came steaming into the station, a
small, quaint-looking figure descended to the platform and
was greeted by the waiting crowd with 'Three cheers for
Richard Wagner! Hurrah, hurrah, hurrah!'

" 'Herr Jesses!' cried the newcomer in a pronounced Saxon dialect, 'do you take me for a prince!'

"His first greetings were for the numerous members of the newly-organized Wagner Society, to whom he related that the day before he had inspected the building site offered to him by the city of *Bayreuth* for the Festival Theatre, and that the *announcement* of the Mannheim concert had greatly increased public confidence in the Bayreuth undertaking. Shortly after Wagner had made his triumphal entry, the train from Lucerne arrived bringing Frau Wagner from Tribschen. She left the train on the arm of a young man of middle height, with dark brown hair, large mustachios, and the high, broad forehead of a scholar and a thinker. Spectacles added to this scholarly aspect, which was nevertheless contradicted by his careful grooming, his almost military bearing and his high clear voice. He was presented to the executive committee of the society: 'Gentlemen, Prof. Friedrich Nietzsche!'

"The day following we learned that he had come to Mannheim to be present at the concert; he never missed a rehearsal and was one of the few present who was familiar with the *Siegfried Idyll* to be given publicly for the first time, at this concert.

"We learned further, that he was not only an enthusiastic disciple of Wagner but also an extraordinary personality in his own right, having been called to the university of Basle at the age of twenty-four, that his lectures on Hellenism had attracted the attention of no less a personage than Jakob Burckhardt, and that his ideas also met with lively sympathy in Tribschen where he was *persona grata*.

"My father and the small circle of friends by whose invita-

90

tion **Wagner** had come to Mannheim, had frequent opportunity of listening to conversations between **Wagner**, Nietzsche and Frau **Wagner**, which in profundity and seriousness of thought could not have been equalled at that time elsewhere in Germany."

The program chosen for the Mannheim concert was as follows:

1. Overture to *"Magic Flute."*
2. A Major Symphony (Beethoven).
3. Lohengrin Overture.
4. Vorspiel to the *"Meistersinger."*
5. Vorspiel and Liebestod to *"Tristan and Isolde."*

At the rehearsal, the *"Siegfried Idyll"* otherwise called the *"Staircase Music"* was played twice to a very select company of listeners, these favored few, aside from Frau Wagner and my brother, including Alexander Ritter and his wife, Emil Heckel and the executive committee of the Mannheim Wagner Society, and further, Pohl, Nohl, Friedrich Wengler and Handloser, the conductor.

This concert made a deep impression upon my brother and he wrote to Rohde: ". . . The experiences I have had this week with Wagner in Mannheim, have been the means of increasing my knowledge of the music to a marvellous degree, and of convincing me of its complete justification. Ah, my friend! To think that you were not able to be present! What are all previous artistic memories and experiences compared to this my most recent one! I was like *one* who sees his dream go into fulfillment. For just this is *music,* and nothing else! And it is precisely this, and nothing else, that I mean by the word *'music'* in describing the Dionysian art! But when I think that only a few hundred people of the next generation will have *the same* that I have from this music, I anticipate an entirely new culture! . . .

". . . A feeling of disgust and aversion is created in me at times by everything that cannot, in some way, be brought into relationship with music. And I was filled with an overwhelming abhorrence of everyday realities upon my return from Mannheim, just because they no longer seemed to me to *be* realities, but hallucinations!"

My brother spent a lonely Christmas in Basle that year, as he needed time and solitude for the working out of his six promised lectures: "*On the Future of Our Educational Institutions.*"

His latest work, "*The Birth of Tragedy out of the Spirit of Music*" had already come from the press and he was eagerly awaiting the first copies so that he might send one to Wagner as a New Year's greeting.

CHAPTER X.

(1872.)

ON New Year's Day, 1872, my brother received his first published work, and, with a heart beating high, he wrote in his own copy:

> "*Schaff das Tagwerk meiner Hände,*
> *Grosser Geist, dass ich's vollende.*"

He then hurried off a copy to his dear friends in Tribschen.

Friedrich Nietzsche to Richard Wagner.

"Most revered master!

"At last, I am sending you my Christmas gift and New Year's greeting in one. This gift is very much belated, to be sure, and yet without any blame being attached either to Fritzsch or myself, as the post, at times unreliable, belongs to 'the powers of fate' over which we have no control.

"The package left Leipzig on December 29th., and I have awaited its arrival hourly, in order that I might send the book together with my blessings and good wishes.

"May this work, in some slight degree, repay the extraordinary interest you have shown in its genesis, and if I believe

93

that in the main I am right, that only means that you, *in your art*, must be right through time and eternity. On every page you will find evidence of my gratitude for everything that you have given me, but I am haunted by the terrible doubt as to whether I have always proven myself properly receptive of your gifts. Perhaps I shall be able to do many things much better later, and by 'later,' I mean the time when the Bayreuth art period is ushered in. In the meantime, I am filled with pride at the thought that I am branded, so to speak, and that henceforth, my name will ever be associated with yours. May God have mercy upon your souls, my philologians, if you are still determined to learn nothing!

"I should be overjoyed, revered master, if upon the threshold of the new year, you will graciously accept this book as an auspicious and friendly omen. I hope soon to be able to send bound copies for you and your wife.

"With all good wishes for you and yours and with deep gratitude for all your tokens of friendship, I am, as I was and shall be

"Yours faithfully,

"Basle, January 2, 1872.   FRIEDRICH NIETZSCHE."

Richard Wagner to Friedrich Nietzsche.

"Dear friend!

"I have never read anything more beautiful than your book!

"It is simply glorious! I am writing you in great haste, as my excitement is so great at the moment that I must await the return of reason before being able to read it

94

carefully. I have just said to Cosima that you stand second only to her, then, for a long time, there is no one until we reach *Lenbach* who has painted such a striking portrait of me! Consider well what she has written, but cultivate indifference as far as the rest of the world is concerned!

"Adieu. Run over at the first opportunity and we shall have a veritable Dionysian feast!

"Yours,

"R. W."

At first, Cosima only wrote a brief note of acknowledgement with a list of names to whom the book was to be sent. But later she wrote in a strain of deep emotion:

". . . Oh, how beautiful your book is! How beautiful, and how deep—how deep and how daring! Did I not feel that you must already have found your highest reward in your conception of things, I would ask, with the deepest concern, where are you to find it? And if you feel this sense of reward, you will be able to bring your own mood of splendid exaltation in harmony with the outer world in which you live and work; 'wie ertrug ich's nur, wie ertrag ich's noch?' Perhaps the day and the 'New Year's Echoes' will help somewhat, will they not, dear friend?

"With this book you have exorcised the evil spirits which I had begun to believe had nothing to do but wait upon our master. You have thrown the most resplendent radiance over two worlds, one of which we do not see because it is too remote, and the other we do not apprehend because it is too near. We now comprehend the beauty which we only half-suspected, and understand the ugliness which came very near stifling us. Like a consoling spirit, you illuminate the future for us, this future which to our hearts is the present, so that we can hopefully pray that in the end 'good may conquer.' I cannot tell you how uplifting your book seems to me and how successful you have been in gaining an insight into problems which so simply and truthfully establish the tragedy of our existence. I have read this work as I would a poem, notwithstanding the fact that it deals with the most profound problems, and, like the master, I cannot lay it aside, for it furnishes an answer to all the subconscious questions of my being. You can imagine how moved I was by your mention of *'Tristan and Isolde.'* In this work, as in no other, I have been made to feel most keenly the idea of destruction through the music and salvation through the drama, as you describe it. Hitherto I have never been able to express this, so that you have now thrown an illuminating light upon one of the most powerful impressions of my entire life.

"And what a beautiful idea, and how beautifully expressed, that of representing Schopenhauer as Dürer's knight, but what will the librarians and proof-readers have to say to this? Nothing at all, I imagine ('in fact, I understood nothing at all about it,' in the words of the honest Kothener). But all this is a matter of no importance, the thing which most concerns us is you yourself. Are we to learn nothing of your lectures? This is the theme of *your* Reformation, and we should like to know more about it. Many thanks for your shipment of books. I fancy that Baroness von Schleinitz already has a copy, and the good R. P. was really superfluous, as his Mannheim *'Lamentations'* were nothing but mischievous rubbish—the good man does not know as much as he imagines he does, in fact, there seems to be only one person who understands Wagner perfectly, but I shall not say who this is. . . ."

Again Wagner felt inspired to renewed creative effort by my brother's ideas and sentiments, just as was the case in 1870 when Nietzsche's new world of thought as expressed in the two Greek lectures, first thrust itself upon the master's consciousness. Cosima writes in regard to this: "The master spends the entire forenoon working and you should hear the second song of the Rhine Maidens. In the evening we read Schopenhauer aloud, in the afternoon we read the *'Birth of Tragedy'* separately, and during dinner discuss the performance of the *'Ninth Symphony'* which is to be given on the evening of the cornerstone laying. The co-operation of the musicians of Germany will be needed for this. Yes, Bayreuth! (Tribschen etymology: *'beim Reuth'!*) 'we are now to become tragic personages!' God knows, whether or not this latest idea will prove a success, but after all, that is a matter of comparative indifference. We have acted to the best of our knowledge and ability and should it succeed, we shall experience in Wilhelmina's historic theatre, that to which you invite us in your book. Has the master told you that the burgomaster and a member of the town council were here? They arrived quite unexpectedly, bringing building plans with them and we had a remarkable day in Tribschen."

My brother was deeply affected by the letters of his friends, some of whom expressed greatest enthusiasm for his book, while others, although well disposed towards him, expressed pained surprise and professed to have had experienced the same "mild shivers" described by the reader of the Engelmann firm.

A fresh breakdown was the result of this strain, and for a time we feared a repetition of the condition of the previous year, but haply our fears proved groundless. But this made it necessary for my brother to decline another pressing invitation to Tribschen, which he could not have accepted in any case, owing to the pressure of work in connection with his forthcoming lectures on the *"Future of Our Educational Institutions."*

Wagner hardly knew how to explain my brother's conduct as he had fully expected him to hasten to Tribschen upon learning of the stormy admiration his book had aroused. Suspicious as he ever was, Wagner construed this to mean that my brother had already regretted having written the work, or at least, to having had it published. This is to be seen from the following letter:

Richard Wagner to Friedrich Nietzsche.

"My Friend:

"How difficult you make it for me to prove the delight I take in you. I was most painfully impressed by the news of your illness. You must forgive us for having frequently observed, and always with a feeling of the deepest anxiety, certain recurring symptoms, not in your growth, but in the fixation phases, so to speak, of your professional career, in so far as these have an effect upon your inner, soul life. From the beginning of our friendship, we have observed disquieting symptoms, of which it is true, you have frequently offered an explanation, but which have then repeated themselves at such regular intervals, as to arouse in our minds the most serious misgivings as to the possibility of maintaining our intimate and friendly intercourse.

"You have now given to the world a work which is unequalled. Every outside influence that has been brought to bear upon you, has been rendered practically negligible by the entire character of this work, and above all, your book is characterized by an assurance so consummate, as to betoken the most profound originality. In what other way could my wife and I have realized the most ardent wish of our lives, which was that some day something might come to us from without and take full possession of our hearts and souls! Each of us has read your book twice—once alone during the day, and then aloud in the evening. We fairly fight over the one copy and regret that the promised second one has not yet arrived. I must have it in order to get myself in the proper mood for working after breakfast, as I am again hard at work on the last act since reading your book. Whether alone or together, our reading is always punctuated by exclamations. For my part, I am still somewhat dazed by the thought of having been vouchsafed an experience of this kind. This is the way matters stand with us! Then we turn to you—and are consumed with anxiety! And just when the most remarkable suspicions have taken hold of us, and we have almost arrived at the conclusion that the publication of the book—if not, indeed, the entire conception of the same—had plunged you temporarily, at least, into a frame of mind strangely resembling regret—you suddenly break your long silence and inform us that you have been ill.

"These illnesses of yours have already caused us great

anxiety, not because they arouse any serious fears as to your physical condition but rather as to the state of your emotional life. If you would only reassure us by writing us a comforting word, or better still, by a visit, even though it be of necessity, a short one!

"Friend! What I am now saying to you is of such character that it can not be put away with a laughing assurance. You have a profound nature and there has been nothing in our intercourse which could lead you to believe that my own feelings are of a superficial character. I also understand you as you reveal yourself in the musical composition with which you so thoughtfully surprised us. It is difficult, however, for me to acquaint you with my sympathetic comprehension, and it is just because I feel conscious of this difficulty that I am all the more embarrassed in expressing myself.

"And furthermore, my friend, what could I say to you that you do not already know, and could say quite as well to yourself did you speak from your innermost consciousness? You see and perceive everything, so that it has been a hitherto undreamed-of delight to be permitted to see and perceive through your eyes.

"I have also gained a much better understanding of many things now engrossing your attention in connection with your vocation—for example, with your ideas in regard to pedagogy, some of which you had already intimated to me. Through you, I have gained a wide and sweeping perspective, and immeasurable vistas of promising activity open up before me—with you at my side!

"But you are ill! Are you also discouraged? If so, how gladly would I do something to dispel your despondency!

100

How shall I begin? Are you not satisfied with my unqualified praise? Did I feel compelled to doubt this, I should be, indeed, miserable! Nevertheless, I can do no other than lavish my praise upon you. Accept it, at least, in a friendly spirit, even though it leave you unsatisfied!

"Heartfelt greetings from
"Yours,
"Tribschen, Jan. 10, 1872.   RICHARD WAGNER."

In reply to this warm-hearted, but nevertheless, somewhat suspicious letter, Wagner received a truly touching reply from my brother, which as Wagner later said, "completely dispelled all doubts." Furthermore, my brother took pains to send copies of his book to all of Wagner's friends, among them Frau von Muchanoff, Baroness von Schleinitz, Liszt, Bülow, Richard Pohl and others, and this he most assuredly would not have done had he already regretted having published the work.

He made only one reservation and that was in the case of the king of Bavaria, to whom he did not wish to send a copy directly as Wagner had requested. His reason for this lay in his inherent feeling for style, which rebelled at the so-called "curial style of letter-writing." As children we had always been obliged to use this in writing to my father's former pupils, the Grand Duchess Constantine, the Grand Duchess of Oldenburg and Princess Therese of Altenburg, and it had ever been a source of intense irritation to my brother. However, Wagner found a way out of this difficulty and my brother was relieved of the necessity of writing this much-detested formal letter.

Richard Wagner to Friedrich Nietzsche.

"Dear friend:

"Just two words in regard to the 'green-gold tree of your life'! Have you still a few copies of your book on hand, and can you, or will you, in this case, intrust them to me for discreet distribution? If not, then I shall naturally apply to Fritzsch.

"After taking the matter into serious consideration, I would advise you not to write to the king personally, but to

> *Court Counsellor, L. Dufflipp,*
> *Court Secretary to His Majesty the King*

begging him to give the work to the king and referring to my communication in regard to the same. You will thus be spared the absurdity of using the curial style, the mere suggestion of which, in your case, makes me indignant.

We are rejoiced at the news of your recovery and also over the promised copies of your book which reached us safely. The 'register' filled me with alarm in all the dimensions of my innermost being.

" 'Der Menschheit ganzer Jammer fasst mich an' (Mankind's collected woe o'erwhelms me!)—etc. Come to us soon —quite unannounced—and convince yourself of our affection for you.

"Yours,

"Tribschen, Jan. 16, 1872.   RICHARD WAGNER."

On the sixteenth of January, my brother delivered the first of his two lectures on "*The Future of Our Educational Institutions,*" and met with tremendous success. "Emotion, enthusiasm and hate nicely combined."

After delivering this lecture he went over to Tribschen, where a truly royal welcome had been prepared for him. Upon his return to Basle, he was received by a delegation from the student corps, announcing that the university wished to give him an ovation in the shape of a torch-light procession as an expression of appreciation of his refusal to consider a call to the Greifswald university. Although he had discussed this matter with no one in Basle it had some-how leaked out, and his decision was received with great enthusiasm.

Instead, my brother recommended Erwin Rohde for the Greifswald post and in writing to his friend said: ". . . Great sympathy was created in Basle by my refusal to con-sider the position, despite my protestations that it was not in the nature of a formal call, but only a tentative feeler put out by the university board. Notwithstanding this, the student corps wished to organize a torch-light procession in my honor, intending thereby to express their appreciation of my Basle activities. However, I refused to be thus honored."

No one was more genuinely delighted at my brother's decision than Jakob Burckhardt, who had taken the greatest delight in the *"Birth of Tragedy"* and the *"Future of Our Educational Institutions."* Referring to this, Frau Cosima wrote: ". . . I imagine his opinion weighs more with you than that of any one else." And this was not far from the truth, as my brother placed a high value upon his inter-course with this eminent scholar, and the cordial reception accorded him when he came to Basle.

My brother became exceedingly "popular" in Basle that winter, public interest in him having been heightened by his

103

decision to remain at the university and by his two successful lectures. In writing of these lectures, he said: ". . . I am extremely well satisfied with the results; they attracted the most serious listeners, both men and women, and practically the best element among the student corps was always to be found in my lecture room."

Moreover he was fêted and feasted by the old patrician families of Basle, and during that winter he was often the only German to receive an invitation to the exclusive dinners and balls. He danced so energetically that, at the close of the season, he wrote us that his evening clothes were in so dilapidated a condition that he would be obliged to order a new suit for the approaching festivities in Bayreuth.

After reading the chapter which follows, disclosing, as it does, the inner conflicts and doubts with which my brother was struggling during this winter, the reader will be all the more surprised to find that he could maintain the character of a pleasure-loving young professor, delighting in nothing so much as a round of balls and dinners.

Nor must it be forgotten, that these conflicts were to lead to decisions directly connected with the fate and fortunes of his dearest friends, and that he was made both proud and arrogant at the thought of being permitted to stake his very existence for these friends.

CHAPTER XI.

BY the end of January my brother found himself plunged into the inner conflicts to which reference has been made. Wagner had been called to Berlin by the news that some well-wisher in that city had conceived the idea of collecting the sum of 200,000 thalers, in order that work might be begun at once on the Festival Theatre and Wagner's own residence in Bayreuth without delaying matters until funds for this purpose had been raised by the Wagner Society.

I beg to be forgiven should I make any mistake on this point, but I am relying entirely upon what was told me later by Baron von Gersdorff, who was well informed on everything that took place at that time.

It was with great reluctance that Wagner accepted this invitation to Berlin, as he placed but little confidence in the proposed plan and was, moreover, deep in the third act of his *"Götterdämmerung."* On his way to Berlin, he stopped off in Basle and poured out his heart to my brother, indulging in passionate complaint of the cares and anxieties by which he was oppressed. During this conversation, many hitherto concealed causes for dejection came to the surface, one of them being that "everything rested upon his shoulders" and that he "had no one upon whom he could depend in

105

such matters," etc. My brother was shaken to the depths of his being at the sight of the suffering of the beloved master and he did everything he could to console and encourage him. Strangely enough, my brother had faith in the fantastic proposition that had come from Berlin, and had he been free to follow the promptings of his own heart, would have preferred to have accompanied Wagner on his journey. But as this was out of the question, he wrote to his friend Gersdorff, saying: ". . . You will be surprised to see Wagner suddenly appear in Berlin. I implore you to *do*, and to *see*, and to *feel* everything that could be of the slightest service to him in this momentous matter. I transfer to you my own feelings for him during the period of his Berlin visit, and charge you to act, in every instance, as I would were I there."

Gersdorff entirely fulfilled my brother's confidence in him and Wagner telegraphed: "The Alexandrian Gersdorff has made himself indispensable to me!" (Gersdorff lived at Alexander Platz in Berlin.) Highly gratified, my brother wrote his friend: "Whatever you do, bear in mind, that we two are called upon to fight in the front ranks of a cultural movement the full significance of which will not be revealed to the larger masses of the public until the next generation, possibly not until a much later period. Let this thought fill us with pride; let it give us courage. On the whole, I have always felt that we were not born into this world to be happy but simply to perform our duty, and we may consider ourselves thrice blessed if we know and realize just where this duty lies."

"*Duty*" was always the first and most solemn consideration with my brother. But was it really his duty to throw everything overboard—his position and his life work—in order the better to consecrate his strength and talents to Richard Wagner and *his* life work?

In the following letter is to be found my brother's answer to this question, as he here gives the first direct intimation of his readiness to sacrifice everything for the beloved master:

Friedrich Nietzsche to Richard Wagner.

"My revered master:

"Scarcely an hour has elapsed since you left Basle and a letter is already on the way to your wife, so that I have hopes of the good news reaching her by tomorrow morning.

"It seems to me that the moment has come for tightening up the bow so long unstrung. But must this task also fall upon you! Must everything rest upon your shoulders! I feel that my present existence is a reproach and I ask you frankly if you can make use of my services. Aside from this inquiry, I know of nothing worth reporting at the moment, but many things, *very many things* that are worth wishing for and hoping for, my honored master.

"Faithfully yours,

"Basle, Wednesday.   FRIEDRICH NIETZSCHE."

Wagner had ignored an earlier suggestion of this sort, partly because he liked the idea of having a university professor as an intimate friend, and partly out of genuine fatherly interest in my brother and reluctance to tear him away from his own life work. But now that the Bayreuth idea had begun to assume a concrete shape, the situation passed into a new phase, and Emil Heckel of Mannheim had earnestly advised Wagner to send some friend of the cause on a lecture tour throughout Germany. In view of the tremendous enthusiasm always created by my brother's lectures, and the added prestige he now enjoyed by reason of the publication of his *"Birth of Tragedy,"* Wagner was convinced that only Nietzsche could succeed in awakening the public to a clear understanding of the Bayreuth idea, and the plans by which it was to be carried into fulfillment. And as we have seen, my brother was ready to make this sacrifice and strike the death-knell of his own professional career. Just imagine what this meant at a time when he had finally succeeded in compelling the respect and recognition of academic circles in Basle!

It was not without a heavy heart that my brother decided upon taking this step, but believing that he was nearer to the beloved master than anyone else, he felt under the strongest obligations to sacrifice everything for Wagner's cause. Under the stress of these feelings, he wrote to Rohde: "Why do we live so far apart? For it is impossible for me to say to you in a letter all that is on my heart today and tell you of my plans for the future. I have formed an alliance with Wagner. You can have no idea how close we are to one another and how all our plans coincide.

"I have been obliged to listen to such incredible things about my book that I shall say nothing more about it. . . . What do you think about the whole matter? In view of all the things I have heard, I am made deeply sensible of the gravity of the situation, and can form a clear idea of the fate of all the other things I have in mind. On the whole, life is not going to be an easy matter with me."

Wagner was in high spirits when he returned to Tribschen

and one of his first letters was to my brother, and from this it is to be seen that the intimations he had made while in Basle were really an expression of his innermost hopes and wishes, but that his affectionate interest in my brother made him hesitate about accepting this supreme sacrifice.

Richard Wagner to Friedrich Nietzsche.

"My dear friend:

"As your letter was the first to greet me upon my arrival in Berlin, you shall now be the recipient of my first greetings upon my return to Tribschen (at noon today). I am fairly frightened at having made myself so plainly understood that day in Basle.

"Gersdorff will have told you everything as he was fully informed in regard to all that was taking place. Of Bayreuth, however, he knows nothing. Gratifying marks of esteem were bestowed upon me there, and I now realize clearly that as far as the material side of the undertaking is concerned, Bayreuth will prove to be one of the happiest inspirations of my life. If I could only talk this over with you!

"Everything has been arranged in the most satisfactory manner, and my régime has been inaugurated.

"You offered me your services and I shall now proceed to take immediate advantage of this offer. I am confronted by many days of the most complicated correspondence. Come to my aid. Request Fritzsch *in my name* to fill the following order:

"1 *'Birth'* to Dean Dittmar.

"1 'Ditto' to Rector Grossmann.

further—1 *'German Art and Politics'* to Councillor of the Consistory, Herr Krausse.

"1 'Ditto' to Professor Fries.

"All of them to Bayreuth.

"Everything at my expense.

"Further!——

"Friend, I have no connections at all with the *Augsburg Allg. Z.* The *Nord. Allg.* is at our disposal. Would it be agreeable to you to send Rohde to them?

"Have I made myself clear? I am very tired today after the night trip. Tomorrow I have to make arrangements for the *'Ninth Symphony,'* and this will require the writing of something like 10 letters. The date is fixed for the twenty-second of May. Nothing remains to be done but to look about for the 'elite' orchestra.

"I am very happy today and announce this to you, first of all, dear friend.

"Many cordial greetings from

"Yours,

"Lucerne, Evening of Feb. 5.   RICHARD WAGNER."

Wagner's hesitation about accepting the sacrifice my brother was ready to make had caused the projected tour in Germany to be indefinitely postponed. But now my brother conceived the idea of making this plan serve a double purpose, by having Rohde appointed as his substitute during the winter semester in Basle; the latter would be relieved from his irksome duties as lecturer at a Germany university, and at the same time my brother would be free to conduct the propaganda for the Wagnerian cause. He was highly elated at the thought of being able to serve two friends at once.

On the face of it, the Berlin proposition looked very promising, and Wagner set out for Bayreuth to confer with Feustel, the banker, and burgomaster Muncker, and to get everything in readiness for the festivities connected with the ceremony of laying the cornerstone set for the twenty-second of May. But it soon became evident that the entire Berlin scheme was illusory and that in consequence it would be injudicious to mature plans for the preliminary festival. Wagner conducted himself admirably even in the face of this bitter disappointment. This capacity of his to bear failure and disappointment with fortitude, his tenacity of purpose, his unshaken belief in himself and his cause, the intrepid, courageous and dignified manner in which he met discouragements—were all qualities which so endeared the master to my brother. Wagner will ever remain an inspiring example for those who have high ambitions and ideals. It is a matter of indifference as to whether all the paths he trod in his efforts to achieve this goal were wholly commendable or not, as such things must not be weighed by common standards. It was only Wagner's staunch belief in himself, which induced men like Heckel, Feustel and Muncker—men accustomed to looking facts squarely in the face, in the transactions of everyday life—to espouse his cause and patiently endeavor to remove all the obstacles to the realization of the Bayreuth idea. It may not be amiss to say here that my brother and I always had the greatest admiration for these men who thus clung to Wagner through thick and thin.

With the transference of his interests to Bayreuth, Wagner began to feel the necessity of abandoning his beloved

111

Tribschen and resuming his proper place in the world. Soon came the leave-taking from the spot, which my brother always called the "enchanted isle" and the magic of which clung to him through life.

Upon arriving in Tribschen one day in the early spring, my brother found Frau Cosima deep in the task of packing. While she moved from one room to another, he sat at the piano, weaving into his improvisations all his grief, his inexpressible hopes and fears, his precious memories and the acute realization that something irretrievable was being taken from his life. The strains, now jubilant, now mournful, echoed through the dismantled rooms, conjuring up ghosts of past joys and sorrows.

Many years later, after there had been a complete rupture in their relations, Frau Wagner often referred to the fascinating and beautiful fantasy which she called my brother's "Farewell to Tribschen." Writing to Baron von Gersdorff, my brother said: "Last Saturday I performed the melancholy duty of taking leave of Tribschen. We walked about as if we were in the midst of ruins, the air was heavy with emotion, the dog refused to eat, and the servants broke into unrestrained weeping every time they were addressed. Together, we packed the manuscripts, the books and letters—ah, it was all so inexpressibly sad!

"What would my life have been without these three years spent within reach of Tribschen, where I made twenty-three visits! Without them, what would I have been! I am made happy by the thought of having crystallized the Tribschen world in my book."

Did this little volume bear the title of "Richard Wagner and Friedrich Nietzsche at the Zenith of their Friendship", it would have to close here, as my brother's deepest feelings for Wagner were always associated with Tribschen, although the following year, 1872, was also included in the Tribschen period. With a mournful attempt at a joke, he said later: "Bayreuth did not begin for me until the year 1873."

But the title is more comprehensive and stretches over the period of the decline in the friendship of the two men, a period which my brother always characterized by the one word *"Bayreuth."*

Nowhere can we obtain a better idea of the high place Tribschen held in my brother's affections, than in the passage from his *"Ecce Homo"*, quoted in the foreword to this book: "In speaking here of the vivifying influences of my life, I feel that I must express my gratitude for that which, above all other things, has refreshed me most heartily and profoundly. This, unquestionably, was my intimate intercourse with Richard Wagner. All my other relationships with men I treat quite lightly but at no price would I have blotted from my life those days spent at Tribschen, those days of mutual confidence, of cheerfulness, of sublime flashes—of *profound* moments. . . . I do not know the experiences others may have had with Richard Wagner, I only know that no cloud ever crossed *our* Heaven."

And this is quite true, as the clouds of misunderstanding did not appear until after Wagner had taken up his residence in Bayreuth and were not clearly discernible until the year 1873.

After the agitation and anxiety connected with the first Festival, which as the world knows, fell far short of the beautiful anticipations, Frau Cosima looked back upon the Tribschen days with a feeling of melancholy regret, and as late as New Year's 1877 she wrote: "Just think of it, Richter spent twenty-four hours of his three-days' holiday with us, saying that he could no longer endure the separation. On New Year's Eve, we reviewed our entire life at Tribschen, sometimes with laughter, sometimes with tears. We recalled your visits and we found that not even the Festival had succeeded in banishing from our affection the charm of this blessed asylum, which in retrospect seems to us a veritable Paradise Lost."

CHAPTER XII.

SHORTLY after the departure of the family from Trib-schen, the ceremonies connected with the laying of the cornerstone of the Festival Theatre took place in Bayreuth. The date of this memorable event was May 22, 1872, but several days earlier there was a foregathering of the faithful supporters of the cause, in this vanguard being the select few who had devoted themselves wholly and passionately to Wagner and the art-work of the future. Among them were Baroness von Schleinitz, Frau von Muchanoff, Countess Krokow, Fräulein von Meysenburg, Countess Döhnhoff (whom my brother found particularly charming) and all the distinguished men who had been active in contributing to the success of the Bayreuth undertaking.

It goes without saying that my brother's friends, Gersdorff and Rohde were also present; in fact, I was the only one of the circle missing as, in a fit of generosity, I had given my seat to Gustav Krug, one of my brother's boyhood's friends.

There was a tremendous and quite unexpected rush and the little rococo theatre could by no means accommodate the crowd. A general introduction of Wagner's friends took place at the final rehearsal of Beethoven's *Ninth Symphony*, and as Rohde jokingly remarked, my brother was taken

115

about and exhibited like some showy *plat de jour*, which my brother amended by saying: "No, we were both on display!" The truth of the matter was that Wagner was very proud of the two, always introducing them as: "My friends, the two university professors!" (Rohde had just been made professor at the university of Kiel.)

It was on this occasion that my brother also made the acquaintance of Wagner's old friend, Matilda von Meysenburg and this was the beginning of a warm friendship. In her book, *"The Letters of an Idealist,"* Fräulein von Meysenburg gives a charming description of this meeting: "During one of the pauses of the final rehearsal, Frau Wagner brought a young man up to me whom she introduced as 'Herr Nietzsche.' Thrilled with joy, I exclaimed: 'Not *the* Herr Nietzsche' whereupon they both laughed and Frau Wagner said: 'Yes, *the* Nietzsche.'

"At last I was given an opportunity of supplementing the striking mental picture I had already formed of this young man, by a still more vivid impression of a handsome presence and agreeable personality; we were speedily on the best of terms."

This memorable twenty-second of May began with a steady downpour, but despite these discouraging conditions, the ceremony of the cornerstone laying was most impressive. In their great enthusiasm the assembled guests forgot the discomfort of the situation and arose to a mood of genuine elation. What must have been Wagner's feelings on this occasion? My brother believed that he possessed the key to his thoughts when four years later, he wrote:

"When on that dismal and cloudy day in May the cornerstone had been lowered into place on the wooded heights be-

yond Bayreuth, under an overshadowed sky and amid a
downpour of rain, a few of us were permitted to drive back to
town with Wagner. He was silent during the entire drive
and there was an indescribable look in his eyes as of one who
has turned his gaze deeply inward. On this day he entered
upon his sixtieth year and his whole past now appeared as
but a preparation for this moment. It is a recognized fact
that in times of extraordinary danger or in all decisive
moments of their lives, men see the remotest as well as the
most recent events of their career with singular vividness.
With one rapid inward glance, they obtained a sort of pan-
orama of a whole span of years in which every experience is
depicted with the greatest fidelity. What, for instance,
must Alexander the Great have seen as he let Asia and
Europe drink from the same goblet? What this self-scrutiny
meant to Wagner on that day—how he visualized his past,
his present and his future—can only be comprehended by
those of us who stand nearest to him, and this only up to a
certain point. Only if we have this Wagnerian vision will
we be enabled to understand his great work and *by the aid of
this understanding, to guarantee its productiveness.*"

The evening performance of the *"Ninth Symphony"* was a
wonderful success. The entire audience was carried away
by enthusiasm for the artist and his work, all were inspired
by the most beautiful hopes for the future, and were made to
feel as if they were participating in the sunrise of a glorious
day containing the promise of a new and triumphant German
culture.

The air was filled with vague memories of Bayreuth's
past glory, and Wagner himself has best described the mixed
emotions of the festival audience assembled on that spring

117

evening in Bayreuth: "Who among those present on that occasion could shake off the thought of past days when the margravian court and its guests, with the great Frederick himself as the oustanding figure—was assembled in this historic house to witness a ballet, or to listen to an Italian opera or a French comedy? Now this selfsame house resounded with the strains of the marvellous *Ninth Symphony* given by *German* musicians gathered together from all the quarters of the fatherland to assist in this festival. From the tribunes where once the gold-laced trumpeters blew a mighty fanfare announcing the arrival of the royal suite, there now arose the voices of distinguished German soloists, calling out to the assembled guests: *'Embrace, ye millions!'*

"Stimulated by this experience, was there any one present who did not have before his eyes a stirring vision of the ultimate triumph of the German spirit?"

In his private correspondence, my brother has left on record the powerful impression made upon him by the *Ninth Symphony*, quite apart from all the external circumstances connected with this historic performance:

"The opening movement strikes the keynote of passion and its course. Without a moment's respite, the music surges forward on its journey through forests and chasms and Nature's prodigious phenomena. In the distance is heard the roar of a waterfall, thundering out an overpowering rhythm as it leaps in mighty bounds, to the valley below.

"We are given a breathing spell in the second movement, (a moment for self-contemplation and self-judgment) and above all our wanderings and our eager, hot pursuits, our eyes catch a vision of eternal rest, smiling upon us blissfully and yet mournfully.

118

"The third movement is a moment snatched from passion in its highest flights. Its course lies under the stars, agitated, comet-like, an *ignis fatuus*, ghost-like, malevolent, a sort of aberration, an inner flickering fire, a fatiguing, exhausting pressing forward, without love or without hope, at times almost mockingly coarse, like a spirit hovering over graves without being able to find a resting place.

"And then the fourth movement! A heart-breaking cry, the soul is no longer able to bear its burden, no longer able to endure the unceasing transports of passion. Even the vision of eternal rest is rudely pushed aside and the soul agonizes, it suffers inexpressible torture. Now it recognizes the curse laid upon it by this soul-solitude, this soul-isolation, for even the immortality of the individual is nothing more than a curse. It is then that a human voice is heard speaking to the lonely soul, as to all lonely souls, and exhorting it to return to the friends and joys of the multitude. This is the burden of its song! At last the song of universal human passion bursts in stormily with its full impetus, reaching heights which it would never have been able to attain had not the passion of the solitary, onrushing individual been of such terrific force.

"Sympathy joins hands with passion, not by way of contrast, but rather as an effect resulting from this cause."

I doubt very much if any one else present experienced the same ardent and passionate feelings in listening to Beethoven's masterpiece as did my brother.

The three friends left Bayreuth filled with solemn resolves and soon thereafter my brother wrote to Gersdorff: ". . . Ah, my friend, we know what we have experienced! No one can rob us of these sacred and inspiring memories. We must

119

go through life solaced by them and, if needs be, fighting for them, but above all, in everything that we do, we must endeavor to prove ourselves serious and high-minded, that we may be deemed worthy of the profound honors and experiences vouchsafed to us."

In the meantime, the *"Birth of Tragedy"* had aroused the most varied and conflicting sentiments throughout academic circles in Germany. The work created the greatest enthusiasm in Wagnerian circles, and Hans von Bülow was also delighted with it as is shown by a passage from one of my brother's letters:

". . . Hans von Bülow, whom I had never met, called upon me here and asked me to accept the dedication of his translation of Leopardi, with which he occupied himself during his leisure hours in Italy. He is so enthusiastic about my work that he travels around with numerous copies to be distributed among his friends."

As may be imagined, my brother was placed in a most embarrassing position by this visit from Hans von Bülow (the first husband of Frau Cosima) occurring, as it did, just at the time when the friendship between Wagner and my brother was at its height. Bülow perceived this at once, and, at the close of their conversation in regard to the *"Birth of Tragedy"*, sought to dispel my brother's embarrassment by voluntarily alluding to the subject of his relations with Wagner and Frau Cosima. He drew the following picture: Cosima was *Ariadne*, he himself was *Theseus*, and Wagner was *Dionysius;* but like all analogies this one also had a weak spot, as in this case *Theseus* had not deserted *Ariadne*, but just the reverse. Bülow, evidently, wished to convey the idea that he had been superseded by a higher being, by a god.

My brother was delighted beyond measure to hear **Bülow** thus investing his own experiences with such an impersonal and mythical character, even though he was not spared a number of Bülow's caustic criticisms of the two beloved friends.

Matilda von Meysenburg has given us a detailed description of her first impressions of the *"Birth of Tragedy"*, as it was her interest in this book that drew forth her delighted exclamation at the time she met my brother face to face, in Bayreuth:

". . . While I was living in Florence in the year 1872, I received a letter from Frau Cosima Wagner calling my attention to a newly-published work from the pen of a young professor at the university of Basle, who, she said, was an intimate friend of the Wagner family then living at Tribschen on Lake Lucerne. The title of this book was '*The Birth of Tragedy Out of the Spirit of Music,*' and the author's name was *Friedrich Nietzsche.*

"Just at that time, I was surrounded by a small circle of highly intelligent friends and we at once began reading the book aloud, our enthusiasm growing as we read. The light thrown upon the two fundamental elements of Greek life, which the author characterized by the names: *Dionysian* and *Apollonian,* disclosed a wealth of inspiring ideas upon this subject, among them being the thought that the Dionysian (the essence of the world 'per se') whose native language is music, generates the art-work of tragedy from the beauty of the Apollonian spirit.

". . . We also learned that Nietzsche was a profoundly scholarly philologian and had been recommended to the university of Basle as professor in ordinary when quite a young man by Professor Ritschl, himself one of Germany's foremost philologians. What attracted us even more than the erudition of this young scholar, who displayed an astonishing familiarity with the classics, was the intellectual depth and poetry of his conceptions, the presaging vision of the poetical soul, which grasped the inner truth of things with the vision of the seer, whereas the pedantic dry-as-dust scholar would have seized hold of the outer husk and believed it to be the inner kernel. It was a genuine delight to feel that such a powerful personality, and at the same time a man of scholarly attainments and a highly endowed creative spirit, should be devoted to the great work now in preparation in Bayreuth under the personal direction of Richard Wagner."

But an ominous silence reigned in philological circles, where, with a few notable exceptions, my brother's ideas were completely misunderstood. The interested reader will find all the details of this question discussed in the big Nietzsche biography as well as in *"The Young Nietzsche."*

Professor Ritschl was one of the few who wrote a letter to my brother, touching in its leniency of judgment. As a matter of fact, this work had also compromised him in the mind of the public, as he had pronounced my brother to be his foremost pupil, thus making himself, to a certain extent, responsible for the fundamental ideas therein contained. How little these ideas were comprehended, may be judged by the pronouncement of one eminent university professor, who dismissed the book as a piece of "absolute rubbish." Ritschl and the good Jakob Burckhardt seemed to be the only ones who surmised something of the real significance of the book. Writing to Rohde, my brother said: "This man (Jakob

Burckhardt) who will have nothing to do with anything philosophical, particularly anything relating to art-philosophy (my own included!) is so fascinated by the apprehension of the Greek character revealed in this book, that he meditates upon it day and night, and in a thousand details, furnishes me with an example of the most fruitful historical adaptation; I shall have much to learn in regard to the cultural history of the Greeks during his summer lecture course, in fact, more than ever, now that I know in what familiar and native soil these fruits have been grown."

Jakob Burckhardt added a special chapter dealing with the marvellous phenomenon bearing the name Dionysian to his work on "*The Culture of the Greeks*", having instantly recognized that this phenomenon, newly perceived, and in a sense, discovered by my brother—would prove an invaluable aid to the understanding of the "still richer, yea, self-exulting Hellenic instinct."

The thick-headed philologians grumbled and waxed indignant at what they considered to be an unclassifiable book published by one of their own colleagues and yet not intended for them. This indignation grew until, finally, the offended German philology arose in the person of the youthful Dr. Ulrich von Willamowitz who came out with a scathing pamphlet addressed to the: "*Philology of the Future: An Answer to 'The Birth of Tragedy' by Friedrich Nietzsche, Professor in Ordinary at the University of Basle.*" This malevolent attack made upon my brother was, in reality, directed against Ritschl, whose many enemies at the Berlin university had undoubtedly prompted young Willamowitz to write the pamphlet. Later, when we came to know the true facts in the case, we were inclined to regard this as a piece of youthful bravado on the part of Willamowitz, and more particularly so, as it was in direct contradiction to the latter's personal admiration for my brother. But, at the time, all of our friends were highly incensed and Rohde immediately announced his intention of taking up the cudgels for my brother. He was anticipated, however, by Wagner who was the first to take up his pen in defense of the work; this he did by writing a circular letter, printed in the "*Norddeutsche Allgemeine Zeitung.*" As this communication may be considered fairly representative of Wagner's own viewpoint at that time, it is reproduced in full in the following chapter.

CHAPTER XIII.

"Esteemed friend:

"I have just finished reading the pamphlet you sent me
written by Dr. Phil. Ulrich von Willamowitz-Moellendorff,
and this reply to your *Birth of Tragedy Out of the Spirit
of Music*' has created certain impressions of which I should
like to relieve my mind by propounding, to you a few questions, which you may deem of a surprising character. I do
this in the hope of moving you to an explanatory answer,
and one as stimulating as your discussion of Greek tragedy.

"First of all, I should like to ask you to explain an educational phenomenon which I have observed in my own case. At
the time I was attending the Kreuz-Schule in Dresden, no
boy could have had greater enthusiasm for classical antiquity
than myself; although it was Greek mythology and history
which interested me most deeply, I also felt strongly drawn
to the study of the Greek language, to such an extent, in
fact, that I was almost rebellious in my efforts to shirk my
Latin tasks. It is impossible for me to judge whether or
not my case was a normal one, but I may be pardoned for
referring to the fact that my favorite master at the Kreuz-
Schule, Dr. Sillig—still living, I hope—was so gratified

125

with my enthusiasm for the classics, that he strongly urged me to adopt philology as my profession. I likewise remember well how my later teachers at the Nikolai and Thomas schools in Leipzig, succeeded in rooting out these tastes and inclinations, and I find no difficulty in explaining this when I reflect upon the general policy of these masters. As time went on, I began to entertain serious doubts as to whether these tastes and inclinations had ever taken strong hold upon me, as they seemed to degenerate rapidly into those of an entirely different character. It was only during my period of later development, that I began to grow conscious of the fact that the regular outcropping of these inclinations, indicated that something had been stifled in me by a fatal system of schooling. Again and again, amid the most absorbing tasks of a life entirely removed from these studies, the only way by which I seemed to be able to gain a breath of freedom, was by plunging into this antique world, however much I was now handicapped by having well-nigh forgotten the language. On the other hand, while envying Mendelssohn his philological fluency, I could but wonder why this philological knowledge had not prevented him from writing his music to the dramas of Sophocles, since I, despite my ignorance, had more respect for the spirit of antiquity than he seemed to display. I have also known a number of other musicians, who could make no use of their knowledge of Greek in their composing and music-making in general, whereas I, strange to say, had worked out an ideal for my musical viewpoints, despite my restricted intercourse with the antique. Be that as it may, I only know there arose in me the vague feeling that the real spirit of the antique was as little apprehended by the average teacher of Greek, for

126

example, as a genuine appreciation of French history and culture is to be presupposed on the part of our French masters.

"But now comes Dr. Phil. U. W. von Moellendorf with the statement that it is the serious aim of scientific philology to inculcate into the mind of the German youth the idea that 'classical antiquity vouchsafes the one and only *Imperishable*, containing a promise of the favor of the muses in its absolute purity and fullness. It is this alone which can imbue the soul with the *Substance*, and the mind with the *Form*'!

"Still thrilled by this magnificent apostrophe of his pamphlet, I look about me in the newly-created German Empire, in search of the blessings resulting from the cultivation of this philological science; these blessings should surely be manifest, for hedged in by their own inviolability, they have hitherto trained our German youth on principles none dared to question. First of all, I was struck by the fact that every one among us who lays claim to the favor of the muses, and this includes practically our whole artistic and poetic world, jogs along without recourse to philology. At all events, that thorough-going knowledge of the languages, which should be made the basis of all classical studies pursued by the philologists, does not seem to have extended its functions to the correct treatment of our German mother tongue. The ever-growing tendency to employ a luxuriant jargon which manifests itself in our newspapers and from there spreads to the works of our writers on art and literature, will soon necessitate racking one's brains every time one writes a word, in order to determine whether this word belongs rightfully to German etymology, or has been borrowed from a Wisconsin stock market report. But however dark things look in the field of belles-lettres, the objection could always be advanced that this had nothing to do with philology, as this branch of science had pledged her services less to the artistic muses than to the scientific. In that case, should we not expect to find her influence manifested among the faculties of our higher educational institutions? Theologians, jurists, and the men of the medical profession, however, deny having anything to do with philology. If this be true, then the philologians will have no one to instruct but each other, presumably for the purpose of turning out more and more philologians—that is to say, more gymnasium masters and university professors, who in turn, will bake a fresh batch of gymnasium teachers and university professors. This I can understand; the idea being to preserve the science in all its purity, and not only to inculcate a profound respect for this science upon the state, but also to bind upon her conscience the necessity of making adequate provision for the salaries of philological incumbents.

"But no! Dr. Phil. U. W. v. M. expressly states that the chief thing should be the training of our German youth by all kinds of 'ascetic processes to attain that one *Imperishable,* promising the favor of the muses.' So, after all, philology must have a high aim and one that strives towards productive culture. This much is to be assumed— at least, so it seems to me. However, this tendency seems to be in danger of complete disintegration as a result of the peculiar process in her present discipline. One thing is evident, and that is, philological science at the present time exerts no influence whatever upon the general conditions of

German culture, whereas on the other hand, the theological faculty supplies us with parsons and prelates; the faculty of jurisprudence with lawyers and judges, the medical faculty with doctors—all of them practical and useful citizens. Philology furnishes us with nothing but philologists who are not of the slightest use to any one but their own little circle. It may be seen from this that the Brahmins of India were not of a more exalted and exclusive rank than our philologians, and that, therefore, we are justified in expecting a word of inspiration from them from time to time, and of a truth, that is precisely what we do expect; we are awaiting the man who shall step down from this marvellous sphere, and without employing erudite terms and terrifying quotations, tell us laymen just what it is that the initiated perceive behind the veil of their incomprehensible researches, and whether it is worth while to maintain so expensive a caste. But we expect of this revelation that it must be something very great, very elevating, and something well worth cultivating, and not merely this elegant tinkling of cymbals with which they seek to satisfy us from time to time, in their popular lectures to 'mixed' audiences. This great and elevating something for which we are waiting, seems to be very difficult of utterance; it almost seems as if a peculiar, uncanny apprehension had taken hold of these gentlemen and aroused the fear that by dispensing with all the mysterious attributes of philological consequentiality, and with all quotations, annotations and fitting mutual felicitations between greater and lesser colleagues—in other words, by letting the light of day illumine the dark recesses, they would thereby be disclosing the depressing poverty to which this particular science had degenerated.

"I can imagine that for any one attempting such a thing, nothing would remain but to stretch forth a hand and forciby seize upon revivifying forces from the inexhaustible fountain-heads of human knowledge, which have, hitherto, waited in vain to be revivified by philology. Any philologian who determined to do anything of this kind would experience the same treatment you are now receiving, valued friend, since deciding to publish your profound treatise on the genesis of tragedy. At the first glance, it was plain to be seen that we had to do here with a philologian who was addressing himself to us and not to his colleagues; for this reason, our hearts beat high, and we regained our courage, completely lost by reading the customary philological dissertations upon Homer, the tragic poets and the like, filled with quotations and empty as to content. This time we had a text but no annotations! Standing on the mountain top, we looked across the spreading plains without fear of being disturbed by the drunken brawls of the peasants down below. But it seems as if we were not to be left in peaceful possession of our acquisition, as philology stoutly maintains that your feet are still firmly planted on her soil, and that therefore, you are not emancipated, but merely an apostate, and that neither you nor any of the rest of us are to be spared a sound cudgelling with annotations. As a matter of fact, the hailstorm has already broken; a Dr. Phil. has hurled regular philological thunderbolts. Fortunately, such storms are of short duration at this time of the year, and so long as one is raging, all sensible persons remain under cover, just as one gives wide berth to an enraged bull. We agree with Socrates in thinking that it is absurd to reply to the hoof of an ass with the toe of a man, and yet, an explanation is

130

due those of us who have followed the trend of events without being able to understand fully just what it is all about. Therefore, I now address myself to you!

"We had not believed that so much rudeness could be committed in the 'service of the muses,' nor that their 'favor' produced such a lamentable lack of polish, as we here perceive in one who claims to possess 'that only imperishable.' Now those who, like ourselves, know nothing of philology, are disposed to defer to the statements of such a man, particularly when these statements are supported by such a formidable array of quotations from the archives of the guild; but we are plunged into direct doubt, not so much by that scholar's wilful non-understanding of your essay, but rather by his inability to understand the very simplest arguments. We refer here to the passage where he attributes to you an optimistic meaning in your quotation from Goethe: '*Behold thy world. A world indeed!*' and indignant with you at not understanding your '*Faust*' better, deems it necessary to explain to you that 'Faust is speaking ironically.'

"What name shall we give this? A question not easy to answer in a communication intended for public consumption. For my own part, such an experience as the one gained from the case in question, is most disheartening. You will remember how zealously I advocated the study of the classics some years ago, in my essay on '*German Art and German Policy*,' and how I predicted a progressive deterioration of our national culture as a result of the ever-increasing neglect of these studies on the part of our artists and writers.

"But what does it serve a man if he give himself infinite pains to acquire philological knowledge? From the studies

131

of J. Grimm I took an early '*Heilawac*,' remodeled it into a '*Weiawaga*' (a form met with today in the world 'Weihwasser') to make it more adaptable for my purpose; I then derived from it the nearly related roots of 'wogen' and 'wiegen,' 'wollen' and 'wallen' and thus built up a root-syllabic melody for my Rhine Maidens something after the analogy of the 'Eia popeia' of our nursery rhymes. What was the result? I am hooted to the very doors of the *Allgemeine Zeitung* by our journalistic street arabs, and it upon this 'proverbial wigala weia,' as he is pleased to call it—that a learned Dr. Phil. now bases his contempt for my so-called poetry.

"Of a truth, my friend, you owe us a word or two of explanation! And by '*we*' I mean those of us who entertain the gravest fear for the future of *German culture*. These fears are increased by a knowledge of the singularly high regard foreigners have for this culture, with the early budding of which they have only recently become acquainted. Unquestionably each nation has its own germ of cretinism. In the case of the French we find their absinthe finishing what the *Academie* began, to wit, an absurd attitude of childish ridicule of everything not immediately understood, and therefore, excluded by the *Academie* from the national scheme of culture. It is true that with us, Philology has not yet acquired the *power* of the *Academie*, nor is our beer so dangerous as absinthe; but the Germans possess other qualities, such as envy and the correspondingly mischievous spitefulness, allied to a degree of insincerity, which is all the more pernicious because it wears the mask of old-time sturdiness. These qualities are so pernicious that they might easily rank as substitutes for the poisons we have not.

Circular Letter from Richard Wagner

"*How do matters stand with our German educational institutions?* This question we address to you in particular, singled out as you were at an early age, by a distinguished master of philology to occupy a university chair where your laurels were so rapidly won as to embolden you to step out from this vicious circle and with a hand truly creative, point out its shortcomings.

"We do not mean to hurry you! No pressure will be brought to bear upon you, least of all by that Doctor of Philosophy who politely invites you to vacate your chair, a thing you most assuredly have no intention of doing merely to oblige this gentleman, and even should you do so, there is not the slightest likelihood of his being chosen to succeed you in the place where you have worked. That which we expect from you can only be the lifetime task of a man sorely needed in high places, a man such as you have shown yourself to be to all those who ask enlightenment from the noblest wellsprings of the German spirit, from the profound seriousness by which it is permeated—as to the form to be taken by German culture if it is ever to help the re-born nation to achieve its noblest aims and aspirations.

"Heartfelt greetings from,   Yours,

"Bayreuth, June 12, 1872.   RICHARD WAGNER."

CHAPTER XIV.

IT is greatly to be deplored that the letter in which my brother expressed his gratitude for Wagner's defense of his work should also have been among those destroyed. He had feared that Wagner, out of affection for him, might write in such a way as would tend to make his position in the academic world even more difficult, but happily, the circular letter turned out far more discreet and diplomatic than my brother had expected. On the other hand, Wagner frankly admitted that Nietzsche had injured himself by espousing the Wagnerian cause, and regarded his article as having done nothing to improve the situation, but had rather made matters worse. Expression is given to these fears in Wagner's reply to my brother's letter of thanks:

Richard Wagner to Friedrich Nietzsche.

"O friend!

"You really cause me nothing but anxiety at present, and this is just because I think so much of you! Strictly speaking, you are the one and only gain life has brought me so far, aside from my beloved wife. Fortunately, Fidi has now been added to my blessings, but there is a gap between us which only you can fill—something like the relationship of a son

134

to a grandchild. I have no anxiety about Fidi, but I am greatly concerned about you and in so far, about Fidi also. This concern is of a rather commonplace character. I wish for nothing so much as your physical wellbeing, since everything else seems to be now assured. Day after day, I have carefully re-read the '*Birth*,' and at each reading, I say to myself: 'If he only regains his health and keeps it, and if everything goes well with him in other ways—*for things must not go wrong with him.*' How gladly would one do something to help matters along!

"This has set me to thinking anew as to how a beginning could best be made, and it this uncertainty which causes my anxiety. But:—hold out a little longer and sooner or later, the right way is bound to be found. I should have unbounded confidence and my fears would be turned into hopes, could I only hear that you had the proper amount of confidence in yourself, that you are encouraged about your health, and that you are in good spirits.

"I have not been able to find anything in my 'letters' to indicate that I have blazed a path for you (as you say) but, on the contrary, it seems to me as if I had done nothing but hang an additional burden about your neck. Nor did I mean to say that it was necessary for you to 'ripen' for your task, but only that your own work will keep you fully occupied as long as you live.

"Nothing but '*Tristan*' will still interest you. But take off your glasses! You must pay attention to nothing but the orchestra. Adieu, dear, well-beloved friend! Shall we not see each other soon?

"Yours,
"Fantasie, June 25, 1872.   RICH. WAGNER."

135

Upon learning of Wagner's intention of writing a public defense of Nietzsche, Rohde believed it was incumbent upon him to retire from the field, but after the publication of the Wagner letter, he was more than ever convinced that a scientific defense was necessary and my brother took the same view of the matter. In re-writing the *"Birth of Tragedy"* and giving a strong Wagnerian inflection to certain chapters, my brother was fully conscious of the fact that by so doing he was jeopardizing his university career, but he was, nevertheless, ready and willing to make this sacrifice for Wagner's sake. But now that an attempt was being made to discredit him by heaping insults and false charges upon his head, he felt the imperative need of defending his position by every academic weapon at his command. Moreover, the knowledge that Willamowitz was endeavoring to dislodge him from the university by attacks upon his philological integrity, had led him to abandon all thought of voluntarily retiring from this post. The entire situation had also undergone a complete change in other respects as Rohde had been appointed professor at the Kiel university, thus relieving him from the soul-wearing duties of instructor, and the great success of the preliminary festival in Bayreuth had made it no longer necessary to travel about making propaganda, as the realization of the Bayreuth idea seemed now assured.

Before going to Basle in 1872, for my customary summer visit to my brother, I made a flying trip to Leipzig, in order to hear from Professor Ritschl's own mouth his opinion of the *"Birth of Tragedy"* and of the stand taken by my brother. I found both him and his wife "incredibly kind and well disposed" towards my brother, who was overjoyed at hearing this. The report I brought back with me also encouraged Rohde to proceed with his polemic against Willamowitz, and thereby prove himself a staunch comrade-in-arms to his friend Nietzsche. Many letters were exchanged on this subject and it was finally agreed upon that this purely scientific defense should be written in the form of a circular letter addressed to Wagner as it was "*the direct allusion* to Wagner and his art in the book, which had given the philologians such a shock and aroused such antagonism." But before proceeding along these lines, Rohde wrote to Wagner asking his permission and received the following answer:

Richard Wagner to Erwin Rohde.

"My dear friend:

"Go ahead! I am delighted to hear of your plans and especially that you mean to address your communication to me. Is anything more than this assurance needed to encourage you to undertake your task with enthusiasm?

"Our friends Nietzsche and Gersdorff were in Munich a few days ago to attend a performance of '*Tristan*'; in fact, I am expecting Gersdorff to stop over in Bayreuth on his way back to Berlin. As for me, I am engaged in finishing off my monstrous opus and am feeling quite well, as is also my dear wife, who joins me in sending you cordial greetings.

"I hope that all goes well with you. Yours cordially,

"RICHARD WAGNER."

Hans von Bülow had invited my brother to come to Munich for a special performance of "*Tristan*"; an invitation which he accepted with the greatest joy. He was·joined there by Gersdorff and the two friends were deeply moved by the beauties of the work. Later my brother wrote to Rohde: ". . . I only wish you could hear '*Tristan*'—it is the most stupendous, the most chaste, and the most astounding work that I know. One fairly floats in bliss and exaltation." Of all Wagner's works, Tristan always exercised the greatest fascination for my brother and from the moment he became acquainted with the music, it remained his favorite music-drama. As late as 1888, after his relations to Wagner had undergone so radical a change, he wrote: ". . . I look about me among all the arts, in vain, for a work of the same dangerous fascination, the same infinite thrill and loveliness as Tristan; all of Leonardo da Vinci's unique qualities lose their charm in listening to the first note of Tristan. This work is, by all odds, Wagner's *ne plus ultra*."

While Rohde was engaged in writing his polemic against Willamowitz, my brother and I spent a quiet, peaceful summer in Switzerland, he devoting himself to his philological and psychological studies of the Greek world, especially to the Homeric contests. He was very happy in this opportunity for quiet, undisturbed literary work, although he worried not a little at the thought of poor Rohde working away on his polemic. On off days, we made delightful little excursions to points of interest in the vicinity of Basle and often strolled along solitary paths singing passages from the Wagnerian dramas.

This conflict with Willamowitz was the means of bringing about a close friendship between my brother and Prof. Overbeck, who had always been one of my brother's most ardent champions. It was he who chose the rather clumsy title for Rohde's little pamphlet

"PSEUDO-PHILOLOGY:
Circular Letter of a Philologian
to
Richard Wagner,
in elucidation of the pamphlet,
'Philology of the Future,'
by
Prof. Ulrich von Willamowitz-Moellendorf, Ph.D."

This little brochure appeared the middle of October and my brother was deeply moved by this touching proof of Rohde's friendship. He writes: ". . . And now your little work, written in a spirit of generosity and courageous camaraderie, comes tumbling down into the midst of the cackling crowd. What a spectacle! Romundt and Overbeck, the only persons to whom I have read it as yet, are beside themselves for joy over the success of your undertaking. They are never tired of pointing out the merits of the work, both as a whole and in detail, and call your polemics *'Lessingesque,'* and you well know what good Germans mean when they make use of this adjective. But what pleases me best of all is the deep, booming ground tone, like that of a mighty waterfall, by which every work of a polemic character must be consecrated if it is to convey an impression of true greatness and is to express love, confidence, strength, grief, hope and victory. Dear friend, I was completely overcome, and when you spoke of the 'friends,' it was some time before I could read further.

What beautiful experiences have been vouchsafed me this year! And how well they have succeeded in dispelling all thought of the calamities that have descended upon my unlucky head from other quarters! I am also proud and happy for Wagner's sake, as your work will signify a remarkable turning-point in his relations to Germany's scientific circles. I hear that the '*National Zeitung*' recently had the cheek to number me among the 'literary lackeys of Wagner'; how great, then, will be the astonishment when you also come forward and acknowledge him!

"That is of still more vital importance than for you to stand by me. Is it not so, dear old friend? And it is just because I see *what you have done for Wagner*, out of friendship for me, that makes this one of the happiest days of my whole life."

Wagner also wrote a cordial letter of thanks to Rohde, saying:

"My dear friend:

"I find that, with and through Nietzsche, I have got into very good company. You cannot know what it means to a man who has spent a long life in the society of inferior or rather stupid persons, at last to be able to say: God be praised, here comes a new type of man, possibly an entire generation. When this happens, one feels compensated for having been obliged to live for half a century in a madhouse. These changed conditions only began after I met Nietzsche. Previous to that meeting, my world swung in no wider orbit than that of Pohl, Mohl and Porges and I cannot tell you how wonderful this change seems to me. Now, please do not ask me to write you anything further. I believe that

140

my wife has already written you—at least, I know that yesterday she wrote to Gersdorff on the subject of the *'Pseudo-Philology'* (dreadful word!). We took the greatest delight in your work and find it a worthy companion piece and complement to the *'Birth'* itself. For us, the chief thing was that we were edified by this dissertation and that, furthermore, we have learned to love and appreciate the 'real man.' Such things should unquestionably be of help to all of us, but personally, I have not the courage to bestow even a glance upon the future morass of the human race. After all, this is a matter we may safely leave to God, and let him arrange affairs to His own honor and glory.

"Accept our cordial greetings and my especial thanks for the great and genuine honor you have conferred upon me.

"Yours sincerely,
"RICHARD WAGNER."

At this time my brother was struggling with many difficulties and discouragements, and as a birthday present to himself (October 15, 1872) he wrote a letter in which he unburdened his heart to Wagner. In reply, the master wrote him in a very affectionate strain, which gives rise to renewed regrets that my brother's letter was destroyed at Wahnfried.

Richard Wagner to Friedrich Nietzsche.

"Dear friend:

"It was really splendid of you to write to me on your birthday, at the same time my wife was writing to you. What you say is very comforting and agreeably expresses the serious mood which seems to have taken possession of us all at present. This mood might almost be called one of apprehension created by our disgust at everything we see and hear. Under the influence of this mood we again ask ourselves the question: What is to be done with this disreputable old world? Liszt has been with us for eight days. We learned to love him anew, but when he left we were filled with the same old misgivings. What *did* we not hear from him of all that is taking place in the world, of which to be sure, we already knew quite enough, but which fairly frightened us to death when thus heard in detail! Knowing that the world classes us together as outcasts, he thought he would be doing us a favor by repeating all sorts of baseness and ingratitude. More and more, I have the feeling that I know but little of my own age, and possibly it is better so if one is writing for posterity. But it is a curious thing, this being made to feel as if I were a novice under constant surveillance. When one is working among the primeval elements, as it were, he comes to realize how imperative is the unbounded solitude of the individual. I am now better able to understand what it was that so often stifled and suffocated you. It was because you looked about you too much in the world. The thing now is to see and yet *not* to see. By abandoning all hope, one can possibly rid himself also of despair. The feeling is growing in my mind that the only possible means a man has of distinguishing himself from the age in which he lives is to become thoroughly conscious of his own strength, and to do this, if needs be, by engaging in a pitched battle with the meanness and pettiness of the age. As far as I am concerned, I have arrived at the point where I do not intend to mince matters, and should the Empress Augusta cross my path she would fare precisely as others do in this respect. Something *must* come of all this, for one thing is certain: *compromise is not to be considered for a moment.* Having got one's self so cordially hated, the only thing to be done is to make one's self feared. . . .

"I think more and more about 'What is German?' and my latest studies on this question have aroused the most remarkable degree of scepticism in my mind, so that I am now beginning to believe that 'being German' is a purely metaphysical conception. As such, however, it is intensely interesting to me, and in any case, is unique in the history of the world, and is to be compared only to Judaism, unless Hellenism can also be made to serve as an historical parallel.

"And then I turn my eyes upon my son, my Siegfried. The boy is growing sturdier and stronger every day and is no less ready with his wits than with his fists. He is a complete marvel to me, and if despair has been chased away by the presence of my beloved wife at my side—I am now learning from the boy what it means to hope again. And so the old dance begins anew but this time to a more vigorous rhythm. It is the boy, my friend, who causes me to turn now to you and inspires me with a passionate desire—from reasons of pure family egotism, it must be confessed—to see all the hopes I have placed in you pushed forward to fulfillment, for the boy needs you—ah! how he needs you!

"But I have said this to you before. You know one is given to repetition as one grows older! It is the same with my expectorations in brochure form with which I have deluged the world, and you in particular. You have doubtless received the essay on '*Actors and Singers.*' This is another way of getting at the matter; this time, I have worked directly through the comedians. And again it has happened that no sooner have I finished, than all sorts of pertinent ideas occur to me thus leaving me a hook upon which to hang a future brochure. But just think of all this being wasted upon the desert air! In thinking the matter over, I have not the faintest idea to whom I could send the gratis copies. Would you like to have some for your colleagues in Basle? Rohde, of course, will receive one. By the way, the reference to your Basle colleagues, reminds me to announce our approaching visit to you and your friends. Early in November we are planning to start out on our voyage of discovery through the German Empire. The first interruption in our regular itinerary will be a visit to the celebrated dentist in Basle whose services can no longer be dispensed with. I imagine that this will take about eight 'ull days, and thus there would be eight evenings which we _ope to spend in the society of you and your friends, and thereby feel ourselves compensated for all the bad treatment we are obliged to endure during the day. As now planned we shall arrive about the third week in November, at which time, we will obtain from you assurances as to the whereabouts and willingness of the American (dentist). Our life here is a somewhat dissolute one occasioned by our removal to the Dammallee. Liszt's visit was the outstanding event, during which the capacity of our present '*salon*' was put to the severest test. As far as such a thing is possible, we have come to a clear understanding with this wonderful man and we regret all the more profoundly that we had— and have—very little hope of being able to do anything for this ruined life. It is still possible that he may decide to settle down with us here in Bayreuth. After hearing your

'*New Year's Echoes*,' he found Bülow's harsh verdict very extreme. Without having heard you play the composition (and this, for us, was the decisive factor) he pronounced a different and much more favorable judgment upon your 'music.' Therefore, let us drop the Bülow intermezzo; it seems to me as if here two singular personalities of the most extreme viewpoints had come in violent contact. All of this I say to you by way of parenthesis, for when all is said and done, the most vital thing is that each one of us must come to a clear understanding with himself, quite independent of outside criticism. Last summer I re-read your book and my wife has devoured it again more recently. I am sure that your ears must have burned just as if they heard very good music.

"At last you will receive a very respectable letter from me. May my chatter fill you with fresh courage, and at any rate, serve to show that in the long run, I am not affected by the baseness and meanness of men and things. A further advantage I gain thereby is that of being able to speak to you in a cheerful strain.

"Greetings from all of us with the hope of seeing you soon in the city of Erasmus.

"Yours faithfully,
"Bayreuth, Oct. 24, 1872.   RICHARD WAGNER."

My brother wrote to Gersdorff telling him of Frau Wagner's comments after re-reading the "*Birth of Tragedy*":

"During her convalescence, Frau Wagner re-read my book and now writes to me that she is 'obliged to marvel anew at the supreme skill displayed in the presentation'; 'you will never write anything better, valued friend,' she

145

continues, 'as I consider any greater degree of perfection than is to be found here as quite out of the question; but you will write other books equally good, on other themes.' Can you imagine my feelings upon reading these words? I was arrogant and abashed at the same time. But above all, I felt myself called upon to aspire to greater, more daring and more ideal aims, if I were henceforth to be satisfied with my own productive work. You wrote of 'simplicity and greatness'—it is as if these words had been spoken from my own heart as they embody my own ideals."

From the following letter it will be seen how the thought of Wagner always filled my brother with joy and confidence:

Friedrich Nietzsche to Richard Wagner.

"Dear master:

"In view of all that I have experienced of late, I have no right to be discouraged, for as a matter of fact, I live and move in a solar system of love and friendship, of comforting assurances and inspiring hopes. But, notwithstanding all this, there is one point which causes me a great deal of momentary uneasiness. Our winter semester has opened and I have no students at all. Our philologians have all remained away. It is really a *humiliation* for me, and one to be carefully concealed from the outside world. But to you, dear master, I have always confided everything and can, therefore, tell you this also. The state of affairs is not at all difficult to explain. I have suddenly been discredited among my philological colleagues and our little university is obliged to suffer in consequence. This distresses me beyond measure, for I am really very devoted and deeply grateful and would

146

not for the world have done anything to injure the interests
of the institution. My philological colleagues, as well as
Dean Fischer are celebrating in a manner never before vouchsafed them in the whole course of their academic careers.
Up until the last half-year, the number of students registered
in the philological department was steadily on the increase—
and now, all of a sudden, they are blown away as if by
magic. All of this corresponds perfectly, to things that
have come to my knowledge concerning conditions at other
universities. It goes without saying that Leipzig is fairly
bursting with envy and conceit, every one condemns me and
even those 'who know me' are unable to rise above a feeling
of compassion for the 'absurdity' I have committed. A
professor of philology at the Bonn university, for whom I
have never entertained a very high regard, settled the matter
once for all with his students, by pronouncing my book
'absolute rubbish' of which nothing could be made; furthermore, that any one who would write such rubbish was
'scientifically dead.'

"I have also heard of a student who intended coming to
Basle, but was persuaded to remain in Bonn, and now has
written to a relative here saying that he thanked God that he
had been kept away from a university where I was teaching.
In the face of all this antagonism, do you really believe that
Rohde's generous deed will accomplish anything more than
increase the hatred and jealousy already existing against
us two? Rohde and I, most emphatically, expect nothing
else. All this could be borne, however, were not the little
university which has shown me so much kindness and placed
so much confidence in me—obliged to suffer on my account.
This distresses me deeply, and will eventually lead to deci-

sions which, for other reasons, I have already had under consideration for some time. By the way, I can make good use of this winter semester, now that I am nothing more than an ordinary school-master and obliged to fall back on pedagogy.

"This then is the 'dark point,' but otherwise all is light and hope. I would be a morose mole, indeed, did not letters such as the one you have just written, cause me to leap for joy. And you are really coming? I praise my lucky stars and the dentist, for I would never have dared dream of such a possibility. Would you not prefer to try the *'Three Kings'* this time? I consider it better than *'Euler'*; my sister and I took our meals there this summer and spent a very jolly day there with Fräulein von Meysenburg and the newly-wedded pair, Herzen-Monod.

"Your splendid essay on *'Actors and Singers'* has again kindled in me the desire to have some one make a comprehensive review from your researches and conclusions in the field of æsthetics, and thereby show what radical changes have taken place in regard to artistic viewpoints,—changes whereby these viewpoints have been deepened and intensified so that practically nothing remains of the traditional theories of 'Æsthetics.'

"I have also been devoting a great deal of thought (while on the Spluegen) as to the part choreography played in the structure of the Greek tragedy, and the relation existing between the plastic arts and the mimicry and grouping of the actors. In considering this question, it came to my mind what a *striking example* Æschylus has given us of the very thing of which you speak, namely, that even in our texts, the symmetry of motion is suggested by the most marvellous metrical symmetry, and your tragedies awaken in me the glorious hope that herein will be found just the right standards, aims and canons necessary for the establishment of a genuinely German style of gesture and plastic realism. With a mind made receptive by the foregoing thoughts, I read your essay as if it were a revelation.

"Then came Rohde's pamphlet. After having read it, was I not justified in asserting that I was in the right even to the smallest side issues? Nevertheless, it is extremely comforting to have this confirmed by a second person. There are times when one grows very distrustful of one's own efforts, especially when one is set upon by the entire profession. It distresses me to think what my poor friend must have suffered while thrashing around with such a 'gang.' It was only the thought of you, dear master, which sustained him and gave him strength and courage to persist in his task. We are now both very happy in having *one and the same* prototype—and do you not think that the world must envy me the possession of such a friend as Rohde?

"By way of curiosity, I must tell you that I was recently approached by a musician, who while ostensibly asking my advice in regard to an *operatic text*, really had me in mind as the author of such a text. I wrote him a very wise epistle, strongly dissuading him from any such plan, but suggesting that he should try his hand at a cantata—perhaps make a new setting of Goethe's *'Walpurgis Nacht,' but a better one than Mendelssohn's!* I am curious to know whether or not he will take my advice. But isn't the whole thing a great joke?

"With the hope that during your pilgrimage through dear, disgraceful Germany you may meet with the same good for-

149

tune which attended you in Bayreuth, and in anticipation of your final wishes regarding your forthcoming visit to Basle, I close for today, with a heartfelt farewell and *Auf Wiedersehen.*

"Ever faithfully yours,

"F. N."

Nothing came of Wagner's projected visit to Basle, but instead he sent a telegram to my brother asking him to meet him in Strassburg on November 21st:

"Changed plans necessitate abandoning Basle visit. Please cancel all engagements. If possible, meet us in Strassburg Friday evening prepared to remain until Sunday. Address Hotel Marquardt, Stuttgart.

"WAGNER."

This meeting with Wagner and Frau Cosima passed off most pleasantly and both were astonished to find my brother in such good spirits, despite all the strain made upon him by professional antagonism, duties of office, composing and travelling. Upon his return to Basle, Frau Cosima wrote: "How delighted we were to find you in such good spirits and health, dear friend! You really exemplify the Goethe-Mazzini maxim and you looked so well and resolute that it was a genuine joy to be with you." And it is true that at that time, my brother seemed to have fully recovered from the nervous breakdown brought on by the war. Professor Holzer had in mind the writings and epigrams of this period when he wrote the following beautiful tribute to my brother:

"It is the early Nietzsche who is speaking to us here—the friend of Richard Wagner and the Nietzsche so dearly beloved of Erwin Rohde. The young Nietzsche, hopeful, confident, looking towards the future with a supreme faith in his ideals and his friends; the combative Nietzsche, who in the early '70's was in the full possession of his powers of body and mind, 'fiery, elastic, and as conscious of his own strength as a young lion' as he appeared to his friend Deussen."

Before closing this chapter, I must mention the fact, that Dr. von Willamowitz replied to Rohde's splendidly convincing and felicitous polemic, but his pamphlet attracted very little attention as he was unable to hold his own against Rohde's scientific arguments.

CHAPTER XV.

(1873.)

WHENEVER Wagner had not seen my brother for some time, he was in the habit of remarking that such long separations could easily lead to painful misunderstandings. My brother took no pains to contradict this statement as emphatically as Frau Wagner evidently expected, and this explains a passage from one of her letters in which she says: ". . . Believe me when I say that there can be no estrangement or misunderstanding between you two. I confess that I have been most uneasy on this score, but am now convinced that such a thing can never happen."

But strangely enough, the year 1873 started in with a misunderstanding of a very serious nature. My brother was at home on a visit and was overjoyed at the thought of being able to work on his Greek book undisturbedly. As his holidays were very brief, he let it be known that he wished to spend all of his time with us, in fact, our dear mother laid great stress upon this as she generously lent me to my brother for six or eight months of the year, and was therefore quite justified in thinking that she saw very little of her children, particularly of her son. In the midst of his vacation, an invitation came from Wagner urging my brother to come at once to Bayreuth and start back to Basle from

152

there. Not wishing to offend my mother, and reluctant to curtail his own period of rest—my brother felt obliged to decline this invitation, but had he understood the interpretation Wagner, at times, placed upon such refusals, he would, possibly, have disregarded all other considerations and gone. It was not until later that he learned of Wagner's having once taken deadly offense at Peter Cornelius for a like indiscretion. It seems that Cornelius had been peremptorily summoned to Munich and had excused himself on the plea that he was obliged to work on his *"Cid."* ". . . Just as if he couldn't have worked on it quite as well here in Munich!" grumbled Wagner indignantly upon receiving this answer. As a matter of fact, Wagner had not the faintest conception of the extent to which his faithful admirers were influenced by proximity to him, and thereby impeded in their own productive work.

As a somewhat belated Christmas and birthday present, my brother sent Frau Cosima five splendid little treatises, which he called *"Five Prefaces to Five Unwritten Works."* The individual titles were: 1. *"The Pathos of Truth."* 2. *"On the Future of our Educational Institutions."* 3. *"The Greek State."* 4. *"The Relation of Schopenhauer's Philosophy to German Culture."* 5. *"The Homeric Contests."* The following dedicatory lines were written in the prettily bound book:

"To Frau Cosima Wagner,
in genuine admiration and by way of answer to many verbal and written questions. This little book was written in a pleasurable frame of mind during the Christmas holidays of 1872."

153

My brother received not a word of thanks for this offering, nor was he the recipient of the customary New Year's greetings, something which he would have been at a loss to explain had he not known that Wagner and his wife had started out on a big concert tour including Berlin, Hamburg and other large cities.

In the meantime, he felt himself called upon to write a little polemic against one of Wagner's enemies, thus giving irrefutable proof of his sincere admiration for Wagner, as nothing was more distasteful to my brother than a task of this sort. Late in the autumn, he had written an indignant letter to Rohde, in which he said: "You know of course, that an alienist has proven 'in noble language' that Wagner is insane, and that another authority has done the same thing in regard to Schopenhauer. You can see from this, how the 'sane' come to each other's assistance; it is true that they do not decree the scaffold for all those *'ingenia'* who prove inconvenient for their scientific classifications, but these stealthy, malicious calumnies serve their purpose better than a sudden removal, as they are designed to undermine the confidence of coming generations."

At the beginning of the new year, my brother was given an opportunity of serving the Wagner cause in a manner more nearly to his liking. The German Musical Society had offered a prize for the best essay, from ninety to one hundred and twenty pages, on the subject of Wagner's Nibelung drama. My brother was one of the first persons to be approached by Professor Riedel with the request that he act as one of the judges. To this he readily consented, but upon learning of the conditions of the competition decided that the amount of the prize money was far too insignificant, and his successful attempt to "screw this up" to three hundred thalers, is the theme of the following letter addressed to Prof. Riedel:

". . . I have had time to consider carefully the various difficulties connected with our undertaking, as I have been confined to bed for several days, and I now hasten to answer your valued letter and submit my views on the subject for your favorable consideration. First of all, let us be very cautious and critical in the choice of the third member of the adjudicating committee. . . . If you will be good enough to listen to a suggestion from me on this point, my advice would be to appoint Herr Hans von Bülow, of whose unconditionally sound judgment and critical severity I entertain the highest possible opinion. Much depends upon being able to present a very high-sounding name, one that will be both stimulating and awe-inspiring, and there is no doubt as to these conditions being admirably filled by the name of Bülow. Are we agreed on this point?

"But now comes another matter of even greater importance. Dear Herr Professor, I find the amount of the prize money ridiculously low, particularly, if one takes into consideration the tremendous importance of the theme and the occasion. At all events, we should be able to compete with the customary prizes offered by any German academy, as anything less than this would seem to me to be unworthy of the name of so great a man and so unique a cause. On the other hand, I would regard any large expenditure on our part as nothing less than a criminal proceeding, so long as the Bayreuth finances are in such a bad way. Therefore, the following plan has occurred to me which is herewith submitted for your consideration.

"Let the Society offer an entire Patron's Certificate as a prize, the money for which is to be raised in the following manner: We already have at our disposal a hundred thalers. We will sell the prize essay to some enterprising publisher for, say, another hundred (about 130 pages, first edition 1000—that is to say, about 13 thalers for a 'Bogen'; this is a very modest and respectable price which should be readily obtainable for a really *good* piece of work. In this way, we would have 200 thalers, to which I will add a personal subscription of 50 thalers, under the condition that some one else can be found to give the remaining 50. (Perhaps the society?) I can assure you that the competition for a whole Patron's Certificate would be a most lively one. We must, by all means, appeal to the very best element in German literary circles and not lose sight of the fact that we have a great responsibility to discharge towards the public. I will only add, that this contest must be conducted in a manner utterly above reproach, and in every way worthy of the great cause."

Having received no communication of any kind from Bayreuth since the beginning of December, 1873, my brother would have had every reason to be astonished at this long silence on the part of his friends had not Rohde written him a detailed account of Wagner's visit to Hamburg. Rohde's letter contained all sorts of messages from Frau Wagner, so that my brother accepted this as a provisory answer and gave no more thought to the matter. Rohde wrote: ". . . I spent three days in Hamburg—Tuesday, Wednesday and Thursday—heard two concerts and attended a most inadequate performance of the '*Meistersinger*,' given in Wagner's honor. The two concerts interested me deeply, despite the deficiencies in the orchestra, as I had never heard certain numbers, such as the *Vorspiel* to '*Lohengrin*,' *Vorspiel* and *Finale* of '*Tristan and Isolde*,' the *Love song* from the '*Walküre*' ('Winterstürme wichen'—) and the *Forging Songs* from '*Siegfried*' given in the right tempo and spirit. In addition to this, I had the gratification of seeing my native city conduct itself in a most exemplary manner. The real *haute volée* arranged a very well-appointed banquet (which I was unluckily unable to attend) with toasts by distinguished citizens—in short, the public displayed at least a trace of appreciation of Wagner's great significance above and beyond such questions as conductors, first and second tenors, and the like.

"I believe that the success achieved here will not fail to bear gratifying fruits from a pecuniary standpoint, at least, so long as Wagner remains the fashion and the good burghers of Hamburg do not allow themselves to be talked out of their inclination by the native 'musicians' and 'critics,' to which, I must confess, they have a deplorable tendency. Personally speaking, the most important thing would have been to have had an opportunity for a quiet talk with our two friends, but this was not to be thought of owing to the everlasting confusion and Wagner's natural fatigue."

He then continues: "In the few moments we had together, your name was often mentioned. First of all, Frau Wagner sends you her warmest greetings and begs you to forgive her long silence in regard to your gift, every moment was occupied in Berlin and things were no better in Hamburg. Of course you received the telegram I sent you in Frau Wagner's name? It read:

" 'While listening to the strains of the *Forging Songs*,

grateful and friendly thoughts go out to you from one who regrets her unavoidable silence . . . Cosima Wagner.' "

In order to keep Wagner informed as to the progress of his philological studies, my brother sent him to Berlin a privately printed thesis taken from the *"Rheinisches Museum"* on the subject of *"The Florentine Tractate on Homer and Hesiod: Their Race and their Contests."* This also remained unacknowledged, until finally, on February 12th, a letter arrived from Frau Cosima, saying: ". . . I begin this letter in a state of the most unusual embarrassment. There is so much that I should like to say to you, dear friend, explain, apologize, congratulate, thank you and give you a report of ourselves. But the truth of the matter is that I returned home yesterday in a state of complete exhaustion to find that my *bonne* has left and there is no one to look after the children but myself. God only knows what success I shall have with this letter. But one thing I know and that is, I would rather send it badly written than not at all.

"You knew full well the delightful surprise you would give me by sending me your book so rich in content. I know of no gift which I would have prized more highly, and you will undoubtedly ask why I did not write at once to thank you, even though it had only been a few lines. This would have sufficed to let you know what was in my heart and had I been obliged to do this without having first read the manuscript, you would, at least have been assured of my deep appreciation of the intention which I valued as highly as I did your significant literary offering. You will also ask why I ignored the arrival of the package and allowed the beginning of the New Year to pass by without sending you, at least a telegram to show you that my thoughts were with you. This is precisely the point upon which I wish to be perfectly frank with you, as nothing less than absolute candor seems to me to be worthy of the pleasure your book has given me and from which I am still drawing my mental refreshment. The master was offended because you did not accept his invitation and by the manner you took of announcing that you could not come. At the time, I could not make up my mind whether to tell you this or not, and finally decided to leave it to time to repair the insignificant breach, and to cause the true feelings to blossom forth again in all their purity.

"Today, I can say that this has come to pass, and when your name is mentioned, I no longer hear the slightest accent of wounded friendship but only those of affection and gratitude for the new pleasure you have brought into our lives. We were indescribably fascinated and impressed by the thoughts expressed in the preface to the '*Homeric Contests*,' but why should this remain a 'preface to an unwritten work'? It seems to me that here you are absolutely at home and in your native element. Would it not be possible to fuse the ideas contained in this preface and those of the preface to the '*Greek State*' into one complete whole? Would it not be a truly 'happy deed,' to make use of this unfelicitous expression, to employ your intimate knowledge, as well as your penetrating discernment, in showing to our age the value of this culture? Nowhere could I find the cheerful Greeks, but the cheerful centaurs, and if Goethe characterizes his Faust as a *tragelaphus*, how then are we to characterize the products of our modern culture—be it men or books? But on the other hand, I think I can understand why you do not wish to write Nos. 2 and 4—you see that I indicate your prefaces by number as a certain pastor of our acquaintance does his children—for a thoroughgoing examination into the stupidity of mankind and the senselessness of existing institutions would not only be a hopeless task, but a perfectly futile one as well. You would be influenced by another reason in not wishing to work out your *'Pathos of Truth'* and this reason you have stated with sufficient distinctness in the closing sentence of the preface. Curiously enough, I have given much thought to questions of philosophy and art and have always endeavored to find a satisfactory explanation for the fact that I am more powerfully affected by the latter. I had finally come to the conclusion that it was because art reflects creation in *her* creations, and that both are as enigmatic as life itself, so that the soul experiences a sense of relief when these two enigmas are brought into harmony. Philosophy, on the other hand, condemned to deal with interpretations, bears about the same relation to the primeval truths as Schopenhauer's allegorical dream does to the dreams that come to us during a heavy sleep.

"I believe that a genuine philosophic knowledge must be the basis of every intellectual task, but I also agree with you in thinking that one should philosophize as little as possible—that is to say, to *speak* of such things as little as possible, but on the other hand, to think and cogitate all the more. From these few lines you will see how inexpressibly stimulating I have found this first preface. The reason is that it agrees so perfectly with my own reflections on the subject, just as No. 5 seems to me to be the approach to that which is my ideal of right. . . ."

Wagner made no attempt to clear away the misunderstanding, but delegated this task to Frau Cosima. His next letter was chiefly one of concern over the loss of the thesis from the *"Rheinisches Museum"* and not until the close of the letter, did he relapse into the old tone of confidential friendship.

Later my mother learned from Gersdorff, who had spent the Christmas holidays in Bayreuth, that Wagner had literally raved and declared in endless repetition, how dear my brother was to him, but that Nietzsche always held back and preferred to go his own way.

Richard Wagner to Friedrich Nietzsche.

"O friend:

"I had bad luck, indeed! But how *could* you send the package containing your philosophic treatise to Berlin? To make a long story short—after I had returned home and had had time to regain my equilibrium, I looked for the brochures, and despite the most persistent search, found nothing but the third volume beginning with page 211. In place of the missing pages, I come across heaps of antiquarian catalogues and brochures of Meistersinger motives and the like, by the dozen. Would it be possible for you to replace the missing parts? It would mean a *great deal* to me.

"Do not demand—or expect anything from me that could, in any way, be interpreted as an expansion of feeling. Last night, I had my first good sleep for a long time undisturbed by disgusting conditions. I have fallen out of conceit with many things. There are moments when I lose myself in deep reflection, and at such times, you usually appear before me—always connected in some way with Fidi. But such moments are of short duration and then Wagner societies and Wagner concerts begin to dance around me in dizzy circles. Therefore—have patience! Just as I am often obliged to have it with you.

"Yours most faithfully,

"Bayreuth, Feb. 27, 1873.   RICH. WAGNER."

Upon the heels of this letter came a telegram, saying: "Brochures packed by mistake with the score of the *'Staircase Music.'* Therefore found, no need re-order. Wagner."

Everything was thus explained, but my brother shook his head dubiously and wrote to Gersdorff: ". . . I have received splendid letters from Wagner and Frau Cosima. I learned what I had not known before, that Wagner was deeply offended because I did not put in my appearance at New Year's. Of this I had not the slightest suspicion, but you knew it, dear friend, and yet kept silent. Now all the clouds have been cleared away and perhaps it is just as well that I knew nothing about it at the time, as there are many things that one only makes worse instead of better. God only knows how often I unconsciously offend the master; each time this is a fresh surprise for me and for the life of me, I cannot get at the bottom of the matter. I am all the happier, therefore, that peace has again been restored. Are you familiar with Wagner's splendid essay on *'State and Religion'* which has just appeared in print although it was written in 1864 as a private manuscript for the king of Bavaria? It is one of the profoundest of all his literary productions and is 'edifying' in the noblest sense of the

162

word. . . . Do tell me what you think of this repeated giving of offense. I cannot imagine how anyone could be more loyal to Wagner in all fundamental matters than I am; if I were able to think of any way of showing this loyalty more plainly, I should certainly do so. But it is absolutely imperative for me to preserve my personal freedom in unimportant secondary matters, and a certain avoidance of a too frequent personal intercourse is for me almost a 'sanitary' necessity. I only do this, however, in order to be better able to preserve my loyalty in the truest and highest sense.

"Naturally, not a word can be said of all this, but I feel it keenly and am thrown into despair when anger, distrust and silence result therefrom. It never occurred to me for a moment that I was giving offense this time, and I fear that a repetition of such experiences will have the effect of increasing my anxiety. Please, dearest friend, let me have your candid opinion on the subject. . . ."

But the friend only consoled him with comforting and sympathetic words so that once more, the "flying gnats" were frightened away.

In the letter from Cosima, quoted above, she said she did not quite know what to make of the words: "in a pleasurable frame of mind" used by my brother in the dedication of her Christmas present. The fact is, that this simple, self-satisfying manner of working, common to philosophers and scholars, was unknown to Wagner, who when engaged in creative work always demeaned himself pathetically—one might almost say, theatrically. Therefore the "pleasurable frame of mind" found neither understanding nor response in Bayreuth. As early as the late autumn of 1872, I accidentally learned how depressed the executive committee in Bayreuth was over the slow progress being made on the Festival Theatre and how slowly the funds for this purpose were coming in. Upon hearing this, I felt called upon to renounce a number of long-cherished plans, among them a trip to Italy which I had arranged to take in company with an English acquaintance. The money I had laid aside for this trip was diverted to the purchase of a Patron's Certificate for my brother, but I frankly confess that the 900 marks sent to Herr Emil Heckel in Mannheim represented an outlay that it was not easy for me to make. This had to be carefully concealed from my mother and my brother was vehemently opposed to my making such a sacrifice. The low ebb of the Bayreuth finances may be judged by the fact that even this insignificant sum (a mere drop in the bucket compared to the total amount needed) received particular mention in a letter Wagner wrote to Heckel on November 28, 1872:

". . . When any payments are made to you, such as the recent one from Fräulein Nietzsche, please transfer the money immediately to Herr Feustel as I know from his latest report that he is made very uneasy in regard to our undertaking when no comforting assurances in the shape of contributions are coming in. . . ." Wagner was so deeply touched by the "sacrifice I had made for his great cause," that he in turn presented me with a Patron's Certificate, purchased out of the special fund contributed by friends of Bayreuth, during his recent concert tour in Germany. He was mistaken, however, in thinking that the money I had spent was in the nature of a deprivation, whereas it was only a passive sacrifice. Wagner wrote to me:

164

"My dear Fräulein:

"You are not the only person who can create Patrons. I can also do this—the money you *saved* by economizing, I *earned* by conducting, and I should like to know which one of us perspired the more?

"At all events, when the time arrives, you will come to Bayreuth as a full-fledged patron. Cordial greetings from my wife.

"Yours sincerely,
"Bayreuth, April 8, 1873.   RICHARD WAGNER."

Determined that no further estrangement should occur between Wagner and himself, and remembering that Rohde had expressed the desire of being alone with Nietzsche in Bayreuth some time—my brother inquired if it would be convenient for him to come with his friend for a short visit at Easter. Wagner telegraphed the following answer:

"Always overjoyed by sensible suggestions, especially when they take the form of announcing a visit herewith heartily welcomed. Expect you Sunday.

"RICHARD WAGNER."

Beside himself for joy, my brother wrote to Gersdorff on April 5, 1873:

"Dearest friend:

"Telegrams are flying back and forth between Heidelberg, Nürnberg and Bayreuth. Just think, I leave tomorrow for an eight days' vacation and will be joined by Rohde day after tomorrow? And where? Naturally, in Bayreuth! I can hardly bring myself to believe it, it has all happened so rapidly and unexpectedly. Eight days ago, neither of us had thought of such a thing. I am already overcome with emotion and my heart is beating high at the mere thought of our meeting at the station in Bayreuth. Every step will be full of memories of last year—of those days which were the very happiest of my whole life. There was something in the very air which I have never felt elsewhere, something quite indescribable but filled with the richest promise. How many things we shall have to talk over, you, of course, among them. My delight today is of a quite irrational sort, for it seems to me that everything is so splendidly arranged that not even a god could wish for anything better. I hope that this visit will atone for the mistake I made in not going at Christmas, and I thank you from the bottom of my heart, for your friendly and energetic intervention. . . ."

CHAPTER XVI.

(1873.)

MY brother's visit to Bayreuth was a disappointment to himself as well as to Wagner. Before going he had written to Gersdorff, saying: ". . . I am taking a new manuscript with me to Bayreuth on the '*Greek Philosophy during the Tragic Age.*'

"It is far from being in shape for publication, however, as I grow more and more critical with myself, and shall allow much time to elapse before I venture on another presentation of this material (the fourth on the same theme). Moreover, I have been obliged to take up the most remarkable studies for this purpose, even mathematics had to be approached, (which caused me no great apprehension) as well as mechanics, theory of molecules, etc. Again I have been splendidly convinced as to what the Greeks are and were. The way from Thales to Socrates is something simply tremendous. . . ."

I cannot say whether any part of this manuscript was really read aloud or not, or whether Wagner manifested no desire to hear it upon learning of its character. At all events, this truly splendid treatise was the cause of another painful experience as Wagner showed his disappointment

167

even more plainly than on previous occasions. He was evidently not prepared for so remote a subject as the *"Philosophy of the Greeks,"* but on the contrary, confidently expected something more directly connected with present problems, with the friends and enemies of Wagner's art and the Bayreuth undertaking. At that time, Wagner's every thought and effort was concentrated upon the Bayreuth enterprise, as it was feared that the entire plan was about to suffer shipwreck. Barely 200 Patron's Certificates had been subscribed, whereas, a thousand certificates—at 300 thalers each—in fact thirteen hundred, were necessary to guarantee the complete success of the undertaking. This situation was viewed very seriously in House Wahnfried, but this only served to display Wagner in the best possible light, as he never rose to greater heights than when confronted by the danger of seeing his life-work wrecked and obliged to fight for his ideals.

As soon as my brother had fully grasped the gravity of the situation, he felt deeply mortified at the thought that he had been dwelling on the distant heights in the company of the Greek philosophers, far remote from the struggles and disappointments of the little Bayreuth following. And yet notwithstanding all this, he felt keenly disappointed at not finding in Bayreuth, as in the dear, old days in Tribschen, the same understanding for his own world of ideas. He was seized with a dread presentiment that in order to remain Wagner's friend he would be obliged to renounce his own path of future growth and development. It was this thought, which, despite the happy reunion with his beloved friend, caused him to look back upon his visit in Bayreuth with a heart full of melancholy misgivings. After taking leave of

Rohde, he wrote: ". . . I spent Monday in Nürnberg, and felt myself as physically fit as I was depressed mentally. And this despite the fact that the good burghers of Nürnberg were running around in the parks dressed in holiday attire, and that the sun was as mild as if it had been autumn. That night I steamed away towards Lindau and crossed Lake Constance at the hour when the night and morning constellations are struggling for supremacy. Arrived in Schaffhausen in time for dinner; fresh fit of despondency, then on home."

Upon returning to Basle, he sadly laid aside his "*Greek Philosophy during the Tragic Age,*" and resolved to fulfill Wagner's expectations by devoting himself more to present-day problems. But before doing this, he subjected himself to the closest self-examination in his effort to decide just how far his obligations to Wagner demanded such a sacrifice. He was greatly concerned about the question as to why so great an idea as the one in preparation at Bayreuth, was not better comprehended by the Germans, and after much thought, he arrived at the conclusion that the German philistines of culture displayed a deplorable satisfaction with the narrow minds of their age, and by so doing had lost all perception for all that was truly great. His reason for choosing David Strauss* as a type of these philistines of culture, lay in the fact that Strauss' new book called: "*The Old Faith and the New,*" had been the subject of much discussion during his Easter visit to Bayreuth, Wagner, in particular, speaking of it with scorn and aversion. A few weeks earlier, Frau Wagner had written my brother: "Everywhere in the

* First "*Thoughts Out of Season: David Strauss, The Confessor and the Writer.*"

German Empire, I met with the greatest enthusiasm for the new book by David Strauss, which on the strength of a quotation from Helmholtz proposes to deliver us from redemption, prayer and Beethoven's music." Such isolated observations led my brother to make a thorough-going examination of the situation, and he began to realize that during the period immediately following the great victories (1870-71), the Germans had grown coarser and more superficial, and that even the academic world—next to our superb military organization, the outstanding element in German life—was resting upon its oars, so to speak, and leaning back with disquieting complacency upon its past achievements.

This was particularly distressing to him in the case of so sharp-witted a scholar as David Strauss, for that reason, he chose him as a type, and began to write with astonishing rapidity, his first "*Thoughts out of Season: David Strauss, the Confessor and the Writer.*" But that this was not animated by any personal animosity against Strauss, but rather out of sheer anxiety for Bayreuth, is shown by the following observations taken from his private notebooks. ". . . Great emotional strain during the genesis of the first '*Thoughts out of Season.*' . . . Anxiety for the genius and his life-work, when compared to Strauss' smug complacency. . . . The most spurious of all intellectual food. . . . The weakening of all conviction! Wavering morality in matters of right and wrong, and the uncontrolled predilection for the commonplace . . . ! A false kind of happiness . . . !"

It would be wrong to deduce from words of this kind that my brother did not cherish the deepest affection for his German fatherland. On the contrary, it is only the indignant

wrath of the deeply loving son, that is voiced in these words:
his passionate desire was to see the German Empire become
truly great, permeated and transfigured by a true culture;
in other words, he wished to evoke a genuine German culture.
The German should not simulate, he should look the truth
squarely in the face, recognize his own imperfections, and
not avoid the struggle with his own weaknesses and the per-
versities of his own nature. And he believed that the German
was capable of doing this, for one of the oustanding qualities of the German is courage. In a letter written to Gersdorff, at the time the latter returned home from the war, my
brother gave expression to the joy he felt in thus placing his
highest and supremest hopes in this development of the German national spirit: "New duties beckon us; and if anything
is to remain from this wild game of war now that peace is
restored, may it be that spirit of sober-minded reflection,
which to my great surprise, I found fresh and unimpaired in
all its early Germanic vigor, within the ranks of our army.
This was a beautiful and unexpected discovery for me; upon
this we can build, and this justifies us in entertaining the hope
that our *German mission* has not yet been fulfilled. I have
never had greater courage than at this moment. . . ."

No sooner was the work well under way, than my brother
wrote to Wagner, and it is impossible to read this letter
without being moved by the manner in which he endeavored
to assume the responsibility for the mild discords which had
threatened to overcloud their relations, and also by the
modesty he displays in calling Wagner's attention to the fact
that he has now written something more closely in conformity with his own ideas.

The Nietzsche-Wagner Correspondence

Friedrich Nietzsche to Richard Wagner.

"Most revered master:

"The days spent in Bayreuth live constantly in my memory, and in retrospect, the newly acquired knowledge and experiences assume still greater dimensions. I can perfectly well understand your not having been satisfied with me while I was there, without being able to do anything to change this. My excuse must be that I learn and perceive very slowly, and every moment spent in your society I experience something about which I have never thought before and am endeavoring to impress this indelibly upon my mind. I realize clearly, dearest master, that such a visit can be no refreshment for you, in fact, that it must almost be unbearable at times. I have often wished for the appearance (at least) of greater freedom and independence, but in vain. Enough! I can only implore you to accept me as your pupil, if possible with pen in hand, and a copy-book spread open before me, and moreover as a pupil with a very slow and not at all versatile *ingenium*. It is true, that I grow more melancholy each day in realizing how utterly incapable I am of contributing anything to your diversion and recreation, however gladly I would be of the slightest service to you.

"Possibly, I may yet be able to do this when I have carried to completion the work I now have on hand, namely a polemic against the distinguished writer, David Strauss. I have just finished reading his '*The Old Faith and the New*' and have been moved to wonderment both by the dulness and commonplaceness of the writer as well as the thinker.

"During my absence, the work of my house-friend, Overbeck on the '*Christianity of Modern Theology*' has made

172

splendid progress. It will be of so offensive a character to all parties concerned, and on the other hand, is so irrefutable and sincere, that when it is published he will also be agitated against as one who has 'ruined his career'—to quote Prof. Brockhaus in my own case. In time, Basle will become most offensive.

"I parted with friend Rohde in Lichtenfels, where we found a bust of you in the restaurant at the railroad station. On Easter Sunday we took a walk to Vierzehnheiligen, about an hour from Lichtenfels. Do you not think that I have splendid friends?

"Today I sent Renan's *'Paul'* to your wife with my best greetings and will send the promised work of Paul de Lagarde together with Overbeck's book when the latter is finished.

"I was so sorry not to have seen the dean. Farewell! Farewell, dearest master, to you and your entire family.

"Yours faithfully,
"Basle, April 18, 1873.   FRIEDRICH NIETZSCHE."

This touching letter was followed immediately by a second, in which my brother inquired of Wagner whether Fritzsch had confided to him the difficulty he was having in the publication of Overbeck's book: *"On the Christianity of Modern Theology."*

Wagner answered both letters at once:

Richard Wagner to Friedrich Nietzsche.

"My dear, good friend:

"Your first letter requires no answer. First of all, you must know yourself how touched I was by it, and therefore, nothing remains to be said except that you are not to allow yourself to be frightened by your own fancies, and that you are to proceed to make yourself 'burdensome' to me as often as you like and in the same way.

"To tell the truth, Fritzsch was embarrassed at the thought of disporting himself as a publisher of theological works, but his hesitancy arose only out of consideration for the author himself, who he feared would not be brought to the attention of the proper public, by a publishing firm such as that of Fritzsch. Thereupon I let myself be heard from in my customary manner of getting at the root of the matter. I pointed out to him the singular destiny he was called upon to fulfill and he seemed to accept his fate in a not ungracious manner. My advice to him was to publish Overbeck's book. We were in Leipzig for a day and thus could discuss everything by word of mouth.

"In regard to your Straussiana, my only feeling is one of impatience to see the work. Therefore, out with it!

"After ten days of turbulent travelling, we returned to the Dammallee yesterday, and hope not to be obliged to leave home again soon. Tomorrow—God and Strauss permitting —I mean to lay the corner-stone of the instrumentation of the '*Götterdämmerung.*'

"The latest story about Fidi is that when I was arranging my books the other day, he stood looking on attentively, and when I called to him: 'Fidi, hand me Creuzer's "*Symbolism*" ' —he handed me Creuzer's "*Symbolism.*" '

"Every one sends greetings. This morning, Eva and Fidi played "*Uncle Nietzsche and Rohde*". Remember me to Rohde. "Yours as ever,

"Bayreuth, April 30, 1873. RICHARD WAGNER."

174

Unluckily, work on the first *"Thoughts out of Season"* did not progress as rapidly as my brother had anticipated, the reason for this being that he was seized with violent pains in his eyes and his short-sightedness made unusual strides. Baron von Gersdorff hastened to his side, and in a letter dated May 24, 1873, described to Rohde the condition in which he had found my brother:

". . . During the past semester, and even earlier than that, Nietzsche attempted such heavy work in connection with his studies for his pre-Platonic philosophy and later, for his Straussiana, all of which was done in his small cramped handwriting—that he finally reached the point where he could work no more than an hour and a half at a time before being forced to stop on account of the most violent pains in his eyes. On Wagner's birthday (May 22) I went with him to the oculist who diagnosed his case as weak-sightedness of the left eye thereby forced into inactivity, and in addition to that, acute shortsightedness of the right eye, upon which rested the entire burden of the work.

"He ordered eye douches and a complete rest from reading and writing for a fortnight." Other oculists, who later made an examination of my brother's case, also established his trouble as being the result of over-taxing his eyes. However, this strain did not begin to show any effect upon his general health until his naturally robust constitution, especially his former excellent digestive organs, became impaired as a result of the severe illness he went through with after the campaign of 1870-71. The optic nerves and those of the brain did not receive sufficient nourishment to support so great a degree of intellectual activity, and this re-acted

175

upon his sight. On June 26, Gersdorff continued his sick bulletins:

". . . When the fortnight's respite was over, Nietzsche endeavored to resume his work but all to no avail, as excruciating pains forced him to hasten to the oculist, who then ordered a belladonna cure and a complete inactivity up to the summer vacation. Belladonna is a clear liquid derived from a plant; it is dropped into the eye and soon spreads over the ball causing an extension of the pupil to twice its normal size and producing an almost alarming appearance.

"This liquid could be recommended to vain persons as a means of enhancing their beauty. Scientifically, it has the effect of suspending the activity of the nerves of vision, thus giving them the necessary rest and recuperation. In order to protect the eye from the increased current of light now streaming in smoked glasses of the 'darkest sort,' as the people of Basle are wont to say, have to be worn. Despite all these precautions, Nietzsche suffers greatly from the noticeable intensity of the light here, which seems to me to be genuinely southern in its force. In the meantime, the vision has been somewhat improved by the belladonna cure and the enforced inactivity, so that he is now able to use glasses No. 3, whereas six weeks ago, No. 2 was barely sufficient. His sister is here to console him and we do everything in our power to alleviate his time of trial."

As the result of our joint effort, the manuscript made good progress and was soon ready to be sent to the printer, leaving my brother free to go to Graubunden and continue his cure.

When the first copy of this book was received on August 8, we celebrated the event with modest festivities, concerning which, Gersdorff wrote to Rohde: ". . . The evening was heavenly clear and pure, a never-to-be-forgotten day. And thus we celebrated the *anti-struthiade.** And now let the adversaries come! To the devil with all of them . . .!"

Baron von Gersdorff had been good enough to attend to the correspondence with Bayreuth and was therefore, the first to receive the thanks and expressions of delight from the Wagners in regard to the book. Finally my brother felt himself equal to the task of attempting a long letter, and it goes without saying, that the first of these was addressed to Richard Wagner, (this letter is also missing in Wahnfried) which Wagner answered immediately:

Richard Wagner to Friedrich Nietzsche.

"Dear friend:

"It was a delightful surprise to see your handwriting after so long a time. And yet, my first feeling was one of concern, in fact, you cause me more anxiety than pleasure at present and this is saying a great deal, as I know of no one in whom I take greater delight than I do in you. And so the first and most important thing I have to say to you today, is to acquaint you with my solicitude, and it is best that I begin at once to relieve my mind on this subject:

"Did your physician really give you permission to write such a long and closely written letter? As for me, I shall take great pains to write as far apart as possible, contrary to my customary manner, and in this way, to justify myself

---

* This is Gersdorff's way of making a pun on the name of (David) *Strauss,* the real meaning of which is "*ostrich.*" Greek word: "σγξουθός."

for writing at all. If I have refrained from doing this for a long time it has been with a mournful determination, as despite Gersdorff's willing intervention—I was vain enough to believe that you would wish to read my letter yourself, and feared that this would prove injurious to you.

"And yet I am doing this very thing notwithstanding the fact that I have very little faith in the concessions made by your physician, as I know from my own experience just how much confidence is to be placed in these gentlemen. My doctor has assured me, again and again, that I am an indestructibly sound person despite the wretched complaints by which I am plagued day and night. All of these he laughingly dismisses as being the quite customary 'maladies of genius.'

"Now God grant, that your *medicus* is of a somewhat less optimistic temperament and that he may be in the right.

"But one thing was left out of this diagnosis of the 'maladies of genius' and this is the thing, above all others, which causes me the most acute distress. Namely: an incorrigible aversion to expressing myself, particularly in writing (on the other hand, this could be of great advantage to your poor eyes). Since the third of May I have again been hard at work on the instrumentation of my '*Götterdämmerung*,' and how far do you think that I have progressed? That day in which I finish one page of the score deserves to be written down in red ink in the calendar of my life. Scarcely have I seated myself at my work when 'letters' arrive or other delightful news necessitating renewed ingenuity on my part for my intercourse with the world, and then my poor 'genial' fantasy takes flight. And now *you* come with your '*Strauss*' and worse than that, Overbeck

178

with his *'Christianity'* to be imprinted upon *'Theology.'*

"This is enough to set a man crazy; in fact I am reminded of the Icelandic skal, Eigil, of whom I once told you, if I am not mistaken. Upon returning home from a very fatiguing journey, he found that one of his friends had left a magnificent shield in his house. Enraged at the discovery, he cried: 'He has just hung this here in order to force me to write a poem upon it. Has he been gone very long? I will hasten after him and strike him dead.' But he was unable to overtake him, so greatly vexed, he turned back to his own house, took another good look at the shield and—wrote a poem upon it!

"The moral is that Herr Overbeck must come himself if he wishes to have his poem. As far as you are concerned, I repeat the conceit which I recently expressed to my family, namely, that I foresee the time when I shall be obliged to defend your book against you, yourself. I have been reading it again and I swear to you, by God, that I consider you the only person who knows what I am driving at.

"All the rest belongs in the chapter of 'style' about which, as you know, I am incompetent of judging, as I bristle up every time the word 'style' is mentioned, to your great vexation.

"Joyful Wiedersehen on October 31 (Feast of the Reformation) and all other good wishes.

"A thousand heartfelt greetings,

"Yours,

"Bayreuth, Sept. 21, 1873.   RICHARD WAGNER."

CHAPTER XVII.

NIETZSCHE'S APPEAL TO THE GERMAN NATION.

(1873)

NOTHING occurred during the summer of 1873 to diminish the anxiety felt in Wahnfried concerning the erection of the Festival Theatre and the success of the entire Bayreuth undertaking. In fact, a complete fiasco was regarded as inevitable, in many quarters. This belief was strengthened by a remarkable incident which had a painful effect upon my brother's impressionable mind, but unnecessarily so, as it later developed.

While I was visiting my brother in Basle during the summer of 1873, I met a strange-looking, elderly woman on the stairs one day who had evidently called upon him. In reply to my question as to whom this remarkable person might be, he answered in his humorous way: "Lisbeth, that is a ghost who makes me periodic visitations and is in the habit of talking to me in a mysterious manner as spirits are wont to do." I found out that this woman, by the name of Rosalie Nielsen had made two previous calls and had succeeded in greatly disquieting my brother by intimating that the firm of E. W. Fritzsch, his publishers, were really bankrupt and only being kept above water by the support of a few friends. She also made mysterious intimations in

regard to an international company which had under consideration the purchase of the Fritzsch firm, and in this event,
would attach particular value to retaining possession of my
brother's works. Owing to the fact that the *"Christianity
of Modern Theology"* was also to be published by Fritzsch,
Overbeck was vitally interested in the representations of the
mysterious stranger, and it was agreed that the next time
she called, the interview should take place in his room. During this conversation, it came out that the international
company mentioned as contemplating taking over the
Fritzsch business, was really doing so in order to get a hold
upon Richard **Wagner** whose prose writings were published
by this firm. Wagner, so ran her story, was in the direst
financial straits, the funds subscribed for the erection of the
theatre had been diverted to the building of his own residence,
and that it was the intention of the aforesaid international
company to ruin Wagner's entire enterprise. At this point
in her recital, my brother's customary amiability and
courtesy forsook him; his indignation was so great that he
was unable to speak a word, but he took a chair, opened the
door and gave the visitor to understand that the chair was
at her disposal—on the *other* side. But he was unable to
shake off the impression created by the mysterious woman,
as he was already much disquieted by the condition of
Wagner's affairs. Therefore he wrote a letter to Rohde, in
which he gave him a half-serious, half-humorous account
of this mysterious story of intrigue:

". . . In the meantime, there is another matter which has
assumed gigantic proportions and threatens to grow beyond
our control. I can only give you an inkling of it here as it

is not a matter to be discussed openly in a letter. Both Overbeck and I are firmly convinced that disquieting machinations are on foot by which the *International* hopes to get hold of the Leipzig firm of ——. The plans we have made to frustrate this scheme would be rendered futile the moment a syllable of this becomes known. I really wanted to make a hurried trip to Leipzig that I might have a personal interview. I am sorry not to be able to place the entire *apparatus criticus* at the disposal of the astute critic E. R. (I mean the letters and written testimony of the female spook, R. N.) but from everything that is known it has been possible for less well-trained minds to arrive at appallingly definite conclusions." He closes his letter with the humorous words ". . . Is your strong manly heart knocking against your ribs? I do not dare sign my name to this letter so filled with fearsome things.

"We are living in one of Samarow's novels, think only in terms of mines and counter-mines, employ pseudonyms and wear false beards. Hui! Hui! How the wind howls! In the name of the conspirators, Hugo with the spectral voice . . ."

Rohde was right when he insisted that all these uncanny stories originated in the brain of the mysterious caller, and was soon able to inform his two friends that the publisher E. W. Fritzsch had "also thrown out the spook."

In an effort to make an end of the precarious conditions in regard to the Bayreuth undertaking, the executive committee called a meeting of delegates from the Wagner Societies to take place in Bayreuth during August. This meeting was finally postponed until October, and in the meantime, Wagner commissioned Emil Heckel of Mannheim to approach Nietzsche with the request that he work out an appeal to the German nation to be laid before the delegates assembled in Bayreuth.

Heckel did as Wagner requested, and my brother at once turned to Rohde for co-operation in drafting this document:

". . . The latest thing is an invitation I received today to write an appeal to the German nation (a modest undertaking!) in the interest of the Bayreuth work. This request comes from the Committee of Patrons. The very thought of such a thing terrifies me, as at one time, I attempted to write such an appeal on my own initiative and made a most miserable job of it. Therefore, I now turn to you, dear friend, with an urgent plea for assistance; perhaps the two of us working in co-operation, will be able to get the monster under control. The general sense of the proclamation, is to implore young and old, as far as the German language is spoken, to hasten to the nearest music-dealer's and there deposit a sum of money. According to instructions given by Wagner to Heckel (so it seems to me) the German public is to be stimulated to this line of conduct by being enlightened on the following points: 1. Significance of the undertaking; significance of the promoter of the undertaking. 2. Disgrace for the nation, that despite the disinterested and personal sacrifice made by every one connected with this undertaking, it should nevertheless be made to appear as if it were the enterprise of a charlatan. 3. Comparison with other nations: If a man in England, France or Italy who, in the face of all the obstacles placed in his way by the general public, had enriched the national stage by five master works, produced throughout the land and everywhere acclaimed with enthusiasm, should cry out: 'The theatre as it exists today does not represent the spirit of the nation, it is an open disgrace to art; help me to establish a home expressive of the national spirit!' 4. Would such an appeal not meet with an immediate response, even tho' it arose from nothing but a feeling of national pride? etc. etc.

"At the close, it must be stated that all desired information may be obtained at every German book-shop, art and music dealer's (3946 by the count) where subscription lists will also be found. Don't be vexed about this, dearest friend, but go to work on it at once . . ."

Rohde, however, felt himself unequal to this task, as may be seen by the following letter: ". . . Ah, dearest friend, gladly as I would come to your assistance in regard to the appeal, I am not able to do what you wish. What I have in mind seems to give but little promise of success when I think of the multitude to be addressed upon the significance of a man and of a work, of which no one has the faintest idea and which has, therefore, to be presented in a disgustingly popular and superficial manner.

"Just now, when all my time and thoughts are occupied with preparation for my university lectures—too long postponed—all the streams of vigorous popular language seem to have dried up in me. In the meantime, should the spirit move me I shall make another attempt; only under such conditions could the work be successful as nothing is ever gained by painstaking reflection. It is a terrifically difficult matter, because one realizes, beforehand, that the whole thing is doomed to failure. In consequence of this the necessary enthusiasm is lacking, and the only thing that could impel one to attempt it would be a sense of solemn obligation."

Without waiting to hear from Rohde, my brother set to work on the appeal and sent the rough draft for Rohde's approval. He was not kept waiting long for his friend's verdict, who wrote: "Only a few words today, dearest friend, in great haste as I am overwhelmed with official duties. My honest opinion of your *'Proclamation'* is that it will make a strong appeal to the *friends* of the cause, who will find an echo of your sentiments in their own hearts and regard the appeal as expressive of their own vigorous and wrathful feelings. But when it comes to the lukewarm brethren, to say nothing of the enemies of the cause, for whose conversion we are striving—it will scarcely have the desired effect as it now stands, and this is most assuredly true of the tone of the introduction. I do not mean to say that I regard this as a mistake on your part, but only that when the entire thing is subjected to close scrutiny, it becomes evident that it is an impossibility, far exceeding human strength. How is one to go to work so to draft a last and final appeal to the lukewarm and disaffected Germans who have been brought to the point of contempt and active antagonism by long years of hostile criticism, without giving vent to one's own extreme indignation? But, in reality, what is needed is a conciliatory tone such as would be instrumental in converting hesitating souls from the errors of their ways.

"The avowed purpose of this appeal, however, is to convert the sceptics, and having failed to achieve this result, the entire undertaking would be futile—in fact, it would only make matters worse. When it has been proven that the

Bayreuth undertaking—*quod di avertant*—has not a ghost of a chance for success, a suitable moment will always be found for roundly chiding the contemptuous and unwilling souls.

"It seems to me that you have lost sight of the chief difficulty of this sheer impossible task, namely, that of stirring the *canaille* to activity without tickling their vanity. I know you will understand my misgivings on this subject, my dear friend. I regard the entire appeal more in the light of a thousand-fold well-deserved kick for the *xaxoi* than as an enticement for the cur slinking behind the stove, whom the appeal, in the last analysis, is designed to reach."

Rohde was right in his pessimistic estimate of the effect of such an appeal, and later my brother wrote him:

"You were quite right, my dear friend; the appeal has been rejected. Accept my best thanks for the sympathetic words received in Bayreuth. The atmosphere there was warm and cordial and very invigorating, the appeal drafted by Prof. Stern is now appearing in all the papers, and my one wish, by day and night, is that the collection boxes at the German book-dealers, may become veritable depositories of wealth.

"To tell you the truth, Wagner, Frau Wagner and I are convinced of the greater persuasiveness of my appeal, and it seems to us to be only a matter of time until something of this kind will be absolutely necessary."

My brother gave a far more detailed and cheerful account of the meeting of the delegates to Baron von Gersdorff, who had been prevented from coming to Bayreuth: "Well,

I was enroute from Wednesday evening until Monday morning, making the trip to Bayreuth alone and having Herr Heckel's company as far as Mannheim on the way back. About a dozen persons all told, were in attendance, all of them delegates from the Wagner Societies and I the only 'Patron.'

"On the real festival day, we were vouchsafed the same nasty weather made memorable by the Dedication Festival, and the result was that each one of the gentlemen was again called upon to sacrifice a new hat. But mark you well! On the day preceding and following the weather was beautifully bright and clear!

"After making our tour of inspection in mud, fog and darkness, we repaired to the City Hall for an executive session, and it was here that my appeal was politely by firmly rejected by the delegates. I, myself, protested against any attempt to re-write it and recommended Prof. Stern for the manufacture of a new article. On the other hand, Heckel's excellent suggestion that all the book-stores throughout the empire be utilized as collecting places, was unanimously approved. The entire session was a remarkable procedure; half-inspiring, half-realistic and yet creating so strong an impression on the whole, as most effectually to silence all the lottery projects and schemes of that kind which were being held in reserve by some of the delegates.

"A very successful, informal and harmful banquet at the 'Sonne' closed the day with Frau Wagner and Fräulein von Meysenburg as the only two women present. I was given the place of honor between them and by reason of this, was christened *'Sargino, the Protégé of Love'* from an early Italian opera. Batz proposed a toast to Frau Wagner and

187

for some incomprehensible reason united his praise of her with some ideas about snuff-boxes and self-expression. A closing session was held on Saturday morning in Feustel's office, during which Stern's appeal was accepted. You will soon have an opportunity of reading this, as it is to be given the widest publicity. My document, considered by the Wagners to be very good, was signed by important names and may some time be of value in case the present optimistic appeal of Stern's fails to achieve the desired results.

"In the afternoon, we again inspected the theatre, this time under the light of the late afternoon sun. The children were also there; I climbed up to the center of the royal box. The structure looks much more beautiful and better proportioned than we imagined after seeing the plans. It is impossible to view it under a clear autumn sky without being deeply moved. We have a building and this is now our symbol."

From other persons present on this occasion, I learned that Wagner was beside himself that my brother's document was considered too serious and too pessimistic by the delegates; he flew into a terrible rage and fairly stamped his feet. It was my brother who persuaded him that an appeal from Prof. Stern would undoubtedly meet with greater success and that his own could always be brought forward in case the necessity arose. It was only in this way that he succeeded in pacifying Wagner, who in order to show his sympathy and affection for my brother, presented him with nine beautifully bound volumes of his prose writings accompanied by the following dedication:

"Was ich mit Not gesammelt,
neun Bänden eingerammelt,
was darin spricht und stammelt,
was geht, steht oder bammelt,—
Schwert, Stock und Pritzsche,
kurz, was im Verlg von Fritzsche
schrei, lärm oder quietzsche,
das schenk' ich meinem Nietzsche,—
wär's ihm zu was nütze.
                          "RICHARD WAGNER.
"Bayreuth, All-Souls Day, 1873."

APPEAL TO THE GERMAN NATION.

We insist upon being heard, for we speak as an admonisher and the voice of warning has always the right to be heard, whoever may be the speaker and wherever his voice may be raised. On the other hand, you to whom this appeal is addressed, have the equal right of deciding for yourselves whether or not your admonishers are honest and upright men, who speak only because they realize your danger and are frightened at finding you so passive, indifferent and uninitiated. This we can affirm of ourselves, for we speak to you from a pure heart and in so doing, have consulted our own interests only in so far as they coincide with yours— namely, the wellbeing and the honor of the German spirit and the German name.

You have been informed of the festival that was celebrated in *Bayreuth* during May of the past year. The purpose of this festival was the laying of a powerful corner-stone, beneath which were buried forever many fears and misgivings.

At the time, we *believed* that this stone placed the seal upon our dearest hopes, but today we say that we *deluded* ourselves into *believing* this. For alas, there was a great deal of delusion about the matter. These misgivings are still alive, and altho' we have not entirely forgotten how to hope, you will, nevertheless, see from this appeal that our hopes are still exceeded by our fears.

It is you who have given rise to these fears; you do not wish to know what is going on, and out of sheer ignorance are about to prevent a great deed from being accomplished. Such ignorance is no longer justifiable; in fact, it seems inconceivable that any one could still be found who knows nothing of the splendid, courageous and indomitable struggle in which Richard Wagner has been engaged for decades—a struggle which has attracted the attention of practically every nation to an idea which in its highest form and truly triumphant perfection, is embodied in the Bayreuth artwork.

If you are now minded to place an obstacle in the way of his unearthing this treasure he intends presenting to you, what would you gain thereby?

This is just the point that needs to be brought to your attention publicly and urgently, in order that you may be informed in due season and that you may no longer take refuge in playing the role of uninitiated. From this time forth, foreign countries will be the judges and witnesses in this drama you are enacting; a mirror will be held up to you in which you will see the reflection of your own picture as it will some day be painted by a just posterity.

Let us assume that through ignorance, distrust, ridicule or calumny you succeed in reducing to a purposeless ruin the building now being erected on the hill outside Bayreuth. Let us further assume, that prompted by uncontrolled antagonism, you do not permit this work to go into fulfillment, to achieve its due effect and bear witness to its own greatness. The result will be that you will not only be obliged to face the verdict of posterity but will also be put to shame before the eyes of the non-German contemporary world. Let us suppose that a man in England, France or Italy had enriched the stage by five works of extraordinary great and unique style, works which had been acclaimed from north to south, and had then called out to his countrymen: "The stage as it exists today is not representative of the spirit of the nation, it is nothing short of a disgrace to the art it purposes to present. Help me to establish a fitting temple for the national spirit!"

Would not every one hasten to his support, even though this be solely from a feeling of national pride and honor? But what is needed here, is *not* merely a sense of national honor, nor the blind fear of the disparaging verdict of a critical posterity; you should be willing to become co-workers, co-sympathizers, co-learners, and simply by resolving to help in this great work, learn to rejoice with us from the bottom of your hearts. You have generously equipped all your sciences with costly laboratories, and yet when an attempt is made to build such a laboratory for the groping and courageous spirit of German art, you hold yourselves aloof, and will have nothing to do with such a project.

Can you point to a more momentous period in the history of German art, or one demanding the solution of more important problems, such as necessitate greater opportunities for fruitful experimentation, if the idea characterized by Richard Wagner as the *"Art-work of the Future"* is to become a concrete and ocular reality?

Which one of us is sufficiently daring even to attempt to picture to himself the extent of this movement of thoughts, deeds, hopes and endowments to be ushered in when the gigantic Nibelung structure with its four mighty towers, rears itself from the earth to the rhythms imparted to it by its creator before the eyes of the conscious representatives of the German people? Can we foresee the movement that will thus be inaugurated, the promise of which stretches out into the most distant, the most fruitful and the most hope-inspiring future?

At all events, no blame will attach itself to the originators of this movement should the wave soon begin to ebb and the surface again to resume its normal aspect as if nothing at all had taken place. For altho' the completion of the work must be our first and immediate care, we are no less oppressed by the misgiving that we may not be found sufficiently ripe, prepared and receptive to guide the unquestionable immediate effects, on into deeper and wider channels of development.

Wherever it has been, and still is, the custom to take offense at Richard Wagner, we have noticed that there lies concealed a big and pregnant problem of our national culture. But, when this antagonism results only in the most mysterious ridicule and criticism, and only in rare instances is productive of serious thought,—then we must be pardoned for entertaining the humiliating suspicion that possibly this celebrated *"Nation of Thinkers"* has already thought itself out, and that obtuseness of thought has replaced genuine thinking.

By what a distracting task did we find ourselves confronted when we attempted to prevent the Bayreuth event of 1872 from being confused with the founding of a new theatre, and at the same time to explain why the significance of this undertaking was not to be compared to that of any existing theatre? What a tremendous effort was necessary in order to open the eyes of the consciously or unconsciously blind to the fact that the expression 'Bayreuth' did not signify alone a certain number of persons, a group with specific musical tastes, but that it comprised the entire nation; that, in fact, it extended far beyond the borders of Germany and appealed to all persons, wherever found, who were ready for serious-minded and active participation, who had at heart the ennoblement and purification of dramatic art, and had grasped the true meaning of Schiller's wonderful prescience as to the future when tragedy in a nobler form would grow out of the opera.

Surely, everyone who has not forgotten the art of thinking, (be this only from a sense of honor!) must regard as a remarkable phenomenon, *morally* speaking, an artistic undertaking that is to be advanced and promoted by the sacrificial spirit and disinterestedness of all the participants; which is to be consecrated by the solemn convictions of all those who think deeply and seriously of art, and arouses hopes for the most significant development of our national life, when German music and its transfiguring influence upon the popular drama, has stamped it with genuine German characteristics.

We believe in something still higher and more universal:

193

namely, that the Germans will only appear worthy of respect and be able to exercise a salutary influence upon other nations, when they have shown how formidable they can be, and yet *will succeed in making the world forget how formidable they have been by the intensive manifestation of the highest and noblest artistic and cultural forces.*

We regard it as our solemn duty to remind you of our duty as Germans at a time when we are called upon to rally to the support of the great art-work of a German genius. We may expect a quick and sympathetic response from those persons, or groups of persons, who have been able to preserve their serious turn of mind during the agitated period of our national history; the German universities, academies, and art schools, in particular, will not be appealed to in vain to support the projected undertaking, each according to the measure of its ability, just as the political representatives of German prosperity in the *Reichstag* (Imperial Parliament) will have serious cause to reflect upon the thought that, more than ever before, the nation is in need of the purification and re-consecration to be brought about by the ennobling magic and majesty of German art. In fact, they will be compelled to do this, if the powerfully awakened impulses of our political and national passions and the new traits stamped upon the physiognomy of our national life, are not to wring from posterity the humiliating confession that in the chase after fortune and pleasure, we Germans lost ourselves, just as we had, finally, found ourselves again.

I must here add a few words in regard to this appeal of my brother. As already stated, it was rejected and never again mentioned, but neither could any great measure of success be claimed for Prof. Stern's appeal, as may be judged from the following passage taken from Chamberlain's Wagner biography: ". . . I will here give a little fact in illustration of the intense neglect with which Wagner's great work—now redounding to the everlasting glory of the German spirit—met with throughout the German empire. Dr. Stern's *'Report and Appeal,'* written at the request of the Wagner Societies, was sent to four thousand book and music dealers toward the close of 1873. Not a solitary one of these four thousand took the slightest notice of the matter, and only a few thalers were subscribed by some students in Giessen."

CHAPTER XVIII.

(1874)

WHILE my brother was occupied with his second *"Thoughts Out of Season"* at the close of the year 1873, the family at Wahnfried was oppressed with increased anxiety in regard to the success of the Bayreuth undertaking. The appeal had met with no success, and Wagner's efforts to secure the necessary funds from King Ludwig II seemed also doomed to failure. At first everyone was at a loss to find an explanation for this: it was a bitter disappointment to Wagner and he seriously considered writing a circular letter disclosing to all those interested in the enterprise, the shipwreck of his plans. He was prevented from doing this, however, by Emil Heckel of Mannheim, whose faith in the ultimate realization of the Bayreuth idea never faltered. He hurried to Bayreuth and met all of Wagner's complaints and resolves with the one word: "That must not be!" It seems that this splendidly energetic man first made an appeal to the Grand-Duke of Baden, requesting him to undertake the office of mediator at Berlin, with the view of inducing the government to appropriate a part of the required sum in return for which, the performance of the Nibelung drama in Bayreuth would be given in commemoration of the fifth *Peace Anniversary* in 1876. After a tremendous effort 100,000 thalers were finally collected by private subscription, and this sum, up to the very last penny, was expended in paying the debts already accumulated. But a further 100,000 thalers were necessary if there was to be no suspension of the preliminary preparations, of the building activity and the artistic plans. The Grand-Duke refused to act as mediator, knowing full well that Wagner's wishes and plans would meet with absolutely no response in Berlin. After a period of great suspense and anxiety, it was again the King of Bavaria who came to the rescue of his artist friend, whereupon it came to light that the king's unwillingness arose from the following cause:

Felix Dahn had written an ode to King Ludwig, and the latter instructed that this be sent to Wagner with the request that he set it to music. Not aware of the fact that this request came from the king, Wagner refused to comply, thereby incurring the displeasure of his royal patron. One of the gentlemen-in-waiting who was on friendly terms with Wagner, explained the matter to the king, who then declared himself ready to come to Wagner's assistance in his usual munificent manner. However, the 100,000 thalers from the king's treasury were only in the nature of an advance, which caused my brother to shake his head and say be could not comprehend where Wagner ever expected to get hold of the money to pay back these loans.

Upon my brother's return to Basle, at the beginning of the year 1874, he was met by the disturbing news that the Bayreuth undertaking was on the point of failure. The news came from Gersdorff who was most unhappy and pessimistic about the whole affair. How my brother passed this

197

miserable period of suspense, we learn from a letter written much later to his friend Rohde:

". . . I have been in a desperate frame of mind since the beginning of the new year from which I was finally able to rescue myself in a truly remarkable manner. I set to work to investigate the reasons for the failure of the undertaking; this I did in the most cold-blooded manner, and in so doing, learned a great deal and arrived at a far better understanding of Wagner than I ever had before." I must confess that I was frightened when I read this statement and said to my brother: "Were you really able to regard the matter so coolly at that time?"—"Not always", was his reply, "it was only now and then that I forced myself to look the truth squarely in the face."

In his note-book of this period, appears the sentence: "In my student days I said, Wagner is a romanticist, not of the art in its zenith, but in its last quarter: soon it will be night! Despite this insight I was a Wagnerite; I *knew* better, but I could not do otherwise."

There was nothing my brother desired more passionately than to find some being whom he could revere, and he, therefore, allowed himself to be carried away by Wagner's splendid energy and superb work ("*Meistersinger*" and "*Tristan and Isolde*") to a point where he was willing to ignore everything in Wagner's art of which he did not approve. But although my brother invariably treated Wagner with the utmost courtesy and respect, there must have been times when he unconsciously betrayed his inner doubts and antagonism, and on such occasions, Wagner was given to making suspicious remarks which had the effect of increasing my brother's inner scruples. He confided to no one this continual conflict with himself, and it was not until the year 1874 that he seemed to have fully sensed this lack of harmony between them and to have formulated the reasons for this. It is quite characteristic of my brother that although he suffered inexpressibly by the threatened failure of Wagner's plans, he did not give way to endless lamentations and reproaches, but went courageously to work to investigate the reasons for this lack of success. He forced himself to make a cool and sober examination of the facts, and thereby endeavor to find a solution for the failure of the undertaking in the very things he himself had felt and thought, but had hitherto loyally suppressed out of love and admiration for Wagner. No stronger proof has ever been given of my brother's sincerity and uncompromising love of the truth than in thus accepting the challenge of his conscience, altho' this meant the shattering of one of his most beautiful illusions.

The notes he made at this time seem to have been intended for publication, as the headings of chapters and the large number of aphorisms bearing on this subject, would seem to indicate that he had in mind a book, which strangely enough, was to bear the title of the fourth *"Thoughts Out of Season; Richard Wagner in Bayreuth."* But I can not think that he seriously entertained this idea and at all events the following notes were not incorporated into the work eventually bearing that title.

(The material here alluded to, ten heads of chapters and numerous aphorisms, was eventually published in Volume X of the Complete Edition of Nietzsche's Works, or Volume II of the Posthumous Works. Isolated aphorisms appear in the English edition of Nietzsche but not all have been previously translated. Translator's note.)

    I. *Reasons for the failure. Above all, the antagonistic element. Lack of sympathy for Wagner. Difficult. Complicated.*

    II. *Wagner's Dual Nature.*

    III. *Passion. Ecstasy. Dangerous.*

    IV. *Music and Drama. Parallelism.*

    V. *Arrogance.*

    VI. *Late Manhood. Late Development.*

    VII. *Wagner as Author.*

    VIII. *Friends. (Arouse fresh suspicions.)*

    IX. *Enemies. (Awaken no respect.) No interest in their contentions.*

    X. *Antagonistic Element explained. Perhaps eliminated.*

"Wagner endeavors to achieve the renaissance of art by proceeding from the only existing basis, namely, the theatre. Here the masses are genuinely moved and are not obliged to resort to pretense as in museums and concert halls. To be sure, this is a very crude mass, and as yet, it has been demonstrated to be an impossibility to weaken the domination of the theatre. Problem: Shall all art continue to live isolated and segregated? Is it not possible to achieve sovereignty for art? Herein lies Wagner's significance. He endeavors to tyrannize by the aid of the theatre-going masses. There is not a shadow of doubt in my mind but that Wagner would have succeeded had he been an Italian. The German has not the faintest conception of opera, and has always regarded it as something imported and un-German. In fact, the entire stage is not taken seriously by the Germans."

"There is something comical about the whole situation. Wagner cannot persuade the Germans to take the theatre seriously. They remain cold and unresponsive—he becomes impassioned as if the whole salvation of Germany depended upon this one thing. Now all at once, when the Germans believe that they are occupied with graver matters, they regard anyone who devotes himself so seriously to art as a cheerful fanatic."

"Wagner is not a reformer, for so far, everything remains as it always was. In Germany each one is inclined to take his own cause seriously, and therefore laughs at any one who claims a monopoly of seriousness."

"Influence of the money crisis."

"General uncertainty of the political situation."

"Doubts as to the wise leadership of Germany at present."

"Period of art agitation (Liszt etc.) now over."

"A serious nation will not permit all levity to languish, hence the attitude of the Germans towards the theatrical arts."

"Chief thing: the significance of an art such as Wagner represents does not fit into our present social and economic conditions. Hence the instinctive aversion to an undertaking that is considered untimely."

"Wagner's chief problem: Why am I not able to make others feel what I feel myself? This leads to a criticism of the audience, the state and society at large. He places the artists and the audience in the relation of subject and object —this is most naïve."

"One of Wagner's chief characteristics: lack of discipline and moderation. Carries everything to the extreme limit of his strength and feelings."

"The other outstanding characteristic is a born talent for the stage, which has been diverted from its logical course and turned into the next most available channel; voice and figure are both lacking and he does not possess the requisite modesty."

"Wagner is a born actor, but like Goethe, a painter without hands. His gifts seek and find other mediums of expression."

"Now let us imagine all these denied impulses working in harmony."

"Wagner brings together all possible effective elements at a time when popular taste is dulled and demands extremely crass and vigorous methods. Everything is employed—the magnificent, the intoxicating, the bewildering, the grandiose, the frightful, the clamorous, the ecstatic, the neurotic. Prodigious dimensions, prodigious resources."

"The unexpected, the extravagant splendour creates the impression of opulence and exuberance. He knows what our age likes; moreover he still idealizes our age, and thinks much too highly of it."

"Himself possessing the instincts of an actor, he wishes to imitate mankind only in the most effective and realistic manner. His extreme nature sees only weakness and insincerity in any other methods. Painting for effect is an extremely dangerous thing for artists. The intoxicating, the sensual, the unexpected, the ecstatic, the being-moved-at-any-price. Alarming tendencies."

"Wagner unites everything that still has charm for us modern Germans. Character, knowledge, all go together.

He makes a determined effort to assert himself, and to dominate in an age antagonistic to all art. Poison is an antidote to poison. Every sort of exaggeration is polemically arrayed against the forces hostile to art. Religion and philosophical elements are introduced, aspirations for the idyllic—in short, everything, everything."

"One thing should be remembered: Wagner's art speaks a dramatic language; it does not belong in a room, *in camera*. It is the language of the folk-epics, and even in its noblest passages, is not intelligible without being grossly exaggerated. It is meant to be heard from a distance, and to weld together the chaos of the masses. For example the *Imperial* (Kaiser) *March*."

"Wagner has a dictatorial nature. He overlooks many minor circumstances and does not occupy himself with small matters but disposes of things in 'a grand style.' Therefore, he is not to be judged by isolated details—such as music, drama, poesy, the state, art, etc. The music is not of much value, likewise the poetry, and the drama even less. The dramatic art is often only rhetoric, but taken as one comprehensive whole it maintains itself at the same great level."

"He has *the feeling of unity in variety;* and for that reason I consider him as one of the world's culture-bearers."

While my brother was unburdening his heart after this fashion, he suffered intensely from the fear that Wagner would never be able to carry out his plans. When, however, news reached him of the success of the undertaking, he regarded it as nothing short of a "miracle" and wrote to Rohde:

". . . If this miracle be true, the result of my investigations will nevertheless, remain. But if it be really true, let us rejoice and make it a feast-day."

He added: "We know from Frau Wagner—and this is a secret shared only by the friends of Bayreuth—that the King of Bavaria has again come to the rescue with a loan of 100,000 thalers, so that work on the stage machinery and scenery can be pushed forward rapidly. Wagner himself writes that the date of the festival is fixed for 1876. He is full of courage and firmly convinced that the undertaking is now on the high road to success. God grant this! This waiting and anxiety is hard to endure, at times, I have really abandoned all hope."

My brother was plunged into a mood of deep melancholy by the result of these investigations. He once said that one of the most important elements of self-discipline was to be able to raise the veil and to draw it down again when it became necessary, and that one's feelings should be the best judge as to whether this had been done at the right moment or not. He felt that the time had not yet arrived for him to lift the veil and disclose his real feelings for Wagner, and upon realizing this, he sorrowfully drew it down again, or at least endeavored to draw it so closely that no one should learn the state of his mind.

CHAPTER XIX.

(1874)

IN the meantime, the second *"Thoughts Out of Season"* on the "Use and Abuse of History" had been finished and sent to Bayreuth, eliciting from Wagner and Frau Cosima cordial expressions of approval. My brother also interpreted their letters as being friendly and sympathetic and informed Gersdorff that he had "received splendid letters from Bayreuth." But somewhat later we learned from Fritzsch that the work had been spoken of in a rather cool and derogatory manner at Wahnfried.

This is not difficult to understand if one keeps in mind that Wagner was engaged in a supreme struggle for the realization of his idea, and at such times, demanded of his friends that they neglect their own affairs and devote themselves heart and soul, to his cause. In other words, he expected them to suffer when he suffered and rejoice when he rejoiced. This my brother did unreservedly, but at the same time, he took the liberty of writing books which had nothing to do with Bayreuth. Privy Councillor Ritschl had once said that Nietzsche was of no use in party factions and to my brother's way of thinking, Bayreuth had already become a party fight, that is to say, a matter for the masses. This

205

explains why my brother, despite his solemn exhortation to the Germans, was unable to manifest the proper degree of zeal and partisanship demanded by Wagner, and also accounts for the unfriendly comments on the book made in the presence of Fritzsch. It is also possible that Wagner was repeating what he had often said: "Nietzsche always goes his own way, and one has to take him as he is." However this may be, the letters acknowledging the receipt of the book, were not lacking in warmth and cordiality:

Richard Wagner to Friedrich Nietzsche.

"Dear friend:

"Eight days ago we received your new work from the bookdealer and have deliberately devoted three evenings to the reading of the same. I wished to write to you while we were reading it, but the worst thing about it was that the thoughts thereby suggested at once mounted into the hundreds of thousands, until they finally reached the proportions of a veritable dissertation and could not be disposed of within the limitations of a letter.

"There was one thing, however, which I should have liked to call out to you, briefly. That was, that I am made very proud by the thought of being relieved of the necessity of saying anything in the future, but can now leave everything to you. Everything 'in the future'? Yes, one takes fright at the very thought, but nevertheless, it is a comfort to know that the subject has been approached in the right way.

"You certainly do not expect praise from me! It would be a fine thing, indeed, for me to presume to praise *your* wit and *your* fire. My wife always finds just the right tone for

206

anything of that sort, for else why should she be a woman? She will not fail to let you hear from her on the subject.

"Now may God bless us all together! Nor will He have a very big task as there are so few of us.

"My big affair will soon be in shape. It will take place in 1876. Full rehearsals next year as it is imperative that we give ourselves plenty of time.

"Our own house will be ready in May, and then your room will always be at your disposal. I hope that sometime you will come here for a good. long rest; there are plenty of mountains nearby.—My wife will write very soon, at present she is suffering with her eyes. That seems to be the fashion now-a-days. Overbeck is the only one who pleases me because he does not wear glasses. Give him my best regards, but Gersdorff will always be revered as the absolute ideal.

"Cordial greetings from

"Yours,

"Bayreuth, Febr. 27, 1874.   RICHARD WAGNER."

Frau Cosima's letter went very much more into detail and therefore sounded more friendly than Wagner's, but later my brother realized that the beautiful words were only sweet-smelling flowers used to conceal the bitter truth that this latest work of his was "inaccessible" not only for the larger public, but also for the master himself.

Frau Cosima wrote: ". . . At first we were greatly surprised, as one is apt to be at present, to find expression given to such deep thoughts, and one involuntarily exclaims: 'Wherefore, for whom is all this meant?' We already know these things and those who do not, have no need of knowing them until we are made to understand by the course of your

207

development why you were obliged to begin in such an abstract fashion. This is not intended as a reproach for your book, but is merely mentioned as one of the difficulties, which will make it inaccessible, I fear, for the larger public. However, this is of no importance, as those who are able to follow you (and to do this requires, I might say, a certain initiation into the secrets of our educational institutions) will not only be grateful to you, but will also be conscious of a certain exaltation at the thought that you have preserved your courage in spite of your keen realization of things as they really are.

"And how well armed you step into the arena, ready for battle, deliberate and sure of yourself, in fact, so much so, that I greatly fear you will find no opponent and will be obliged to content yourself, as did Frithjof, who overturned the idols and set the temple in flames without being given an opportunity for combat.

"But that which personally affects me most strongly in your work, is the certainty, now made clearer to me, that a knowledge of the sufferings of genius has been the means of enlightening you as to conditions in the world at large, and that you now see not alone with the eyes of intelligence, but also with those of the heart. Just as the Indian prince was instructed in the essential character of things by being brought into contact with beggars, old men and corpses, and the Christian is made a saint by the sight of Christ on the cross—so your sympathy with genius has made it possible for you to gain an all round view of our present-day world of culture. It is this which invests your work with its marvellous warmth, a warmth which it will retain, I am firmly convinced, long after our petroleum and gas stars have been extinguished.

"I think it possible that you would not have been able to have felt with us so deeply, had you not had so complete a mastery over the manifold phenomena of life. Your irony and humor also spring from the same source and create a much deeper and more powerful impression by being projected upon this background of compassion and sympathy, than were they only the result of your play of intelligence.

"But now, who is going to read the 'History'? I greatly fear that you have interfered with the circulation of the same by having given it too elegant a binding, as those who would gladly pay fifteen silver 'groschen' for the *'Beethoven'* may not be able to find the thaler necessary to have unrolled before their eyes the uses and abuses of history, however great their enthusiasm for the subject. You should not be compelled to look for your reading public among the circle of the well-to-do culture-philistines, but rather among the 'literary nomads' who today, as in days of yore, preserve the genuine German spirit. But be that as it may, you have written a very beautiful treatise and as for the rest—'let Hans Sachs take care of that,' and by 'Hans Sachs,' I mean the German nation. I say this as one who has both great hopes and great fears. We have so often discussed form and style when we were together, that I should like to say something to you on this subject, although I realize that it is the most difficult of all questions if one hopes to make one's self perfectly intelligible.

"One recognizes in your work the influence of aristocratic surroundings, but misses a note of complete freedom. In this respect, I believe that the classic models remain inimitable, from the very fact that they imitated no one but aspired to the beautiful as it was *in* and *around* them. Moreover, a certain carelessness is apparent to me in your great artistic intention, such as, 'where did he get that'; this seems to me to be too familiarly expressed to fit into the tone of the whole, and I further notice a somewhat too intentional avoidance of the relative pronoun 'which.' You nearly always say, 'he *that* does this or that,' 'or that work *that* pleases.' Why do you do this? And finally, can one say of himself that he is a *'classical philologist'*? Would it not be better to say 'professor of classical philology?' But while I am putting these unimportant criticisms on paper, I am reminded of the splendid moments of your work irrespective of the contrast between the inner and outer qualities of the same, and I find it very foolish to be thus inflicting you with my purisms without having half adequately expressed my delight at the richness of your thought and the striking originality of your point of view.

"It is ever thus when one is chatting with an intimate friend; one is apt to cling to a discussion of some minor point and not touch upon the true greatness of the work, simply because one has been pleasantly stimulated by agreement on the main issues under discussion.

"But you understand, do you not, my dear friend, just how much pleasure you have given by what you have written? . . ."

I must add here that Cosima always found something to criticize in my brother's writings from a standpoint of style. And despite his profound admiration for her intellect and his gratitude to her for pointing out his faults, he could not refrain from smiling at her comments, as strictly considered, Frau Cosima was a foreigner. Moved thereto by criticisms like the above, my brother once made the heretical remark that if she were so keen about achieving an improvement in German literary style, it would be well to direct her energies, first of all to Wagner's well-known transgressions in this respect.

It was weeks before my brother was able to overcome the depression resulting from the self-examination to which he had subjected himself in regard to his feelings for Wagner's art. Now that he no longer considered Richard Wagner and his art as representing a transcendent ideal, and no longer felt it to be the one and only purpose of his life to work for this ideal—he began to look upon himself and all his previous efforts as utterly futile. He began to feel as if he had been moving around and around in a circle of ideas, and had been lacking in the ability of seeing and creating a wider and greater field of activity. It was in this strain that he wrote to Gersdorff:

". . . Dear faithful friend:

"You have much too good an opinion of me. I am firmly convinced that the day will come when you will be keenly disappointed in me, and I now start the work of disillusionment by declaring that to the best of my knowledge, *I deserve not one whit of all your praise.* Could you only know what discouraged and melancholy thoughts I entertain *about myself* as a productive being! I long for nothing more than a little freedom, for the genuine breath of life. I am both angry and rebellious when I think of how really fettered I am. There can be no question of real productiveness so long as one is conscious of constraint and weighed

211

down by the burdensome feeling of suffering and oppression. Will I ever be able to achieve this feeling of perfect freedom? Doubt is piled upon doubt; the goal is too remote and by the time one has reached the goal, his strength has been exhausted by the long struggle. One achieves the wished-for freedom and is thereby as exhausted as a day-fly when night comes. I have such a haunting fear that this will happen to me. It is a misfortune to be conscious of this struggle so early in life. Nor have I any deeds to show for it as has the artist or the ascetic. How wretched is this everlasting mire-drumming complaint! For the moment, I am heartily sick and tired of the whole thing.

"As to my health, it is excellent—you may be quite reassured on that point. But I am very much dissatisfied with nature, who should have endowed me with somewhat less intelligence and given me instead a stronger heart. The best thing is always lacking with me and the realization of this is nothing short of soul-torment. Routine work in any profession is a good thing, for it brings with it a certain degree of mental torpor and thereby one's suffering is reduced. . . ."

He also wrote in the same melancholy strain to Bayreuth, and Frau Cosima replied saying that Wagner would like to start at once for Basle and take my brother off home with him. I must explain here that Frau Cosima firmly believed that the atmosphere of Basle was chiefly responsible for my brother's despondency. She wrote: "For a long time I have wished that you could get away from Basle, notwithstanding the fact that I fully appreciate the many good qualities of this little world and the advantages you gain by remaining

212

there. But on the other hand, I also am familiar with the gloomy, calvinistic atmosphere and know how little calculated it is to help anyone in meeting a difficult situation. However worthy they are of our highest respect, and whatever sense of their peculiar characteristics is felt by the good people themselves, they nevertheless lead an empty life, and are like ghosts moving about in their own peculiar garb so that intercourse with them produces the strangest sort of melancholy."

My brother entertained quite different feelings towards Basle and Wagner also displayed a far greater understanding of the situation, ascribing Cosima's animosity to the place to a disagreeable experience she once had there. Wagner wrote a pleading letter to my brother, begging him to come at once to Bayreuth. In this letter he made use of all sorts of joking allusions which he knew my brother would be apt to employ in searching about for an excuse for not going.

Richard Wagner to Friedrich Nietzsche.

"O friend:
   Why do you not come to us?
   I can find an excuse for everything—or whatever
   you like to call it.
   Only don't hold yourself so aloof! If you persist
   in doing this I can do nothing for you.
   You room is ready.
   However—or, on the contrary:
   Nevertheless!
   or yet:

'if it must be'!

Written the moment after your last letter arrived.

More another time.

"Cordial greetings from

"Yours

"Wahnfried, June 9, 1874.   R. W."

This cordial invitation of Wagner's and my brother's inability to accept it would again have given rise to unpleasantness had not there been something so touchingly mournful about my brother's letter that Wagner felt only compassion for the unlucky genius whom fate seemed to be pursuing so relentlessly.

Much of my brother's melancholy arose from his disappointment in regard to Wagner, who had not reached the heights he should have scaled by reason of the irritating antagonism of a contemptuous contemporary age. Nor had Wagner realized my brother's ideal of the artist and the man. It is true that my brother expected far too much from his "ideal," and had been led into the mistake of transforming Wagner into a sort of supernatural being as to endowment and character. He made humorous recognition of this error some years later when he wrote: "Such gifted creatures as I then imagined geniuses to be have never existed."

CHAPTER XX.

DURING this period of doubt and inner conflict, my brother would most assuredly have turned to Rohde for sympathy, had not this well-beloved friend been of a far more melancholy turn of mind than Nietzsche himself, and therefore in constant need of being buoyed up by his friends rather than asked to share their burdens. Rohde had written the following appealing letter to my brother: ". . . I implore you, dear friend, to let me have frequent tokens of your friendship and sympathy, without which I could neither live nor breathe. . . A horrible lack of self-confidence renders futile all my plans, hopes and wishes, so that often I awake suddenly in the night, as if oppressed by a terrible nightmare. At such times, I seem to be wandering about in a desert, without friends, unbeloved of all men, and even my very existence seems so uncertain as to make any serious attempt to formulate hopes or plans for the future appear like a veritable absurdity. . . I know these are all delusions of the brain and not borne out by actual conditions; and yet to one who has had the misfortune to be born under an unlucky star—it is just these thousand and one little things which become entangled in a magician's snarl, and form a source of endless irritation and hindrance to one as sensitive as I am. At such times, any insignificant

215

disappointment can be made to appear as a symbol of a life wholly wrecked. . . ."

In an effort to comfort his friend, my brother describes the means he employed to extricate himself from similar depressing experiences. This he did, first of all, by composing and then by submerging himself into a creation of a new literary work. He writes: ". . . I have made good use of my time during the last six weeks by finishing my 'Hymn to Friendship' and writing it out carefully for four hands. This song breathes hope and courage and was sung for all of you. If this mood can be preserved, I believe that all of us will be able to endure the world for some time to come. And No. 3 of my *'Thoughts Out of Season'* is so well along, that I am only waiting for a warm, fructifying rain to see it shoot up like a stalk of asparagus."

As a matter of fact, this third *"Thoughts Out of Season,"* entitled *"Schopenhauer as Educator,"* proved the greatest consolation to my brother during this period of doubt and dissatisfaction. In this work he portrayed in manifold forms and disguises, the conflict through which he was passing, and his deep yearning to invest his own life with permanent and significant values. In a way, it is an attempt at self-justification for having placed himself solely at the service of Schopenhauer and Wagner, regardless of his own unique gifts and intellectual needs. In a passage of wonderful beauty, we find the following expression of feeling concerning his future development:

". . . In what way may your life, the life of the individual, retain its highest value and deepest significance? And how may it be least squandered?

"Forsooth, only by living for the good of the rarest and

most valuable types; but not for the betterment of the ma--jority, who taken as individuals, are the most worthless types. And it is precisely this way of thinking that should be implanted and cultivated in the mind of youth; he should be taught to regard himself as somewhat of a failure of Nature's handiwork, but at the same time, as a testimony to her larger ideas. 'She has made a mistake,' he should say, 'but I will do honor to her great idea, by placing myself at her service, in order that she may succeed better the next time.'

"Animated by this resolve, he consciously enters the charmed circle of that culture, which is the child of every man's knowledge of self and dissatisfaction with self. Every one who acknowledges this culture thereby confesses: let every one help me to achieve this, as I will help all those who know and suffer as I do, to the end, that finally that man will appear, who feels his love and insight, his vision and power to be complete and boundless, and who in his universality, lives *in* and *with* Nature, as the judge and appraiser of all human values.

"It is difficult to impart this feeling of indomitable consciousness of self to anyone, because it is impossible to teach love, and it is from love alone that the soul gains not only the clear, analytical, understanding vision of itself, but love also creates the desire to get out of one's present self and search, with all one's might, for a higher and nobler self, still latent. Therefore, it is only by clinging with devotion to some great man (as a prototype!) that the individual is vouchsafed the first consecration of culture. He may know this by his sense of mortification without resentment, by his hatred of his own narrow-mindedness and warped vision, by

217

his sympathy with genius ever rearing its head from the murky wastes of mediocrity, by his prescience for all that is nascent and struggling, and by the innermost conviction that Nature in distress is everywhere to be met with, as she presses closer to man, as she feels anew a sense of failure, and at the same time, sees the success of her marvellous conceptions, forms and designs. The men in whose midst we live, therefore, are to be likened to the fragments of those precious plastics, who cry out to us: Come and help us, piece us together as we belong, for we have an inexpressible longing to be made complete.

". . . The sum total of these processes I have called the 'initial consecration into culture.' I have now before me the infinitely more difficult task of describing the effects of the 'second consecration.' This is the transition from the inner life to the valuation of outer processes and manifestations. From now on our look is turned outward to search through the great world of thought and action for that culture known to us from our own earlier acquisitions. The individual must utilize his own strivings and aspirations as an alphabet whereby he will be able to interpret the strivings and aspirations of humanity. Nor can he rest here, but must rise still higher. Culture demands from him not only these inner processes, and the true valuation of the outer world in which he lives and moves, but primarily and finally —action. That is to say he is called upon to fight for culture, and to oppose all those influences, customs, laws and institutions, in which he does not find his own goal— namely, the creation of genius."

Every one who reads this passage will be forced to admit that Nietzsche ever remained consistent in his views. His goal was the perfection of mankind, and for him humanity's genuine salvation and worth were to be found only in the highest types. That which he here calls "genius," making it the supreme type of human aims and aspirations, he later characterized as the "Superman."

A large part of "Schopenhauer as Educator" was written during a delightful spring sojourn we made at the Rhine Falls near Schaffhausen, one of the most beautiful spots in German Switzerland. Superb weather and a holiday mood prevailed, and my brother's melancholy was gradually banished by the auspicious influences. Until now, he had suffered from inordinate modesty, a trait also established by the graphologists, who had made a study of his handwriting. He conceived his first duty to be a whole-hearted service to Schopenhauer and Wagner, but in the joy of creating this new work, he felt for the first time a marvellous presentiment of his real worth and the true significance of his creative powers.

We wandered about in the magnificent country surrounding the Rhine Falls until we found a cozy nook where my brother could write diligently in his note-book, while I passed the time reading Gottfried Keller. We were in the best of spirits and fond of indulging in the childish pastime of using only one verb in our conversation, my brother explaining humorously, that it was quite unnecessary to take so much trouble about acquiring a large vocabulary, as a comparatively few words suffice to make one's meaning clear. The verb we chose for this game was "snuffle" ("schnobern"), the persistent use of which gave rise to no end of jokes and misunderstandings. We got the idea from Wagner who had

219

once signed a letter relating to executive matters, with the words:

"RICHARD WAGNER,
(ever snuffling around to find a trace of the German spirit!)"

"Snuffling" was finally advanced to the dignity of a noun, and ever little nook and corner in the magnificent forest bordering the Rhine, which became associated with my brother's studies and writings, was christened the "chief snuffling place."

But whatever we did, whether we walked about talking, or sat silent, each of us occupied with his own thoughts, we were always conscious of the deep, booming organ tones of the falls, which formed an accompaniment to all our thoughts, and sent us a faint echoing greeting even when we strayed far a-field.

While my brother had succeeded in dispelling the feeling of depression, Frau Cosima and Gersdorff, who spent a great deal of his time at Bayreuth—continued to worry about him and take counsel among themselves as to the best way of helping him. Frau Cosima insisted that he should leave Basle, but as no other university found favor in her sight, the friends hit upon the amusing plan of marrying my brother off to some rich woman, whereby he would be enabled to come and go as he liked and choose his own place of residence, which Frau Cosima never doubted would be Bayreuth.

My brother found this idea of a marriage council very diverting and wrote in this strain to Gersdorff: ". . . It is really a delicious idea to picture you and the Bayreuth friends sitting in a sort of marriage consideration commission. Yes-s-s—but! I must say to that, particularly when the deliberations end with the advice that there are plenty of women in the world, but that it is my business to find the *right* one. Am I then to fare forth like a knight of the Crusades in quest of the promised land of which you speak? Or did you mean that the women were to come to me to be inspected, and let me decide which one of them was the right one? I find this theme a trifle impossible, dear friend; or why do you not make a personal application of the efficacy of this theory?"

My brother was really much annoyed that so much should be said about his depression which he had entirely shaken off under the inspiration of creative work. He wrote repeatedly saying that he was not depressed and that his letters had apparently created a false impression, but all his protestations were to no purpose and finally he was obliged to write to Gersdorff: ". . . My dearest, best and very best friend, I am really somewhat annoyed that none of you will believe me when I say that I am well, uncommonly so, at least, as well as I have any right to expect. I cannot say that I am 'very well,' (censor No. 1) but what is one to expect here under the changing moon? But who knows, perhaps I shall even bring my health up to No. 1 just to spite all of you."

Although no unpleasantness had arisen from my brother's failure to accept Wagner's invitation, he came very near falling out with Gersdorff, who was on an intimate footing in Bayreuth and consequently felt himself called upon to reproach my brother for his non-appearance. In fact, he went so far as to threaten to absent himself from the reunion

221

of the friends in Basle, if my brother did not come immediately to Bayreuth. Not even his most intimate friend had a suspicion that Nietzsche was then struggling with inner doubts and misgivings, and a strong letter was necessary in order to put an end to Gersdorff's persistent reproaches:

"I got no further than good intentions. In regard to Bayreuth; it seems to me that their home and their life is in such a state of unrest that a visit from us would be untimely. I trust that all of you are now satisfied as to the state of my health as you seem to have outdone each other in pessimism. I can think of nothing else, at present, but of finishing my No. 3 to my satisfaction. By the way, my dear friend, how did you hit upon the droll idea of attempting to force me to Bayreuth by using a threat? You almost make it seem as if I did not wish to go there voluntarily, although I was there twice last year and had two meetings with the Bayreuth friends the year before, making the trip from Basle, despite the inconvenient arrangement of our holidays. We both know that Wagner is naturally very *suspicious*, but I should not have thought it a wise thing to encourage this feeling. Finally, I beg of you not to lose sight of the fact that I have obligations towards myself, and that these obligations are difficult to discharge on account of my none too robust health. Really, no one shall force me to do anything. . . ."

Believing that Wagner was genuinely offended at my brother, as otherwise Gersdorff's intervention seemed utterly incomprehensible, my brother begged me to write to Frau Wagner and first of all, to ease her mind in regard to his health, and then explain to her how dearly he would have welcomed an opportunity of seeing his beloved friends, had he not felt compelled to finish his third *"Thoughts Out of Season"* before granting himself this pleasure. Frau Wagner replied at once in a most cordial tone, from which it was plainly to be seen that Gersdorff's representations had been made without their knowledge. One thing revealed by this correspondence was that Gersdorff had so endeared himself to Wagner and Frau Cosima, that as the latter wrote: "He is absolutely the only person at whom one can never take offense."

My brother did everything he could to re-assure me, but I, nevertheless, felt a certain apprehension kept him from going to Bayreuth, and this reluctance will be well understood if one bears in mind the private memoranda made at this time. It is true that he had drawn a heavy veil of forgetfulness over these soul-searching observations, but a certain degree of uneasiness remained, and there was the ever-present danger of betraying his change of heart. And this really did happen when we went to Bayreuth in August. In the spring, we had heard a performance of Brahms' *"Song of Triumph"* in the minster at Basle, a work that made a deep impression upon my brother. He bought the score and took it with him to Bayreuth, without having the faintest idea (as I then thought!) that this would be mis-interpreted by Wagner. But later I came across this sentence in my brother's note-book: "The tyrant admits no individuality other than his own and that of his most intimate friends. The danger is great for Wagner when he is unwilling to grant anything to Brahms or to the Jews."

From this it will be seen that my brother wished to make

an effort to induce Wagner to be just and generous towards Brahms. This Wagner must have suspected, as the "*Song of Triumph*" created an extremely painful scene, in the course of which, Wagner indulged in an uncontrollable fit of temper quite out of keeping with the insignificant cause. Wagner, himself, described the entire scene to me some months later, in the rare way he had of speaking ironically of himself: "Your brother laid the red-bound book on the piano, so that my eye fell upon it every time I came into the room and enraged me as a red rag does a bull. I knew perfectly well that Nietzsche wished to say to me: 'See here! Here is some one else who can also compose something worth while!' I stood it as long as I could, and then one evening I let go of myself and how I did rage!" Wagner laughed heartily as he recalled this scene.—"What did my brother say?" I asked anxiously. "Not a word," was Wagner's reply, "he grew red in the face and stared at me with a look of astonished dignity. I would give a hundred thousand marks all at once if I were as well-bred as Nietzsche; he is always the aristocrat, always dignified. Such deportment is of the utmost value to any one."

This is the truth of the story which certain Wagnerians have embroidered into the following romance. My brother showed Wagner an opera he had composed, whereupon Wagner, enraged, had replied: "It is a worthless piece of work." My brother was deeply offended, and his apostasy dated from that episode. But *la bêtise humaine* can find no other explanation for a change of mind except wounded vanity and therefore, invents such unpsychological fables.

As a result of my brother's "well-bred behavior" this episode had no unpleasant results, as Wagner always made an especial attempt to be agreeable when he found that he had offended Nietzsche, and when agreeable, was always irresistible.

It has always remained a mystery to me why my brother did not tell me of this incident. It must have been because he took it much more to heart than Wagner would have me believe. When I later questioned him about it, he was silent for a moment and then said softly: "Lisbeth, at that moment Wagner was not great!"

To all intents and purposes, the friendly feelings still remained unchanged, but little scenes such as that just described throw a strong light upon the state of my brother's mind. I have already mentioned that Wagner's indifference and adverse criticism of the second *"Thoughts Out of Season"* had a depressing effect upon my brother at Easter 1874; it was then that he said to himself with a heavy heart: "It has become plain that my only value lies in my being a Wagner commentator: I am to be nothing more. I am permitted to admire only *that* which is stamped with the seal of Bayreuth's approval."

Was there ever a great spirit willing to have its course circumscribed and mapped out by another? At that time, the current of my brother's development was flowing in broader and deeper channels than ever before and was he now to permit it to be dammed up into a corner? This thought agitated and rankled—and yet all the time was urging him to greater freedom. In June of 1874, I plucked up my courage and spoke to Fritz of his hidden grief, whereupon he answered emphatically: "Ah, Lisbeth, each one of us has a worm gnawing at his vitals, and I am no exception." And in a letter dated July 9, he wrote to Gersdorff: "Many things are fermenting in me, among them much that is extreme and daring. I should like to know just how far I should be justified in communicating these things to my best friends, naturally not in writing."

Cold superficial souls will not be able to comprehend the inner conflict with which my brother had been struggling during the past four years. What do such persons know of a passionate friendship such as bound my brother to Richard Wagner, what of the agitation of a loving heart all a-quiver with pain at the thought of the heart-breaking hours preceding the final farewell? My brother was not only grieved at the thought of what this break would mean to him but of the distress he would, thereby, be causing others; but it is possible that he had an exaggerated idea of Wagner's feelings on the matter.

Upon returning from Bayreuth to Basle in August of 1874, my brother at once set about re-writing a part of *"Schopenhauer as Educator."* Apparently other and newer thoughts had come to him during his sojourn in Bayreuth and it is therefore, most regrettable that the first draft of the work is no longer available, so that a comparison might be made, with a view of establishing the changes made out of affection and deference for Wagner. On the twenty-fourth of September, he wrote to Gersdorff: ". . . The closing weeks of our summer semester was a difficult time for me, dear friend, and I draw a deep breath now that it is over. In addition to all my other work I was obliged to re-write a comparatively long section of my No. 3, and the inevitable fatigue and soul-exhaustion attendant upon such studies came very near upsetting me, and I have not yet entirely recovered from the child-bed fever. But at all

226

events, I can console myself by the thought that something worth while has been brought into the world, and a work in which you will take the keenest delight."

The forthcoming publication of the third *"Thoughts Out of Season"* was also announced to the friends in Bayreuth, as is to be seen from a draft of a letter found in an old notebook. The letter itself, like so many others, was destroyed in Bayreuth, but the replies of Wagner and Frau Cosima indicate that the rough draft agrees in the main with the letter as it was finally written.

Friedrich Nietzsche to Richard Wagner.

(Draft of Letter written about Oct. 10, 1874.)

"The summer has now come and gone as well as my autumn vacation, and nothing came of the meeting of my friends arranged to take place at this time, or rather it all turned out quite different from what we had planned. Gersdorff was expected from day to day and finally arrived just as I was in the thick of my heaviest school work; Rohde had even worse luck during the fortnight he spent in Basle as we were all over-run with work to an almost unendurable degree and were consequently unable to do much for my friend. Krug passed through Basle with his wife, Deussen was also here, but young Baumgartner deserted me to absolve his year of military service with the Hussar regiment in Bonn. We three friends in 'Baumann's Cave' take long walks together but not without that feeling of making ourselves ridiculous that always attaches itself to an isolated trinity. As evening comes and we see our three long shadows stalking along near us, the thought of the *'Three Just Comb-*

227

Makers' (the title of one of Gottfried Keller's novels) occurs to us and we laugh ourselves to death.

"Within the next few days, I hope to send you my No. 3 which I recommend to your sympathetic good-will and consideration. The average reader will think that I am talking about the man in the moon, but in the long run, I only care about 6 or 7 readers. The work must now take its course and I know of nothing more to say about it. In the meantime, ideas for the succeeding number are already pressing in upon me, but heavy duties, particularly in the way of Greek literature, make it seem highly improbable that I shall be in a position to put my hand to this task."

Copy of a telegram sent by Richard Wagner to Nietzsche upon receiving the above-mentioned copy of his *"Schopenhauer as Educator"*:

"Deep and great. Presentation of Kant boldest and most original idea. Verily, only intelligible for those who are possessed. I can picture to myself the three just men. May they cast long shadows in the sun-land of the present.
"Yours,

"R. W."

This third *"Thoughts Out of Season"* was greeted with enthusiasm in Bayreuth, and made the subject of much rejoicing. It was received with quite different feelings from the second which had provoked only a moderate degree of approval, not unmixed with antagonism. Frau Cosima wrote a wonderful letter on the subject:

"This is *my 'Thoughts Out of Season,'* my dear friend, and I thank you from the bottom of my heart for the pleasurable stimulation the book has given me. The feelings, thoughts, ideas, intuition, power and knowledge therein displayed, have amazed me and I have warmed my soul at the fire of your enthusiasm,—here burning so bright and clear—just as I did in the case of your *'Birth of Tragedy.'* And how beautiful and characteristic is your language! It is easy to see that here you had a concrete and inspiring theme which you were able to grasp in its entirety, and the depths to which you have moved me are only to be measured by the strength you have displayed in your comprehension of this theme. I find your introduction extraordinarily beautiful and artistic; it suggests those magnificent introductions employed by the master musicians in leading up to their *Allegri.* And you could not have introduced the name of Schopenhauer more effectively and beautifully, and at the same time, done more to arouse the interest of the reader, than by expounding to us, first of all, the debt we owe to culture. I find it particularly beautiful that you write here subjectively, for as you say later on, the effect of Schopenhauer's genius is almost uncanny, and for that reason it is of the utmost importance to learn the personal testimony of one of the elect.

"The comparison with Montaigne, the distinctive qualities of cheerfulness, in the case of greater and lesser men, the three elements comprised in the impression created by Schopenhauer completely satisfied my curiosity as to how you would succeed in characterizing this powerful genius. Your very correct discrimination between Kant and Schopenhauer brought to my mind a picture, in which the former in his life, works (and quite abnormal genius!) was to be compared to Bach, while Schopenhauer could only be compared to Beethoven; Beethoven also certainly prized his own music more highly than did his contemporaries. But the most beautiful thing of all—in fact, that part of your essay which moved me to tears—was your presentation of the three dangers by which genius is confronted, and more particularly the picture you draw of the third danger. I feel that your eloquence and illuminating prescience has furnished me with the key to Luther's visitations, and when you affirm that you take no pleasure in the German language, you are magnanimously punished by the noble muse, who has endowed you with a gift of persuasion and impressiveness, to be attained through the medium of no other language, in this particular field of thought. Do you not see, dear friend, that this *is* German (not national), that it is *felt* as a German would feel it, *spoken* as a German would speak it? Having arrived at this point, I should like to ask you if you do not think that nations, as well as individuals, are unique, and that therefore, Germany is not to be treated as only one little corner of the earth (compared to larger territorial areas) for she is unique both in her good and her bad qualities, and our only wish should be that her development may not be retarded by the worms and caterpillars gnawing at her vitals?

"Personally I do not share the feeling of impending danger upon which you touch; I regard our democracy as so miserable a thing, that to me, it seems to be very far removed from Rousseau's 'Image of Man,' nor do I think that it will ever be able to achieve the same results. I can imagine that one fine day the Socialists will have vanished, as you so splendidly forecast in regard to the professors of philosophy (in many ways, one of the most beautiful passages in your entire essay). Socialism is disharmonious, as is everything, of necessity, that is achieved by force, and will disappear from the moment it is no longer fortified by genuine non-German support. But you are right in saying that anxiety on this score, whether justified or not, has a most demoralizing effect. The Goethe man is very correct and beautiful, however incapable we are in youth of appreciating this image of man, and would like to place a *sword at his left*. Even more beautiful was your portrayal of the 'platonic idea' in Schopenhauer's philosophy. Hail to you, dear friend, for your capacity of establishing the innermost nature of genius thereby rescuing this treasure from the dark shaft of knowledge, and bringing it again to the clear light of day. Your penetrating vision, your firm resolve, your assured boldness of action (I call your writings 'acts') are abiding qualities whether recognized or not by the world, at present. It is said that there are persons, who, wandering about at random, are able to establish for a certainty the presence of minerals or water in the ground upon which they are treading, and in the same way, you seem, quite intuitively, to have apprehended the nature of genius. You not only understand the language of genius, but your perspicacity bores through the deep shaft of moral values and the infinitely deeper one of the sufferings of genius. I was deeply moved when I read what you say of the degeneracy of the sensitive natures in Germany, as this is the one thing about our Fatherland which grieves me inexpressibly. What shall I say further of your presentation of Nature in her so-called extravagant mood, of your wonderful picture of the relationship existing between animals and men, of the aim and abuse of culture, of the present-day philosophers, who read newspapers and attend concerts in their leisure moments, and of the relations between philosophy and the state! Should I attempt to do this, there would be no end to this letter, and I should most probably not succeed in making myself clear or intelligible; what I have already written will surely suffice, despite its cursory character, to give you a picture of the impression created upon me by the reading of your book. On the whole, it seems to me that in none of your previous works, have you so fully proven yourself a master of form and content, and as a consequence of this, your wit and humor flow more freely in this essay. It is also 'cheerful' as you say of Schopenhauer's works, and I am of the opinion that it will cut a deep furrow, did not things look as they do with us! But who would dare indulge in a prophecy under the present confused conditions? You will completely win over the 6 or 7 for whom you write, and in the long run, this minority will also have a word to say. . . ."

This splendid letter of Cosima's is not to be regarded merely as an expression of her own personal expression on *"Schopenhauer as Educator,"* but also reflects Wagner's views on the subject. Wagner himself once told me that when Cosima was reading the book aloud to him, she kept a note-book and pencil at hand, and jotted down his comments. Every one of my brother's works was read aloud and commented upon in the same fashion. Therefore, Cosima's letters containing discussions of my brother's books are to be regarded as of particular value, mirroring, as they do, an accurate picture of Wagner's mood at the time of reading.

On the other hand, I should not like to state positively that my brother expressed himself as candidly in his letters to the Bayreuth friends. There were several reasons for this, one of them being his desire to avoid everything that could possibly give offense to his dearly-beloved friend, and furthermore, his regard for the formalities of polite intercourse. My brother often carried this delicacy so far as to express adverse opinions of men and things, if he thought that by so doing, he would please the person to whom he was writing or speaking. For example, attacks upon the Jews are often to be found in his letters to Wagner which expressed Wagner's views on the subject rather than his own. This hyper-courtesy was often a great burden to him and he was angry with himself with yielding to this feeling. The knowledge that he was not able to keep up the same freedom of intercourse with Wagner and his family as he had done in the happy Tribschen days also added to his depression and it is easy to understand his feelings when he writes:

". . . Ah, we lonely, free souls. We see that we continually seem to be other than we really are; while wishing for nothing so much as to be honest and sincere, we are caught in a net of misunderstandings and despite our most passionate desires, are unable to prevent a haze of false meanings, compromises, and erroneous innuendoes from obscuring our real deeds and thoughts. A cloud of melancholy settles on our brow, for the thought that speciousness is a necessity is as hateful to us as that of death, itself. . . ."

Without a knowledge of the above-mentioned reasons, it would be impossible to understand why my brother wrote such melancholy letters to Bayreuth during the winter of

1874-75. Otherwise, he was in fairly good spirits; his *"Schopenhauer as Educator"* had convinced him that he was on the right road, his health was excellent and great activity reigned in Basle social circles that winter. A few of the German professors and their wives had formed a little circle, in true German fashion, with a fixed date for reunions. To this belonged the philosopher Max Heinze, the political economist, von Miaskowski, Immermann of the medical faculty, Professor Overbeck, Dr. Romundt and my brother. The time was passed in music-making, readings, tableaux and even dancing. Frau Miaskowski has published passages from her correspondence at that time, which would have seemed quite incredible to the friends in Bayreuth had they compared it with Nietzsche's letters to them of the same period. She says: "One evening, we took along a young woman who happened to be our guest at the time. Upon reaching home, she remarked that she had never been in an atmosphere of such innocent jollity, and the queerest part of it all was that the two chief fun-makers were Nietzsche and Overbeck, both of them known throughout Germany as the worst sort of pessimists and Schopenhauerians."

High spirits also reigned in Bayreuth where Christmas was being celebrated for the first time in Wagner's new home, christened *"Wahnfried."* The Christmas tree, placed in the large reception hall, stretched out its branches until they reached the golden gallery. Frau Wagner wrote us a detailed account of the festivities and described how she stood in the gallery, taking the part of the "dear God" to the young musicians of the *Nibelung* "Kanzelei," who were climbing up and down the ladder disposing of the decorations according to her instructions, while Wagner in the

role of Jacob, but not a sleeping one, attended to matters
at the foot of the ladder. My brother's letter of birthday
greeting to Frau Cosima introduced a minor strain into
this symphony of gayety and Christmas cheer, and so annoyed Wagner that he replied at once and took this opportunity of airing all the grievances he had been cherishing
for the last year:

Richard Wagner to Friedrich Nietzsche.

"Dear friend:

"Your letter has given rise to renewed uneasiness about
you. My wife will write you at length on this subject in
a few days, but I happen to have a free quarter of an hour
on the second holiday and this I am going to devote to
you, possibly to your annoyance. I must let you know
what we have been saying about you; one thing was that
never in my entire life did I have such opportunities for
masculine companionship as you seem to have in Basle;
but if you are all determined to be hypochondriacs, then
this intercourse will be of no value to you. There seems
to be a lack of young women, but as my old friend Sulzer
used to say, 'Where can we get them unless we steal them?'
I should say that in a case of extreme necessity, one would
be justified in stealing. Of one thing I am firmly convinced,
and that is that you must either get married or write an
opera. One would do you just about as much good—or
harm!—as the other. But of the two, I advise you to marry.

"In the meantime I can recommend a palliative, but you
are so in the habit of looking after your own apothecary
that it is impossible for any one to prescribe for you. For

example, when we built our house, we made arrangements to offer you an asylum at any time, such as was never offered to me even in the time of my direst necessity. The plan was for you to spend your entire summer vacations here with us, but no sooner has winter set in than you cautiously announce your intention of spending the summer on a high and remote peak of the Swiss Alps. Can that be otherwise construed than as a refusal of our invitation in advance? We could be of great help to you. Why do you scorn this assistance on every occasion? Gersdorff and all the others always enjoy being here. There will be a great deal going on here. All of my Nibelung singers will be passed in review, the scenic painter will be at work, the machinist will be busy fitting up the stage and all of us will be head over ears in the matter. But—every one knows this and other peculiarities of our friend Nietzsche.

"I shall say nothing more on this subject, however, as I realize that is not of the slightest use. For Heaven's sake, do marry a rich wife! Why was Gersdorff born a man? Or go off on a long trip and enrich your mind with all the beautiful experiences which make Hillebrand so versatile and enviable (in your eyes!) and then—write your opera which I know will be scandalously difficult to perform. What Satan made a pedagogue of you? You see how radical I have become under the influence of your letter; but God knows, I cannot look on and remain quiet.

"By the way, Dr. Fuchs gave me great pleasure by quoting a passage from Overbeck's book, which interested me so much that I am now re-reading it.

"For the second time, by the way! Full rehearsals next

summer (with orchestra) in Bayreuth. The Festival in 1876. We cannot be ready before then.

"I am taking daily baths, because I can no longer endure the misery in my abdomen. Do you also bathe, and eat meat?

"Heartfelt greetings from

"Yours faithfully,

"Second Christmas Day, 1874. R. W."

The mention of Prof. Hillebrand of Florence refers to a disagreement my brother had with his friends in Bayreuth the preceding year. My brother wrote to Gersdorff: "Here is a splendid piece of news. Order immediately from Görlitz *Twelve Letters From an Aesthetic Heretic*,' published by Robert Oppenheim, Berlin, 1874. You will take unbounded delight in this book, but I shall leave you to guess the name of the author. New courage is ever springing up in my heart and our little 'Society of Hopeful Ones' seems to be steadily increasing."

The book to which reference is made here, was written by Carl Hillebrand, of Florence, whom Gersdorff knew and esteemed very highly. The views therein expressed coincided so exactly with my brother's well-known theories that even Jacob Burckhardt assumed that the author must be an intimate friend of Nietzsche's, possibly Gersdorff.

My brother and his little circle of friends in Basle thought so highly of this book that he sent it to Bayreuth, but despite his warm recommendations, it found but scant recognition from Wagner and Frau Cosima. The latter wrote: "Upon your recommendation, I have read Hillebrand's little work and while some very delightful ideas are expressed

237

therein, I, nevertheless, found much to censure. First of all, a certain diffusiveness and carelessness of form, an arrogant tone, and a conspicuous lack of warmth, depth and humor. I should like to say to him what was said to *Malvolio:* Just because you are virtuous is no reason that there are no cakes and wine in the world. . . . Further, I find that the essay has an entirely erroneous fundament; had he really found the picture given as the *raison d'être* of the letters, then it was plainly his duty to reveal the secret and give the name of it. Even though it were proven later that he had been mistaken, this error would have been condoned as the result of misguided enthusiasm, and in any case, would have been of more service than his coquettish half-veiled allusions. An error of judgment, later confessed, is always a courageous deed. His *constructive* hopes also appear rather insignificant; they were unquestionably influenced by the '*Birth of Tragedy*,' '*Opera and Drama*,' '*Art and Politics*,' etc., but he did not possess sufficient intellectual strength and courage to ally himself to these 'hopeful ones,' but was bent upon reserving a little special niche for himself and his work. To me, this little niche looks very much like a sulking corner. And then his citations—'*Tom Jones*' and '*Orestria*.' . . . And furthermore, to expect the Germans to know what the expression *Tarte à la crême* signifies! Do you think the same thing could be expected from the French had he quoted from the German without giving the name of the author? The result is that the reader recognizes the intention and at once becomes disgruntled. And to my mind, Goethe is quite another sort of universal genius from Molière. On the whole, I found that a great deal of bad taste was displayed in this little book which is forever harping upon the question of taste. . . ."

I can not give the exact reason for Frau Cosima's harsh verdict but only remember that Wagner always displayed a particular aversion to the expressions "taste" and "tasteful" and for this reason the little book (the exemplification of "good taste" in the best sense of the word) found no favor in her eyes. My brother had no particular reason for breaking a lance for Hillebrand, as the latter's criticisms of my brother's writings were not entirely sympathetic. But however that may be, my brother found æsthetic tendencies coinciding with his own and possessed sufficient objectivity of judgment to make acknowledgment of this, irrespective of any personal feeling in the matter.

CHAPTER XXI.

MY brother spent the Christmas holidays of 1874-75 very quietly with us in Naumburg, and we again discussed many "big plans," the most immediate of these being my long cherished trip to Italy where I was to be joined by my brother at Easter. But nothing turned out as we expected. On January 17, 1875, I received a letter from my brother saying: "My dear Lisbeth, this year is going to be quite different from the plans we made at Christmas. See enclosed letter from Frau Wagner as to the plans that are brewing in Bayreuth."

Frau Cosima's letter read as follows: "I come to you with a big request and one that you will think is most unusual, my dear friend. While making preparations for our approaching tour, it has become more and more difficult for me to leave the children behind, although I know that they will be well taken care of here. My first thought was to send the two older girls to the Louisa Institute somewhat earlier than originally planned, but I had no sooner received permission to do this from the prioress than I became frightened at the idea of leaving the younger children alone the entire time, as it will scarcely be practicable to have the others come home for the Easter vacation. I would solve the problem by taking all five of them with me, did I

240

not fear the ridicule of newspaper reporters. **In this**
dilemma, I turned to Fräulein Maier and begged her to come
to my rescue and this she promised to do, but now writes
that there has been a calamity of some sort in her family
which will require her presence at home. Before resorting
to the desperate alternative of sending the children away to
school, I am writing to ask whether your sister would do
us the great favor of coming to us at the beginning of
February and remaining here as a mother to our children
when we leave on our tour the middle of March.

"They have their governess (a good-natured young girl)
and the household consists further of the housekeeper, her
sister Kuni, whom you know, the gardener, and the stable-
boy, all of them most reliable. The whole thing resolves
itself into a moral sedative to quiet my mother heart. I
would introduce your sister to our circle of friends here,
who, no doubt, would do all they could for her during our
absence. I have not written directly to your sister, wishing
to spare her the embarrassment of refusing, and thinking
that you would know best whether this request can be
granted or not. I fully recognize the difficulties with which
every one has to struggle and the restraint circumstances
place upon our movements. That I presume to ask so great
a favor from you and your sister, will most assuredly prove
to you the light in which I regard our relations. . . ."

To this my brother added: "I beg of you unconditionally
to grant this request and I feel assured in advance of our
mother's joyful assent." On this last point my brother
greatly erred, as this plan not only brought to light my
mother's hitherto concealed antagonism against the Wagners
at this time, but aroused her indignation at my brother for

having so freely disposed of me without consulting her. My brother was in the habit of monopolizing me for six months of the year in Basle and it made her very angry to learn that she was to be deprived of my company during the winter months also. A somewhat excited exchange of letters took place between the two members of my family, but finally they came to an agreement and this helped to remove the uneasiness I felt at assuming so great a responsibility. The fact that I had spent the greater part of my life in the company of so superior a person as my brother, had robbed me of the necessary self-confidence. I had come to think of myself as a very unimportant member of society and had acquired the habit of concealing my best and most original qualities as if they were something to which I had no right. On the other hand, no amount of appreciation bestowed upon my brother seemed to me to be unwarranted. This lack of self-confidence led on the one hand to a rather exaggerated self-depreciation and on the other, to all kinds of surprises for others as well as for myself, for, as a matter of fact, when any responsibility was imposed upon me, I suddenly developed qualities and gifts, hitherto unexpected. I only mention this by way of explanation, as it was not the prospect of the stay in Bayreuth that occasioned my excessive nervousness, but only the thought that I might not be able to fulfill my brother's expectations.

Early in February I set out for Bayreuth in high spirits, as it made me very happy to think I could be of service to friends whom I admired so greatly and who had always been so uncommonly kind to me. My brother was even happier than I at the turn affairs had taken, and wrote:

"Dear Lisbeth, I am delighted at your decision. I attach

great importance to this visit, which, in the long run, will be a sort of high school for you. Moreover, I know of no other way by which you could be so thoroughly initiated into my Bayreuth relations, and it is fortunate for future developments that things have so shaped themselves. I am overwhelmed with joy every time I think of it. . . ."

As has been seen from Wagner's earlier letters, he wished to appoint my brother Siegfried's legal guardian, and this will explain my brother's repeated references to the importance of my becoming more closely acquainted with conditions in *Wahnfried*. He once wrote: "When I think of the manifold obligations I shall some day be obliged to assume towards Wagner's family, it seems to me to be of the highest importance that you should also be on a familiar footing with them."

I was given a most friendly reception in Bayreuth and was made to feel perfectly at home there: Cosima took me with her to pay thirty-two calls, as a result of which I was deluged with invitations as soon as the Wagners had set out on their journey to Vienna. I was soon the best of friends with the five well-behaved, lovable children. Daniela, the eldest, was then fifteen and almost a young lady, so that I could take her with me to all the coffee parties given in my honor, but this distressed the other children so greatly that I curtailed my social activities as much as possible. Later Frau Cosima wrote my brother a letter filled with the children's lavish expressions of endearment, and in a letter to Fräulein von Meysenburg, he repeated one of Siegfried's remarks about me: ". . . Siegfriedchen said to my sister, 'I love you more than I do myself' . . ."

I took the children for long, daily walks, and remember

particularly an excursion to the "*Fantasie*," where the little ones were given a special treat in my brother's name. A carriage was ordered for the occasion and the children were allowed to have chocolate and cake to their heart's desire. They enjoyed being the chief personages at the feast and Daniela proposed a very pretty toast in verse to the "Good Uncle Nietzsche." Upon learning of this, my brother wrote: "Thank the children for the dear Uncle-Nietzsche toast at the Fantasie picnic; it gave me a ridiculous amount of pleasure."

I was somewhat surprised to find comparatively little understanding in Bayreuth for Wagner's art, but on the other hand, tremendous interest in all the external circumstances connected with it. I must have written something of this sort to my brother, as he answered: "I perfectly understand your remarks in regard to the good people of Bayreuth; I do not remember ever having claimed that it was an 'enthusiastic' city. But you will surely have noticed that it is a place where we all share in the government, even though this be only the control of gossip; in other words, that one can live there just as he pleases and the people soon adapt themselves to conditions."

But that which gave the greatest pleasure during this sojourn in Bayreuth was the fact that my admiration for Wagner and Frau Cosima increased rather than diminished upon closer acquaintance, as I thus gained a better understanding of their unique qualities of head and heart. Wagner was an ideal head of a family; I have seen him leave his work to play "horse and wagon" with the children, and all difficulties were met with an assumption of cheerfulness.

But he could also manifest great impatience when approached with all sorts of tiresome requests; one thing that was extremely distasteful to him being the examination of new compositions. Some days the mail brought heaps of such compositions and at such times Wagner raged in a manner truly Jovian. One incident of this nature has remained indelibly impressed upon my memory because of the part I took in it. An unusually bulky parcel arrived one day, containing an opera composed by the director of such and such a bank. When Wagner told me this, I said, "Oh, I know his name, as I have some stock in that bank." Wagner raised his finger with a warning gesture, saying: "Little girl, sell those stocks at once; a bank director who writes operas does not pay sufficient attention to business." Thereupon, banker Feustel took the matter up and reassured us as to the liability of the bank in question. But in this instance, the artist's intuition was correct, as the bank later became quasi-bankrupt and my disregard of Wagner's advice cost me several thousand marks. On the other hand, Wagner was always ready to comply with any reasonable request made by his friends whether it were the inspection of manuscripts or the autographing of photographs [tasks for which he had no great fondness]. For instance, my brother asked him for a picture for Frau von Moltke, the sister-in-law of the field marshal, which Wagner sent at once with the following note:

Richard Wagner to Friedrich Nietzsche.

"Dear friend:

"Here is the photograph selected by my wife, and your sister also approved of this one. It does not please me at all, and moreover, I wear my hair much more becomingly at present. But as it is intended for a woman, it is a matter for the women to decide.

"I have now become a regular man of business; that is to say, a theatrical promoter. The thought makes me dizzy, not once in a while, but every day. We are leaving for Vienna day after tomorrow. Delightful thought! The only thing pleasant about it is the opportunity it gives me to play the Götterdämmerung excerpts for my wife. I imagine you receive frequent reports from Wahnfried. The most gratifying news that could come to me from Basle is that you are well.

"Cordial greetings from

"Yours,

"Rich. Wagner."

I shall never forget the quiet evenings, when the children had been sent to bed and we sat together in the library talking of all manner of things. At first, my brother was the chief topic of conversation and I can still see the significant looks exchanged between Wagner and Frau Cosima as I related how cheerful my brother had been during the Christmas holidays and how many diverting things he had to tell us of the Basle "circle." "Then why does he always write us such melancholy letters?" asked Wagner, almost angrily. "Does he do that?" I replied, genuinely astonished, and upon receiving an affirmative, hastened to explain that in writing to Wahnfried he was always made to realize how far away he lived, and could no longer share all their intimate family experiences as in the dear old days at Tribschen. Wagner seemed somewhat mollified, declaring that it did him

246

good to hear this explanation. And of a truth, my stay in Wahnfried did much to dissipate Wagner's distrust of my brother's loyalty, and this in turn, pleased my brother tremendously.

During the course of our conversation, I heard much of Wagner's inward sufferings, and it was from these confidences that I learned of the heavy burden borne by geniuses who, standing as they do in direct contact with all the great movements of thought and culture, are exposed to endless friction. Wagner's wrath at the German people (to which, as far as I know, he continued to give expression to the end of his days) can only be explained by the fact that his entire life, his work and his aspirations had been rendered extremely difficult by the antagonism met with in Germany. When reminded of this, even in the remotest way, he flew into an uncontrollable fit of rage. I often had the feeling that these outbursts of wrath to which Cosima and I were forced to listen, were in reality intended for the spirits of his adversaries hovering about him, to accept a theory once expressed by my brother. Although Cosima never gave the slightest cause for such outbursts, he often turned upon her, and the equanimity with which she endured these injustifiable attacks heightened my admiration for this remarkable woman. On the whole, it must be admitted that being the wife of a genius is not the easiest position in the world to fill.

During my visit a warm friendship sprang up between Cosima and myself and we began to use the familiar "Du" in addressing one another. Great fortitude was demanded of her at this time, as a subtle form of blackmail was employed against her, and although these attacks were repelled with true greatness and dignity, she nevertheless suffered inexpressibly. I endeavored to console her as best I could, without knowing the true nature of these accusations at the time. As a result of these machinations, she was obliged to dismiss a number of the servants who had been in her employ while she was still the wife of Hans von Bülow.

As they were on the whole rather incompetent, they were easily replaced by one reliable man servant and the remaining honest Bavarians of the household were glad to know that this mischief-making element had been dismissed. From this time forth, Wagner's former dissolute household developed into a veritable "idyll," as Cosima later wrote me.

I have often been asked to describe Cosima's appearance and character and I shall here make an attempt to do this. She had a good skin and a wealth of very beautiful hair, a very large mouth and nose, which she inherited from her father, Franz Liszt, to whom she bore a striking resemblance. Like him she was also tall and thin, too much so for a woman. But after all, her appearance was a matter of complete indifference, as she possessed so much charm as to make every one oblivious of her external traits. In fact, no one would have wished her to look other than she did, as her entire appearance was admirably suited to her character and dominating personality. For me, Cosima was the personification of "will to power" in the noblest sense of this term; so long as Wagner lived, she exercised these powers by and through him, by which I do not mean to say that she ruled him, but only that *his* art, *his* fame, *his* greatness, and *his* puissance, were her instruments of power. It is only since his death, at least so it seems to me, that her eminent gifts have been given their fullest expression. To judge Cosima by any other standards would be to misunderstand her splendid character, her abandonment of Bülow for Wagner, her entire rich and full life and her later evolution into the "*Margravine of Bayreuth*," as my brother jokingly christened her.

A German writer, sadly lacking in psychological instincts, started the absurd report that my brother had entertained a grand passion for Cosima. Wagnerians, who were indignant with my brother for his apostasy to Wagner (entirely overlooking the fact that this was done from purely artistic and philosophical convictions) endeavored to make capital out of this invention by misrepresenting the entire origin of the relationship existing between Wagner and Nietzsche and the causes leading up to the final rupture. Any one who has followed the course of these relations from chapter to chapter in this little book, will be convinced of the absolute absurdity of this gossip.

My brother always spoke in terms of the greatest respect of Frau Wagner and pronounced her "the most sympathetic woman," in fact, "the only woman possessing the grand manner" whom he had met during the course of his whole life. Any thought of an alleged "grand passion" would most assuredly have seemed ridiculous to him.

In one of his aphorisms, my brother has very clearly described how a feeling of great love arises in a man. (Naturally he was speaking here objectively.) ". . . Whence springs this deep and sudden passion of a man for a woman? Least of all from sensuality but rather when the man discovers weakness, dependence and at the same time, pride in some woman. His soul as it were, boils over, he is at

249

once touched and yet resentful, and it is in this moment that love springs up in his heart."

The attributes here described are fundamentally different from those possessed by Cosima: "Weakness, a clinging nature, pride"—I am moved to laughter at the thought of the very opposite qualities awakening the grand passion in my brother.

It was a great delight to my brother to learn so many details of the life in Bayreuth from my letters and later verbally, and all that I told him only strengthened his belief in Wagner's friendship. Gersdorff confirmed these reports so that my brother had no reason to doubt the absolute sincerity of those feelings. Gersdorff was on a very intimate footing at Wahnfried, and Wagner looked upon him as the only person to whom he could confide his thoughts about Nietzsche. This is shown in the following letter:

Richard Wagner to Baron von Gersdorff.

"My faithful friend:

"You do me a great honor in regarding my opinion as of such vital importance to you in your decisions. I should be very well satisfied with myself, did I really think that I had exerted so great an influence upon you, as you carry out your resolves with such manliness, energy and persistence that I should like to be able to say that I had been of assistance to you. On the other hand, close contact with another friend seems to have only a confusing, in fact an injurious, effect. By this I do not mean solely our beloved Nietzsche, though I must confess that I cannot see how he would have been any happier had he never met me. Be that as it may, he came across my path in a field of life that could easily have become a quagmire had we not been able to fly away at the right moment. You on the other hand, tread upon firm ground, bear fruit and introduce a stimulating current into our lives. Upon closer scrutiny, I believe that I am nearly always stuck in the mire, but I affect not to notice it and this I attribute to my peculiar gifts. But best of all is my ability to make my dearest friends think that I am floating in the air, and this is your doing.

"Therefore, good luck to your speedy and honorable discharge from Hohenheim. I can already picture you to myself on your carefully cultivated estates where all of us will be assembled for a rural festival, myself attired in Don Quixote's arcadian costume.

"Things are going fairly well with us, in fact, the children are too well and positively rampageous. The devil will soon be to pay here, and then you must not fail us!

"Cordial greetings. 'You are my well-beloved friend, in whom I take great delight.'

"That sounds like the dear God speaking.

"Yours,

"Bayreuth, May 31, 1875. Richard Wagner."

"P.S.—In six days we celebrate the sixth anniversary of Nietzsche's first visit to Tribschen."

I will add here a few words of explanation in regard to Gersdorff, who after the death of his two older brothers fell heir to entailed estates of his father. Hohenheim, alluded to in Wagner's letter, was an agricultural college where, by Wagner's advice, Gersdorff was taking a course of training preparatory to assuming the active management of his properties.

When I met my brother in Baden-Baden at Whitsuntide, 1875, there was no end to our exchange of confidences and ideas in regard to Bayreuth. The big rehearsals for the Festival were to take place during the summer of 1875 and he was beside himself with joy in anticipation of this event. During the winter he had written me: "Are you not delighted that my summer vacation fits in so well with the Bayreuth rehearsals and festivities? To me, it seems nothing short of a miracle." But again fate intervened. Without any particular warning my brother fell very ill, and as it was his stomach this time that revolted, he was told by his physician that the hotel cuisine was responsible for these conditions and that he must set up his own menage where a prescribed diet could be followed. The doctor also forbade my brother going to Bayreuth, as he deemed such an exertion far too strenuous both for his eyes and his general nervous system. Gersdorff was chosen as the friend to apprise Wagner of this fatal news, the letter in which my brother appointed him as his mediator, reading as follows: ". . . Under these circumstances it has become imperative to establish my own home with the help of my sister. We have taken an apartment near the former one and expect to move in just after the summer vacation. In spite of everything, I have managed to keep up my studies and lectures, not allowing anything to interfere with these tasks except on the very worst days when I am forced to remain in bed. My plans for the summer depend upon the success of the cure I am now taking, but in any case, it will be some *spa*. I have great faith in this new domestic arrangement with my sister and we shall endeavor to live very systematically. To prove to you that I have not entirely lost heart, I must tell you that I have just finished drawing up an outline for my university lectures for the *next seven years*. But life has many vexations, and aside from that, there is something so undignified about sicknesses of all sorts, as they cannot even be regarded as accidents.

"Will you prepare the friends in Bayreuth for my not coming in July? Wagner will be very much annoyed, but not any more than I shall be. . . ."

I did not believe that it would be possible for my brother to remain away from Bayreuth, as he had been living for years in anticipation of this event and the friends had planned to have a reunion there. Gersdorff was also of my opinion, and my brother seriously considered disregarding the advice of his physician. With this in mind, he wrote to Gersdorff: "I am almost of your opinion in regard to Bayreuth. It simply will not do; I could not endure to be the only one absent. Let us wait a little! I shall surely be able to find some way out of the difficulty."

It was also an inexpressible disappointment for me to give up the rehearsals, but after discussing all the pros and cons of the case, my brother came to the conclusion that it would be folly for him to attempt it.

From Steinbad, near Bonndorf in the Black Forest of Baden, he wrote to Rohde: "Dear friend, all of you are assembled in Bayreuth today and I am the only one missing from our circle. My half-formed plan of appearing suddenly in your midst one day, and refreshing my soul by the sight of my friends, has proven an impossibility. It can not be! I can say this today with conviction. I have just had a long conversation with **Dr.** Wiel about my condition, as I was kept in bed yesterday by a violent headache and during the afternoon and night had several spells of vomiting. The lesser trouble, dilation of the stomach, has yielded somewhat to the cure I have been taking for the past fortnight, but much more time will be required before any positive results will be seen in the nervous affection of my eyes. The only thing to be done is to observe the régime very strictly and have an infinite degree of patience. I had a few very good days, the weather was fresh and cool and I roamed around in the forests and mountains quite alone, but I cannot tell you how cheerful and agreeable it was. Nor would I dare to put into words all the hopes, plans, and possibilities upon the realization of which I have set my heart. Almost every day is made memorable by the receipt of dear, affectionate letters; the thought that I belong to you and that you belong to me, beloved friends, always fills me with pride and emotion. If one only had a little happiness to *impart!*

"That which causes me the greatest anxiety and impatience is the thought of being absolutely good-for-nothing, and of being obliged to let things take their course, however pitiless that may be. And again, at other times, it seems to me as if I were a sort of lucky upstart who had escaped all the severest knocks and blows of fate.

"I have not dwelt sufficiently on the stupidity and maliciousness of fate, and am not at all worthy to be classed among the host of the truly unfortunate. In other words, I am trying to say that after all, I have some happiness to give to others, if I only knew how. . . ."

Poor Rohde was involved in a very unfortunate love affair

at this time, and took a more melancholy view of the situation than was, perhaps, necessary. Knowing this, my brother was now prepared to share with his friend some part of his own good fortune. In this we find an unconscious admission that he had not been made inconsolable by his enforced absence from Bayreuth, but on the contrary, regarded it as a sort of fortuitous escape from some disagreeable experience by which he was threatened. Other friends besides Rohde were also in trouble, until suddenly he gave his own case a serious examination and then wrote to Rohde: ". . . Desperation on all sides! and I am *not* desperate. And yet I am not in Bayreuth. Can you tell me how to construe this? I can find no explanation for it. And yet I am there in spirit at least three or four times every day and like a ghost my thoughts are continually hovering around Bayreuth. Tell me more about it, dear friend. You need have no fear of arousing desperate soul-longings. When I am out walking, I conduct long passages (all those that I know by heart) with my walking stick and sing the music as best I can. Remember me affectionately to the Wagners."

My brother came back from Bonndorf in good spirits and enthusiastic about his new domestic arrangements. Gersdorff and Rohde paid him a visit in the autumn and once more plans were made for a visit to Bayreuth and again frustrated.

One day I said: "Fritz, you will not have been in Bayreuth once during 1875." He replied quickly: "But *you* were there for a long time and so was Gersdorff. Besides all of the friends met there during the summer."

"Oh, Fritz," I said, "do you honestly believe that all of us put together could take your place in Wagner's affections?" "No," Fritz softly replied, "Nor can any one else take Wagner's place in *my* affections."

CHAPTER XXII.

(1876)

CORDIAL letters received from his friends in Bayreuth during the summer of 1875 again revived my brother's old love and admiration for Wagner and for the time being his severe criticism of Wagner's art was relegated to the background. By referring to my brother's notebook of that period, it would seem that the following aphorism was written only for his own private gratification:

"I know of no other way by which I could have been vouchsafed the purest, serenest delight than through the Wagner music, and this, despite the fact that it by no means speaks always of happiness, but more often of uncanny subterranean forces, of human conduct, of suffering in the midst of happiness, and of the finiteness of all human happiness. The enchantment, therefore, that radiates from this music must lay in the manner in which it speaks to us. It is not difficult to realize what manner of man Wagner is and what his music means to him, if we consider the scenes, conflicts and catastrophes in which he seems to take the keenest delight. No poetry in the world contains anything more beautiful than Wotan's relations to Siegfried, his love, the obligatory hostility and the joy in pure destruction. All

257

of this is symbolical of Wagner's own nature: love for that by which one is redeemed, judged and annihilated, but the whole conceived in a truly god-like manner."

Professor Holzer once said of this aphorism: "Wagner himself would have been god-like in his nature, had he been able to feel towards Nietzsche as Wotan did towards Siegfried. But between the lines of Wagner's and Cosima's letters one can read the paltry fear that Nietzsche could outgrow Wagner. He was always being metaphorically 'ducked', and there is scarcely one of Cosima's letters in which she does not give some intimation that Nietzsche's real vocation should be to place himself completely in the service of Wagner's genius."

This statement is exaggerated, but be it as it may, I can only state with the utmost confidence, that at no time during this period did my brother ever maintain that he bore the same relation to Wagner as Siegfried did to Wotan, nor that he was obliged to fight him in order to be absolutely loyal to him. On the contrary, he was never weary of recalling the sixteen years of inexpressible delight that Wagner's art had brought into his life, as well as the beatific hours of close friendship by which they were bound during the Tribschen period, and he always confessed how poverty-stricken his life would have been without the friendship and art of Richard Wagner.

It was in this mood that he began to write his fourth *"Thoughts Out of Season: Richard Wagner in Bayreuth."* This title was originally intended for the fifth *"Thoughts,"* and *"We Philologians,"* at that time practically finished but never carried to completion, was to be published as No. 4.

"Richard Wagner in Bayreuth"

My brother worked on his Wagner essay from August until October, and the greater part of the manuscript was read aloud to me. Suddenly, he declared that he could proceed no further with the work, as it did not please him, and early in October, he wrote to Rohde: "My essay on Richard Wagner will remain unpublished. It is almost finished, but it falls so far short of the standard I have set for myself, as to possess no further value than that of a new orientation upon the most difficult point of all that which we have hitherto experienced. I do not stand sufficiently above the matter and I am conscious of the fact that I have not been entirely successful with this orientation, to say nothing of the correspondingly trifling value it could have for others."

How dissatisfied he was with his preliminary work on his new "*Thoughts*" may be seen from the draft of a preface which he also read aloud to me and then tore into pieces, accompanying this act by all sorts of humorous and serious observations. After persistent search, this preface has been brought to light in one of my brother's notebooks:

"There are, possibly, a few quite superficial persons who know nothing of Bayreuth and the idea associated with this name; and then there is a large class which claims to be initiated into this idea and is given to circulating false impressions of the same. But how colorless are even the sincere and splendid things that remain to be written about it as compared to the feelings of those who are candid enough to confess them, and on the other hand, how inarticulate must those others admit themselves to be, when glowing with the fire of this spirit, they attempt for the first time to speak to the world of their personal experiences.

259

"I, myself, stand midway between those deficient in perception and the inarticulate class. To confess this is neither arrogant nor overly modest, but highly painful, but it is not necessary that anyone should know just why this is so. But just by reason of my middle position, a sense of duty compels me to speak and say certain things more distinctly than has hitherto been done in reference to these events. A feeling of necessity restrains me from giving concrete expression to the various considerations by which I have been influenced. By employing a certain art of subterfuge, it would be a comparatively easy matter to convey the impression of having accomplished something complete and finished, but I prefer to remain honest and say that it has been impossible for me to do this any better than I have done here, however badly it may have been done."

My brother was far too proud to publish anything with which he was not absolutely satisfied. Furthermore, he was occupied at that time, in extending and finishing off his magnificent work on *"Greek Philosophy During the Tragic Age"* and many other alluring vistas of activity were opened up to him during the summer of 1875. As we have already seen he was outlining literary work which would have sufficed to keep him employed for seven years.

This renewed activity had again imposed a great strain upon his poor eyes, and as I have already said, he was the victim of a false diagnosis, as his stomach was believed to be the seat of all his disorders, whereas, the condition of that organ was directly the result of overstrained optic nerves. At the turn of the year (1875-76) my brother was in such a poor state of health that he was obliged to curtail his university work and finally, to go over to Lake Geneva for a complete rest. Gersdorff accompanied him and he returned from this visit very much refreshed in body and mind. Now that so much was being said about the Bayreuth Festival, and definite plans were being made for our participation in this long-anticipated event, my brother felt that it would be impossible for him to keep silent any longer on this subject. Gratitude for all the blissful hours and the untold inspiration that Wagner had brought into his life, impelled him to resume work on his unfinished *"Thoughts Out of Season: Richard Wagner in Bayreuth."*

In the following letter, my brother enumerates very distinctly everything he owed to Wagner and it may be easily imagined that Wagner's reply stimulated him to further effort, as Wagner granted him permission to "look on *in his own way.*"

Friedrich Nietzsche to Richard Wagner.

"Basle, May 21, 1876.

"Deeply revered man:

"Only sentiments of the most intimate personal nature are in place on a day which has the distinction of being your birthday. Every one who has been brought in contact with you has had experiences which have affected him personally, in his *innermost* being. Such experiences cannot be added up into one great total and were this possible, birthday felicitations in the name of the *many* would signify less than the most modest wish of the *one,*

"It is now nearly seven years since I paid my first visit to Tribschen and I know of nothing to say to you on your birthday more than this: since that time, I have regularly celebrated my spiritual rebirth in May of each year. Since that meeting, you live and work in me as unceasingly as a drop of blood, but one which, most assuredly, was not in my system previous to that time. This new element that had its origin in you, incites me, makes me ashamed, encourages me, spurs me on and gives me no rest, so that I should almost feel inclined to be vexed with you for thus disquieting me, did I not feel that it is just this feeling of unrest that impels me and will eventually make of me a freer and better man. For this reason I can only be most deeply grateful to the man who has stirred these feelings to life in me, and my dearest wish for the approaching events of the summer is that you will have the same effect upon *many others*, who seized by this same feeling of unrest, will, thereby, be permitted to participate in the greatness of your character and your career.

"My only birthday wish for you today is that this may come to pass, for where is any other happiness that I could wish you? I beg you to accept this wish in the most friendly spirit from the mouth of

"Your very faithful,
"Friedrich Nietzsche."

Richard Wagner to Friedrich Nietzsche.

"O friend:

"Only get strong and well! The severest calamity that could have befallen us during all the seven years of which you write is that you were so often kept from us by so much outward 'dislocalität' (give me the word, please!) and inward 'dyskolie' (Also good!).

"Unfortunately, I have reached the point where I am only able to rescue myself from the quagmire of existence by calling good and bad jests to my aid. Yesterday we had an improvised banquet in the artists' restaurant near the theatre, and one of the guests proposed a toast to the effect that my reputation would be tremendously increased through the success of the Festival. I replied that I had found a hair in my reputation and was therefore ready to transfer this 'hide and hair' to Albert, the very competent manager of the restaurant. I stormed at my coachman because he did not congratulate me on this witticism! Otherwise everything was very nice, chiefly because it was over with. The 'enterprise,' on the whole, has cost me enough trouble and annoyance, and everyone connected with it fears me as he would the devil.

"When all this is over, I hope to stretch myself out at full length—probably in Italy, where I have resolved to take my ease with wife and child and live on the receipts of my American march.

"But for the present, on through thick and thin! If I feel that you are looking on *in your own way* I shall know that the trouble has not been in vain. *'Natura nihil facit frustra,'* said Schopenhauer to me recently and this was a comforting thought.

"Remain full of courage and in good health and give our best greetings to the little sister. It will not be long before we shall see each other again.

"It is something quite extraordinary for me to write so long a letter—as a usual thing, I only write telegrams.

"Yours most sincerely,

"Bayreuth, May 23, 1876. RICHARD WAGNER."

263

My brother at once set to work on his book, to which he added three closing chapters (Parts 9 to 11), written during a sojourn in Badenweiler. It came from the press about the end of June and was therefore ready to appear in good time for the Festival which was to open the middle of July.

Strangely enough, my brother feared that the book would meet with Wagner's disapproval, and as a matter of fact, it contains many passages which reveal something of the contradictory feelings with which my brother was then struggling. But in my opinion, Wagner was too much absorbed at the time to read carefully between the lines. Drafts of my brother's letter accompanying the author's copy of this book, and also that of his letter to Cosima, have happily been preserved, and I will first quote two passages from the rough copy not to be found in the final letters. I do this, because they show very distinctly my brother's state of mental agitation at the time these words were written:

"It is as if I had once more put everything to the venture. I implore you, let bygones be bygones, and vouchsafe your compassionate silence to one who has never spared himself. Read this essay as if it had nothing to do with you and as if I had not written it. As a matter of fact, my work should not be spoken of among the living, as it is only for the shades.

". . . In looking back over a year filled with suffering, it seems to me as if all the really good hours had been spent in conceiving and working out this essay, and it is a matter of pride for me today to be able to produce the fruits borne during this period. This might not have been possible, notwithstanding the very best intentions on my part, had I not

264

been carrying around with me for the last fourteen years the thoughts of which I have now dared to speak . . ."

Although the two letters which follow exist only in rough drafts, there is no reason for supposing that there is any deviation from the exact text of the letters finally dispatched by my brother to his friends in Bayreuth.

Friedrich Nietzsche to Richard Wagner.

(Original Draft.)

"July, 1876.

"Here, dearest master, is a sort of Bayreuth Festival sermon. It has been impossible for me to keep my mouth shut as there were certain things that I felt compelled to say. My pride and my confident hope is that I will thereby increase the joy of those who are now *rejoicing*. But how you, yourself, will take my confessions, it is impossible for me to surmise this time.

"One of the disagreeable results of my literary habits is that each time I publish a work of any kind, some element in my personal relations is called into question, and it is only by an expenditure of humor that this can be set right again. I should not like to give articulate expression as to the degree in which I feel this quite particularly, today. I grow fairly dizzy with embarrassment when I consider what I have dared to do this time, and I appear to myself like the '*Horseman on Lake Constance.*'

"In one of the very first letters you wrote me, however, you said something about your firm belief in *German freedom* of thought; and it is to this belief that I address myself today. It is only by keeping this in mind that I have found the courage to do what I have done.

"With a full heart,

"Yours humbly,

"Fʀ. N."

Friedrich Nietzsche to Frau Cosima Wagner.

(Original Draft.   July, 1876.)

". . . There is no need to assure you that the thoughts of all the friends of Bayreuth are now turned to you with sentiments of the greatest sympathy. Which one of us but wishes to prove in some way his deepest gratitude to you at the present moment? It is in this spirit that I crave your indulgence for the attempt I have made to give you some slight degree of pleasure, by sending you and the master two festival copies of my latest work. (Under the pressure of the heavy cares and burdens you are carrying you will have neither time nor inclination to read the same until the summer is past and gone.)

"But you will see from this little work that I could no longer endure the thought of remaining in my remote solitude and preparing myself for the stupendous and overwhelming occurrences of the summer, without giving vent to my joy. My only hope is that here and there I have divined something of your joy and given expression to this along with my own. I can think of nothing more beautiful to wish for."

Both Wagner and Frau Cosima replied immediately.

"Richard Wagner in Bayreuth"

Richard Wagner to Friedrich Nietzsche.

"Friend:

"Your book is simply tremendous! Where did you learn so much about me? Come to us soon and accustom yourself to the impressions by attending the rehearsals.

"Yours,

"R. W."

Frau Cosima to Friedrich Nietzsche.

(Telegram.)

"July 11, 1876.   Prof. Nietzsche,

"Schutzengraben 49,

"Basle.

"To you, dear friend, I now owe my sole refreshment of mind and elevation of spirit, aside from the powerful artistic impressions received here. May this serve to express my thanks.

"COSIMA."

CHAPTER XXIII.

(1876)

UPON receiving these words of warm commendation from Wagner and Frau Cosima, my brother began to make the most enthusiastic preparations for going to Bayreuth. We see from his private correspondence that his doubts had been completely banished and he hoped to fall under the old spell in listening to Wagner's music. For example, he writes: ". . . I could wish for such a degree of rhythmic, visualizing endowment as would enable me to survey the Nibelung work in its entirety, as I have, at times, succeeded in doing with the single dramas. But here I anticipate rhythmical delights of a very special kind and degree. For instance: the scene of Siegfried and the Rhine Maidens in the second act of the last drama; the scene between Alberich and the Rhine Maidens in the first act of the first drama; the love rhapsodies of Siegfried and Brunnhilde upon finding each other in the last act of *'Siegfried'*; the parting rhapsodies of the lovers in the first act of *'Götterdämmerung'*: the scene of the Nornes at the beginning of the first act (Vorspiel) of the *'Götterdämmerung'* and so on."

It was with anticipations of this nature that Nietzsche

set out for the Bayreuth Festival, devoutly hoping for new revelations by which he would be brought more closely to Wagner's art.

I wish that a benign fate had kept my brother away from Bayreuth so that he might have clung a little longer to the belief that he was to find there the fulfillment of his most beautiful dreams. In a few words he expresses his feelings: "I made the mistake of going to Bayreuth with an ideal in my breast, and was, therefore, doomed to suffer the most bitter disappointment. The preponderance of strong spices, the ugly and the grotesque thoroughly repelled me."

I shall not attempt to describe here the external happenings of the Festival of 1876, as these have been told elsewhere, and in any case, it was not these tragi-comical occurrences, having no direct bearing upon the performance that so disheartened my brother, but the inner conflicts which arose between Wagner and himself and between the art-works and the audiences.

First of all we must ask ourselves the question: What did Nietzsche expect from Bayreuth both for himself and for other like-minded natures? No better answer could be found to this question than a passage from his fourth *"Thoughts Out of Season"*:

"Bayreuth signifies for us the morning sacrament on the day of battle. No greater injustice could be done us than to suppose that it is only the art of the thing we are concerned about, as if this art was to be looked upon merely as a means of healing or stupefying us and thus ridding our consciousness of all the misery about us. In this tragic artwork at Bayreuth we see rather the struggle of the individual against everything which seems to bar his path—

269

against irresistible necessity, power, law, tradition, conduct, and the entire established order of the universe.

"There can be no more beautiful life for the individual than to hold himself ready to sacrifice himself and to die in the fight for love and justice. The look vouchsafed us from the mysterious eye of tragedy neither lulls nor paralyzes. Nevertheless, she demands tranquillity so long as her gaze is fastened upon us, for art does not serve the purposes of war, but is merely for the rest pauses before and in the midst of the conflict and for those moments—when looking back and yet dreaming of the future—we seem to understand all that is symbolical, and experience the same feeling of relaxation as that resulting from a refreshing dream. Day dawns, and the fighting begins; the sacred shadows disappear and art seems very remote, but her sweet ministrations hover ever over the fighter."

As will be seen, my brother made the mistake of expecting to find only kindred spirits assembled in Bayreuth, all looking forward to the Festival as something by which their entire life was to be consecrated. That such a unique audience was possible had been proven at the ceremonies of the laying of the cornerstone in 1872. On that occasion, the elect of Europe had come together, all of them idealists who had been working for years for the success of the Bayreuth idea and now stood on the threshold of the consummation of that idea. To them Wagner could say, as the cornerstone was being lowered into the ground: "May this building be consecrated by the spirit which inspired you to listen to my appeal, and gave you courage to have the fullest confidence in me and my undertaking, despite the prevailing scepticism; by the spirit which could speak directly to you because it found a response in your own hearts; and by the German spirit which shouts a youthful morning greeting to you across the centuries."

Of this earlier body of listeners my brother had written: "In Bayreuth, the spectators themselves are worthy of being seen. A wise, contemplative sage passing from one century to another for the purpose of comparing the cultural movements, would most assuredly find much to interest him here. His sensations would be those of a swimmer who suddenly comes upon an unexpected warm current of an entirely different temperature from the surrounding water, and he would say to himself that this current must have its origin in other and deeper sources. Just so, all those participating in the coming Bayreuth Festival will be regarded as men born out of season, whose explanation must be sought for elsewhere than here and now."

My brother failed to take into consideration the widely differing conditions existing at the preliminary festival of 1872. At this earlier event, the participants were all invited guests known to Wagner and his co-workers as persons of like ideals and aspirations. On the other hand, any one able to pay the sum of 900 marks for the twelve performances was free to come in 1876, and the result was that Bayreuth became the rendezvous of the customary "first night" audiences from the larger centers, for the most part people who came to be seen and boast of having been present.

Thus it was not the rare souls of 1872 who gave the cachét to the Festival of 1876, but this new and objectionable element, and unfortunately, this was not only true on the Festival hill, but also at Wahnfried, where my brother came in contact with people who had not the vaguest idea of the ideals lying at the bottom of the undertaking. In fact, it almost seemed as if these ideals had been lost sight of by the chief personages concerned, which explains the bitter words my brother wrote later: "It was not only that I then became convinced of the illusory character of Wagner's ideals, but above all, I saw and felt that even those most closely concerned with the success of the undertaking, no longer regarded the 'ideal' as paramount, but laid chief stress upon quite other things. Added to this, was the tiresome company of 'Patrons,' both men and women, all very much enamored with each other, all very much bored and all unmusical to the point of nauseation !"

It seemed as if the entire leisure rabble of Europe had met here and everyone was free to go in and out of Wagner's own house as if the entire Bayreuth undertaking was some new and fascinating sort of sport. And as a matter of fact, it was scarcely anything more. This class of rich idlers had found a new pretext for idling, this time "grand opera" with obstacles, and Wagner's music, by reason of its concealed sexuality, was found to form a new bond for a social class in which everyone was bent upon following his or her own *plaisirs*.

I do not mean to say that there were not many refined, highly intelligent persons present, but they were entirely lost sight of in the flashing brilliancy of this world of elegant toilettes and splendid jewels. Only once did I have the feeling that among the Bayreuth visitors were to be found people quite differently constituted from the customary hydra-headed public. One morning I went to make a call at Wahnfried and was waiting in the small reception room, as the large hall was crowded with visitors. I looked in and saw about forty persons, conductors, young artists and authors who were waiting for an audience with **Wagner**. (Owing to the rush of visitors, Wagner was obliged to hold these audiences, en masse. On the opening day of the Festival, alone, five hundred cards were left at Wahnfried.) While waiting for the servant to announce me, I had an opportunity of observing these interesting artist heads and fine intellectual faces; the older men spoke together in subdued tones and the younger ones listened with a beautiful expression of reverence on their eager young faces. *"The Ring of the Nibelung"* should have been performed before an audience of genuinely artistic people and the right of free discussion should have been granted the listeners at the close of the performance. How much greater would thereby have been the influence exerted by Bayreuth upon the development of art. I do not mean to say that this audience should have consisted solely of fascinated young Wagnerites as not much could have been learned from persons too carefully trained in partisanship, despite the fact that, at one time, Wagner and my brother regarded such persons as the "ideal type of listener." The incurable Wagnerites, for the most part members of the various branches of the Wagner Society, were to be found assembled every evening in Angermann's tap-room. But these were not the most delectable type of visitors, as they beat upon the table with their fists, raised their beer glasses threateningly on high and were ready to engage in a hand to hand fight with any one who presumed to express a thought that could be regarded as the slightest deflection from the strict Wagnerian code. Wagnerites of this kind seemed to my brother to be a parody on themselves.

It is not difficult to imagine how this "human, all-too-human" reality affected my brother. Moreover fate had willed that his two most intimate friends, Gersdorff and Rohde, were both involved in love affairs which, as every one will agree, not only makes the best of men unbearable, but also utterly indifferent to things otherwise regarded by them as being of the highest importance.

My brother was thus compelled to lock up in his own breast his most intimate thoughts and feelings. He wrapped himself in that deep pythagorean silence to which he had admonished his readers in his fourth *"Thoughts Out of Season"* and wandered around like a man in a dream. Many years later he wrote of this: "Any one who had the faintest idea of the visions which even at that time had flitted across my path will be able to judge of my feelings when one day I suddenly came to my senses in Bayreuth. It was just as if I had been dreaming. . . . Where was I? Nothing seemed familiar to me, not even Wagner himself. It was in vain that I turned the leaves of memory! Tribschen—remote isle of bliss; not a shadow of resemblance! The never-to-be-forgotten days of the cornerstone laying; the *small company of the elect* which participated in this event, all of them persons far from lacking fingers for the handling of delicate things; not a shadow of resemblance!"

I recall one evening when we had given our seats to relatives as the performances had proven so exhausting to my brother. Our guests had taken leave of us and the streets were filled with the noisy crowds on their way to the Festival Theatre. Carriages rattled by on their way up the hill, returning in a slower tempo, until at last an almost uncanny silence spread over the little city. We discussed a multitude of things that lay remote from our real thoughts, until I finally ventured to say: "How strange that we two should be sitting here alone on the evening of a festival performance!" With a peculiar intonation, my brother replied: "This is the first really happy hour I have had since I came." I knew that he was deeply moved but could not trust himself to put his feelings into words.

Nothing was more painful to him than to be obliged to discuss his latest work: *"Richard Wagner in Bayreuth."* One day a very discerning woman said to me: "Tell me, why does your brother avoid all mention of his last work?" When I repeated this to him, he said with some passion: "Why can not people let these old stories rest?" to which remark I gave the astonished answer: "But Fritz, the work only appeared five weeks ago." "It seems five years to me!" was his only reply.

Somewhat later, he made a careful comparison between the two works *"Schopenhauer as Educator"* and *"Richard Wagner in Bayreuth,"* and discovered to his great joy that the third *"Thoughts Out of Season"* represented the first step towards his own emancipation. . . . "The *Schopenhauerian man* drove me to scepticism towards everything I had previously respected, cherished and ' defended (even towards the Greeks, Schopenhauer and Wagner); towards genius, sacred things, the pessimism of knowledge. By this *devious route*, I came out on the *heights* where fresh winds were blowing. My work on Bayreuth represented a pause, a falling back a *breathing spell*. Here for the first time I realized that Bayreuth was no longer *indispensable*—to me."

Bayreuth was no longer necessary for him! It will not be an easy matter for the world of today to realize what this meant to my brother. But far greater than the disappointment he felt in the festival audiences was that created by the art-work itself. He sensed nothing of the long-anticipated revelations nor of the irresistible fascination of the Wagner music, but only the depressing confirmation and justification of all his inner doubts and scruples. But I shall here let my brother speak for himself by quoting a series of observations he made later upon Wagner's art as expressed in the "*Ring of the Nibelung.*"

"This music is addressed to inartistic persons; all possible means are employed by which an *effect* can be created. It is not an *artistic effect* that is achieved, but one operating solely upon *the nerves.*

"Wagner has no genuine confidence in *music*, in order to invest it with the quality of greatness, he calls to his aid related emotions. He tunes himself to the key *of others*, and first gives his listeners an intoxicating drink in order to make them believe that they have been *intoxicated by the music itself.*

"His soul does not *sing*, it *speaks*, but always in highly impassioned accents. *Naturally*, tone, rhythm and gesture are primary essentials to him; the music, on the other hand, is never quite natural, but is a sort of *acquired* language, with only a limited vocabulary and a *different* syntax.

"Just listen to the second act of the '*Götterdämmerung*' detached from the drama. It is inarticulate music, as wild as a bad dream, and terrifyingly distinct, just as if it were trying to make itself heard by deaf people. *This volubility with nothing to say* is distressing. The drama comes as genuine relief. Can it be interpreted as *praise* to say that this music is only intolerable when heard alone (with the exception of intentionally isolated passages)? Suffice it to say that this *music when detached from the drama* is a perpetual contradiction of the highest laws of style governing the earlier music, and he who becomes thoroughly *accustomed* to it, loses all feeling for these earlier laws. But has the drama, on the other hand, *gained* anything from this adjunct? It is true that a *symbolical* interpretation has been added, a sort of philological commentary, by which restraint has been placed upon the *inner, free fantasy* of the imagination—it is tyrannical! Music is the *language of the explicator,* who, however, talks all the time and gives us no breathing spell. Moreover, he uses a language so complicated that it, in turn, demands an *explanation.* He who has mastered, *step by step,* the drama (the language!), then transformed this into action, then studied out the symbolism of the music until he has gained a perfect understanding of its intricacies—will then be prepared for enjoyment of an uncommon character. But what an *exacting task!* It is quite impossible to do this, save for a few moments at a time, simply because this ten-fold intensive application of the eye, ear, intellect, and feeling—the highest activity of all the senses, without a corresponding productive re-action —is far too exhausting!

". . . Only a very few are capable of such application. How then shall we explain the effect that this music has upon *so great a number?* Simply because they give it only *intermittent attention*—that is to say, they are unreceptive for whole passages at a stretch, listening now to the music, now to the drama, or watching the progress of the stage action— in short, they are *dissecting* the work.

"But by so doing, the *type* we are discussing is destroyed;

277

not the *drama*, but merely a *moment* of it is the result—
or an arbitrary selection. It is just here that the creato
of a new genre should be on his guard; the arts should n(
always *be served up together*, but he should imitate t:
moderation of the ancients which is truer to human nature.

"The length of the work is at variance with the violence
of the emotions aroused. This is a point upon which the
author himself can not be considered an authority: having
taken a long time in the construction of his work, he ha:
gradually accustomed himself to its length. It is quite
impossible for him to put himself in the place of the receptive listener. Schiller made the same mistake, and th(
pruning-knife had also to be used on the works of the earlier
classicists.

"Apparently, Wagner wishes to create an *art for all*,
which explains his employment of coarse and refined means.
And yet he was bound by certain laws of musical æsthetics,
namely by moral indifference.

"Wagner's Nibelung cycle, strictly speaking, are *dramas
to be read* with the aid of the inner fantasy. *High* art genre,
as it was with the early Greeks.

"*Epic motives* for the inner fantasy: many scenes, for
example, the dragon and Wotan—lose very much in effect
when visualized.

"We have no point of contact with wild animals displaying sudden paroxysms of sublimated tenderness and wisdom.
Think of Philoctetes, by way of contrast.

"Wotan, in a rage of disgust: let the world go to pieces.
Brünhilde loves: let the world go to pieces. Siegfried loves:
why bother himself about the means of subterfuge. (Wotan
like-minded.) How it all disgusts me.

"Certain tones of an incredible realism, I hope never to hear again; if I were only able to forget them (Materna).

"Wagner has made the *dangers of realism* very acute. An effort to employ the terrifying, the intoxicating, etc., for *its own sake.* But there is an undeniable wealth of material.

"Paroxysms of *beauty:* scene of the Rhine Maidens, flickering lights, exuberance of coloring, like the autumnal sun; nature in her varying phases—glowing reds, purples, melancholy yellows and greens, all running into each other.

"I utterly disagree with those who were dissatisfied with the declarations and stage machinery at Bayreuth. On the contrary, far too much industry and ingenuity was applied in captivating the senses, and expended upon material which did not belie its epic origin. But the *naturalism of the attitudes, of the singing* compared to the orchestra. What farfetched, artificial, and depraved tones were to be heard there. What a travesty upon nature.

"Several ways are open to musical evolution (or *were* open, before Wagner's influence made itself felt): one of these was an organic creation in the form of a symphony with a drama as pendant (or mimicry without words?); and then *absolute music*, to which the laws of this organic creation were applied, and using Wagner only as a steppingstone—a preparation. Or again, to *out-Wagner* Wagner, *dramatic choral music. Dithyrambic music.* Effect of unison. . . .

"The trend of evolution has been disastrously interrupted by Wagner, and the path cannot be regained. I had visions of a drama *over-spread* with a symphony. A form growing out of the *Lied.* But the alien appeal of the opera drew

Wagner irresistibly in this other direction. All possible resources of art here brought to the highest climax.

"We are witnessing the death agony of the *last great art:* Bayreuth has convinced me of this."

It must not be forgotten that all this criticism was directed against the Nibelung Tetraology and its author, and not against Tristan and its creator. At that time, Tristan had practically been relegated to the background, or made the object of scathing criticism by some of the most fanatic Wagnerians. Even in Wahnfried, Tristan was seldom mentioned, and due courtesy and respect was also withheld from that noble woman, Madame Mathilde Wesendonck, who, as all the world knows, was the direct inspiration of the work. Had Tristan been the work chosen for performance at the first festival, it is quite certain that my brother's criticisms would have been of quite a different character and his disappointment by no means so keen.

Having gone this far, we may as well go still further and ask: Was Wagner, himself, a disappintment for my brother? He has given us the answer to this question: "I no longer recognized Wagner, or rather I realized that I had been cherishing in my mind an ideal portrait of the Wagner I *thought* I knew." Mournfully, he wrote in his notebook: "I must bear the fate of all idealists, who see the object of their adoration tumbling from its pedestal. Ideal monster: the real Wagner shrinks away to nothing.

"My mistaken estimate of Wagner has not even the merits of individuality, as there are many others who have said that my picture is a correct one. One of the outstanding characteristics of such natures is their stupendous ability of deceiving the painter and we are apt to commit an error of justice as much by our goodwill as by our illwill."

From the writings of a Frenchman, M. Ed. Schuré, we may get an idea of Wagner as he appeared at that time to his other admirers. "Wagner, a youthful Wotan despite his sixty-three years, enjoyed the legitimate triumph of having created a new world and set in operation a colossal enterprise in which he was called upon to manipulate thirty-five principals, including gods, goddesses, dwarfs, nymphs, men and women, to say nothing of the chorus, the stage machinery, and the orchestra.

"During the brief hours of respite snatched from this herculean task, he gave free rein to his buoyant gayety, to that exuberance of wit and humor which was like the foam of his genius. Before being able to transmit his spirit and his thoughts into these creatures of flesh and blood, he was obliged to turn actor and stage manager, and by no means the least formidable part of this task was the endeavor to preserve the *amour propre* of his ensemble and to maintain an equilibrium of the passions and rivalries of his regiment of actors and actresses.

"Ever a subtle charmer and subduer of the fair sex, he always gained his point by employing a judicious admixture of violence and caresses, and never once lost sight of his goal whether indulging in outbursts of choleric temper or sincere emotions. Living thus in the midst of the whirlwind which he had conjured up and was now called upon to reduce to a system, he was unable to give but a divided attention to his disciples and admirers.

"Confronted by the prodigious artistic deeds accomplished under our very eyes every day, none of us took this to heart, thank God! but only experienced the same feeling of astonishment that Mime must have had in the presence of Siegfried when the latter was re-forging the sword broken into pieces by his father, after having first reduced it to filings and cast it into the crucible.

"Did Nietzsche's pride, perhaps, not suffer from being thus treated like an inferior? Were not his acute sensibilities often wounded by certain familiarities and rudenesses on the part of Wagner?"

The closing sentence in these observations is approximately correct, as my brother was not particularly fond of Wagner's witticisms, a fact thoroughly recognized by Wagner, who once said: "Your brother is exactly like Liszt in not enjoying my jokes." But aside from this, M. Schuré was mistaken in regard to my brother, as he was not sufficiently familiar with Nietzsche's relations to Wagner to be able to judge and observe correctly. For example, M. Schuré is absolutely in the wrong when he says that Wagner neglected my brother. The latter had never the slightest cause to feel offended, and as a matter of fact, Wagner seemed eager to single him out and to do honor to him on every possible occasion. It was my brother who endeavored to ward off these noisy demonstrations, as Wagner's boisterous praise was extremely distasteful to him. Moreover, both of them felt that something unexpressed lay between them and there were none of those deep and great moments together which might have bound my brother anew to Wagner. Was not such a moment once very near? I remember quite well that we walked out to Wahnfried one morning and met the master in the garden on the point of going out. I cannot recall just what Wagner said, but I remember that my brother's eyes suddenly lighted up and he fairly hung on the master's words with an expression of the most tense expectation.

Did he think that Wagner would say: "Oh friend, the entire festival is nothing more than a farce! it is not in the least what we both have dreamed for and longed for. My music also should have been quite different; I now see this and I will return to melody and simplicity."

Did my brother cherish the false hope that Wagner would say something of this kind? If his opening remarks gave rise to this hope, it was soon dispelled by the further conversation. The light died out of my brother's eyes, as he saw and felt that Wagner was no longer young enough to take sides against himself.

I shall never be able to convince myself that Wagner, in his innermost soul, was really satisfied with the Bayreuth Festival. He only made a pretense of being satisfied. He could not have entirely forgotten the picture he had drawn of the festival while he was still living in Tribschen. Some of these idealistic plans had been noted down by my brother:

"*Future of the Bayreuth Summer.* Union of all really creative persons; artists to come with their art creations, authors to produce their new works, reformers to present their new ideas. It will be a universal *soul-bath* and a new realm of untold blessing will be revealed there."

One can see from these notes what marvellous visions floated before my brother and I honestly confess that it is one of my dearest and most profound wishes to see established here in Weimar such a festival of great souls. I am waiting for some one to come to me with such plans, as I am not in a position to carry them out in the same sense which my brother had in mind. I am growing old and have neither the means nor the physical strength for such an undertaking. But it is my dearest wish that the time may come when the *Nietzsche Foundation* may be able to carry into fulfillment my brother's vision of the future.

After the first rehearsals, my brother left Bayreuth, or it would be nearer the truth to say that he fled to Klingenbrunn in the Bohemian Forest, there to write down these harsh verdicts. He returned in time for the first cycle—on my account, he said—but if the truth were told because he wished to confirm his impressions and convince himself that his judgment was a final one. But the strain upon his nerves became so unendurable, that before the close of the Festival, he took his departure from the old Franconian town which had been the scene of so many heart-breaking experiences.

"Ah, Lisbeth, and *that* was Bayreuth!" he said to me as he bade me good-bye. His eyes were filled with tears.

CHAPTER XXIV.

END OF THE FRIENDSHIP.

(1876-1878.)

THUS my brother bade farewell to that which the world today calls "Bayreuth." When he set out for the Festival, there floated before his mind's eye a vision of an event in which the art-works presented and the listeners of these works would be equally worthy and admirable. But now all that he had to look back upon was a festival bearing a strong resemblance to the clamor of a Rhenish Music Festival, or the excitement prevailing at the famous Baden-Baden races. And it was for this that he had fought and made soul-wasting propaganda for years! He was seized with a fit of impatience at his own blindness and he longed to be free from outside influences, in order that he might gradually come to his senses and be able to follow his own tastes and inclinations. The period of youthful enthusiasm was over and he had no more time to waste on such extravagances.

Not only had he been disappointed by the musical side of the Festival, but his ethical and æsthetic taste had also been offended. His very soul had been nauseated by the Wagnerian operatic figures with their "erotic obsessions," by the "re-modelling of the Edda myth, by the aid of the perverse traits of French romance" (for example, Siegfried's origin), and by the sultry sensuality which lies at the bottom of all the Wagner music. He longed again for healthy, virile, well-balanced sentiments held in check by joy, pride and the *pleasure in being moderate*, just as the fiery steed is reined in by the powerful rider who takes pleasure in his task. He longed for music full of happiness, pride, high spirits, *limpidezza*, gigantic power, and yet held well within bounds by the highest laws of style. He had expected music of this kind from the Wagner who had created the figure of *Siegfried*, but this was not the music he found in Bayreuth.

Furthermore, my brother's health had suffered greatly from his stay in Bayreuth, and the oculist in Basle, who by this time, had been able to form a clearer idea of my brother's troubles, reproached himself severely for not having protested more vigorously against my brother's participation in the festival. A severe strain had been imposed upon his eyes by being required to look at the stage so intently, as well as by his diligent reading of the score. As my mother insisted that I return home upon leaving Bayreuth, my brother was obliged to get along without me, but as the doctor had commanded an entire rest from reading and writing, he was looked after and assisted in his work by Dr. Paul Rée and the musician, Heinrich Köselitz. Rée read aloud to him and Köselitz took down his dictations; in fact, it was to this friend that my brother dictated the sentences noted down during his stay in Klingenbrunn and afterwards incorporated in his *"Human, all-too-Human."*

Wagner seems to have sensed nothing of my brother's changed feelings, but appealed to him by wire to make some purchases for him in Basle, there being certain articles which he fancied only that city could furnish in the desired quality. My brother's feelings upon receiving these commissions are expressed in the following letter:

Friedrich Nietzsche to Richard Wagner.

"Highly revered friend:

"You have made me very happy by the commission you intrusted to me as it reminds me of the dear old days at Tribschen. At present, I have a great deal of time to devote to thoughts of the past, the remote as well as the immediate, as I am kept in a darkened room by an atropin cure found necessary upon my return. This autumn, following upon *this* summer, is more of an autumn for me than ever before, and I do not doubt that this is the case with many others. Back of the great events, lies a streak of the blackest melancholy, and there seems to be no other way of rescuing one's self from this but by starting for Italy or by plunging into creative work—perhaps by combining the two.

"When I picture you to myself in Italy, I always remember that it was there that you found the inspiration for the beginning of the '*Rheingold*' music. May it ever remain the land of beginnings for you! There you will be rid of the Germans for a time, and this seems to be necessary now and again, if one hopes to be able to do anything to help them.

"Possibly you have heard that I am starting for Italy next month, but in my case it is not to be a land of beginnings, but one where I shall end my sufferings. These have again reached a climax and it is the highest time for me to take this step. My school board knows full well what it is about in granting me a year's leave of absence, despite the

287

sacrifice thereby entailed upon this little community. But had they not seen fit to open up this alternative to me, I should have been lost to them in an entirely different way. Thanks to my long-suffering disposition, I have clinched my teeth and endured agony upon agony during the last few years, and at times it seems as if I had been born into the world for this and nothing else. I have paid tribute in the fullest measure to the philosophy that teaches this long-suffering. My neuralgia goes to work as thoroughly and scientifically as if it were trying to probe and find out just what degree of pain I am able to endure, and thirty hours is required for each of these tests. I must count on a repetition of this research work every four or eight days, so you can see that, at least, I have the malady of a scholar. . . . But now the time has come when I can no longer endure it, and either I wish to live on in good health or not at all!

"A complete rest, mild air, long walks, darkened rooms—all this I expect to find in Italy. I shudder at the thought of being obliged to see or hear anything while I am there. Please do not think that I am morose; it is not sickness but only human beings who are able to put me in a bad humor, and yet I am constantly surrounded by the most helpful and considerate of friends.

"At first I had the moralist, Dr. Paul Rée, and now I have the musician Köselitz, who is writing this letter at my dictation. I must not forget Frau Baumgartner in enumerating my good friends, and possibly you will be interested to hear that a French translation of my last work (R. W. i. B.) from her hand, will go to press next month.

"Did the spirit descend upon me, I would put my good wishes for your journey into verse, but this stork has not built his nest in my neighbourhood of late, an oversight for which he may be pardoned. Therefore, please accept my heartfelt wishes as they are and may they ever abide with you—with you and your revered wife, 'my most noble friend,' to make use of one of the most unpermissible Germanisms of the Jew Bernay.

"As ever faithfully yours,
"Basle, Sept. 27, 1876. FRIEDRICH NIETZSCHE."

It is plain to be seen from this letter that my brother had not taken an eternal farewell from Wagner himself, even though he had renounced his art as presented in Bayreuth. The leave of absence to which my brother refers in his letter was about to begin, and he endeavored to forget all else and occupy himself with his preparations. But whenever this subject was referred to in later years, my brother always confessed how infinitely sad was the period that elapsed between his Bayreuth experiences and his visit to Italy. During this interim period he lived in Overbeck's old *chambre garni* with his former landlady, Frau Baumann, in the so-called "Baumann's Cave" where he had lived for six years. He often declared that during this time, he was "as melancholy as were ever the old cave-dwellers," but in reality, the house was light and cheerful and aside from its arbitrary name, had nothing in common with a cave.

When Dr. Rée saw that he could be of great service to my brother in the way of saving his eyes, he offered to accompany him to Italy, a plan which met with the approval of our old friend, Fräulein von Meysenburg, who was going to look after my brother and had made all the arrangements for his stay in Sorrento. He started for Italy on the first day of October, 1876, stopping on the way at **Bex in the Savoy Alps**, from which place he wrote to me:

"Dear sister:

"It is the day before my departure. The Föhn is blowing from the south and I can hardly believe that I shall be as well off in Italy as I am here. Bex was an excellent choice; to be sure, there has been no marked improvement, and yet the last attack (day before yesterday) did not last as long as usual (possibly owing to a new salve Schiess prescribed to be rubbed on my temples). I also have a slight cold. My heartfelt thanks for all your good wishes. By the way, the fifth *'Thoughts Out of Season'* is finished and I only need some one to whom I can dictate it."

This fifth *"Thoughts"* was never finished and the material collected for the preliminary work was incorporated in *"Human, all-too-Human."* My brother arrived in Sorrento the end of October and was enchanted with the place. He was obliged to make his letters very brief, but verbally he could not say enough of the magic influence of the south and particularly of the Bay of Naples. A touching description of impressions received here is given in the following aphorism:

"I have not sufficient strength for the north. Sluggish and superficial souls predominate there who labor as consistently and urgently upon precautionary measures as the beaver on his house. I passed my entire youth among these people, and this came over me anew as I watched evening fall over the Bay of Naples for the first time, tinging the heavens with tones of velvety gray and red. Thou couldst have died without having been permitted to see this, I cried! I shuddered and was sorry for myself at having begun my life by being old, and I shed tears at the thought that I had been saved at the last moment. I have intellect sufficient for the south!"

When he attempted to describe the happiness and the radiance of the south, his words became music. Listen to the following strophes:

> "The Midland sea lies in white sleep
> Save for a single purple sail.
> Cliff, fig-tree, tower and harbor keep
> Their pagan innocence; the sheep
> Bleat in this peace that does not fail.

> "Weary of the stark North was I
> And of its slow, methodic tread.
> I bade the wind lift me on high
> And learned with all the birds to fly
> And southward over ocean sped."

From this time forth, the south was ever his refuge from the heavy air of the north, but although he made many visits to Italy, he always remembered with peculiar affection this first sojourn on the shores of the Bay of Naples. As late as 1887, he wrote to Fräulein von Meysenburg: "I have retained a sort of longing not unmixed with superstition for the quiet sojourn *down there*. It seemed to me as if I were able to breathe more freely, even if only for a few seconds, than at any other time and place during my entire life. For instance, when we took our very first drive out to Posillippi."

But this paradise of Sorrento was not without its dangers and difficulties. By that I do not mean that the traditional serpent made its appearance, but I am firmly convinced that in that soil grew the tree from which my brother was obliged to pluck the fruit of knowledge concerning Richard Wagner. On the way to Italy, he learned that the Wagners had also chosen Sorrento as their place of sojourn and although frightened by this news at first, he later welcomed the opportunity of coming to an understanding with Wagner.

In leaving Bayreuth, my brother had not broken away from Wagner himself; in fact, he had not yet arrived at any definite conclusions in regard to his feelings of loyalty for the dearly beloved friend and his innermost convictions concerning Wagner's art works.

This is proven by a private observation which reads: "Just at first one has faith in his intellectual sympathies, but when his better judgment begins to make itself felt, *defiance* appears and says, we will not yield our ground. *Pride* says that we possess sufficient intelligence to look after *our own* affairs. *Arrogance* has a comtemptuous regard for this evasion and thinks it arises from a low, faint-hearted standpoint. *Lustfulness* enumerates the joys of pleasure and doubts exceedingly if our better judgment is able to offer us anything more worth while. Added to this is our *compassion* for our idol and his sad fate, whereby we are prevented from examining his imperfections too closely. To a still greater degree, we are affected by our feeling of *gratitude*. But most of all, by the *intimate intercourse*, by our *loyalty* while breathing the same air with our idol, and the sharing of his happiness as well as his danger. And ah! his confidence in us, his letting himself go in our company has the effect of frigtening away any thought of his fallibility as if it were an indiscretion, if, indeed, not direct treason."

At first, both Wagner and my brother gave unmistakable signs of joy at being thus reunited and Fräulein von Meysenburg declared later that they hurried to each other every day as if nothing at all had occurred. My brother never gave me to understand that they met so frequently, but it was quite natural that they should see a great deal of each other, as Wagner was reading the third "*Thoughts out of Season*" of which he had spoken most enthusiastically before leaving Bayreuth. The Festival was a tabooed subject, the reason for this being that it had closed with an enormous deficit and the executive board in Bayreuth was in despair as to how this deficit was to be covered. (160,000 marks was the sum mentioned.) Letters from Bayreuth threw Wagner into a terrible rage and Malvida implored my brother to do everything in his power to prevent the conversation from turning upon the Festival, to which my brother readily agreed as there was no lack of other material for discussion. I am unable to say whether the two friends ever had one of those deep moments so frequent at Tribschen, but I do know that this meeting was marred by a painful incident to which my brother referred again and again in his private correspondence.

It was on the last evening they were together; my brother and Wagner took a walk along the coast and up the hill from which the famous view is to be had of the bay, the coves and the islands. It was a beautiful day, the air soft and mild and a certain melancholy in the light effects which betokened the approach of winter. "A farewell mood," Wagner called it. Suddenly, he began to talk of his "*Parsi-*

fal" and to my brother's intense surprise, spoke of it not as an artistic conception, but as a personal religious experience. Possibly Wagner felt that a *"Stage Consecrating Play"* conceived and written by so pronounced an atheist as Wagner was known to be during the Tribschen days, in fact all through his life—would be regarded as a glaring inconsistency.

My brother's amazement may, therefore, be imagined when Wagner began to speak of his religious feelings and experiences in a tone of the deepest repentance, and to confess a leaning towards the Christian dogmas. For example, he spoke of the delight he took in the celebration of the Holy Communion, meaning, of course, the rather austere ceremony of the Protestant church. Had he had in mind the picturesque ritual of the Catholic church, which always creates a deep impression upon sensitive artistic natures, my brother would have had less reason to doubt his sincerity. (Many years ago, I met a highly intelligent Catholic priest, with whom I discussed *"Parsifal."* "We do that sort of a thing much better!" he said with a sweeping gesture as if brushing *"Parsifal"* to one side.) My brother had the greatest possible respect for sincere, honest Christianity, but he considered it quite impossible that Wagner, the avowed atheist, should suddenly have become a naive and pious believer. He could only regard Wagner's alleged sudden change of heart, as having been prompted by a desire to stand well with the Christian rulers of Germany and thus further the material success of the Bayreuth undertaking. My brother was confirmed in this belief by a remark Wagner made when referring to the unsatisfactory attendance at the first Festival; almost angrily, he exclaimed: "The Germans do not wish to hear anything about gods and goddesses at present, they are only interested in something of a religious character."

While Wagner was speaking, the sun sank into the sea and a light mist came up blotting out the fair scene. This atmospheric change seemed to have awakened Wagner to the change that had taken place in my brother, and he asked: "Why are you so silent, my friend?" My brother evaded the question, but his heart was full of anguish at what he considered the pitiable subterfuge on the part of Wagner. It was this that he had in mind when he wrote:

"It is impossible for me to recognize *greatness* which is not united with candour and sincerity towards one's self. The moment I make a discovery of this sort, a man's achievements count for absolutely nothing with me, as I feel that he is only playing a part and everything he does is based upon insincerity."

Had Wagner frankly said to my brother: "In this age of Christianity, and heightened religious consciousness, there is a great temptation for the artist to put these feelings into musical form." Or had he said with his customary roguishness: "Now I am going to translate the feelings of the age into music," my brother would have had the most perfect understanding of his motives and been in full sympathy with his artistic plans. But this make-believe on Wagner's part and this pretense of having become a naive, pious Christian was more than my brother could stand. He was made inexpressibly sad by the fact that Wagner, who once stood out for his principles against the halloo of the entire world, should now weakly surrender to the spirit of the age and repudiate all his theories of life. I must admit that there is a strong doubt in my mind as to whether the atheistic or the Christian-pessimistic views of redemption expressed the deepest needs of Wagner's own nature. *Lohengrin* and *Tannhauser*, at all events, would seen to confirm the latter theory.

Much time had elapsed before my brother was able to discuss this last painful meeting with Wagner. If we ask ourselves what really took place on this last eventful evening, we find that only one explanation offers itself. Two passionately cherished ideals stood opposed to one another; on the one hand, the Catholic-romantic figure of *Parsifal*, implying negation of life—on the other, the powerful figure of Siegfried, god-like, transfigured, and the personification of life affirmed. To my brother's mind, Wagner had always personified the latter ideal, and hence his bitter disappointment! . . . Malvida was only able to remember that my brother was noticeably sad on that evening and withdrew to his room earlier than was his custom. He seemed to have a presentiment that he and Wagner had met for the last time, and thus the paradise of Sorrento was to live in his memory as the place where he said farewell to the most beautiful dream of his entire life.

He had always hoped that Wagner and he would develop together, in fact, along the lines of Nietzsche's own views. Only in Tribschen where all conditions were most auspicious would this have been possible, as my brother's influence is clearly to be felt in Wagner's essays of that period. As a matter of fact, Wagner, his art and his leaning towards the northern myths, would have fitted in very well with my brother's fundamental views as they gradually developed. But Wagner was too old to assimilate any new thoughts and to take sides against his own earlier views. It is my firm con-

viction that my brother frequently had reason to think that
in his heart of hearts, Wagner was inclined to accept his
new ideas and that he recognized the correctness of
Nietzsche's critical judgment. "Wagner confessed as much
to me more than once during our confidential conversations,"
wrote my brother, "but I only wish that he would do so
openly, for wherein lies true greatness of character if not
in the ability to take sides even against one's self, if truth
demands this?"

Many years later I said to my brother: "How I wish
that Wagner had been twenty years younger when you made
his acquaintance. I am convinced that you would have been
able to have converted him to your way of thinking." "I
also hoped and believed that at one time," answered my
brother, "but then came *'Parsifal'* and destroyed all hope,
yea every possibility of such a thing. In the meantime, I had
recognized the fact that my faith in Wagner was based
upon an error; we were too essentially different in our innermost natures and this was *bound* to cause a separation,
sooner or later."

My brother remained in Sorrento the entire winter of
1876-77 without the expected improvement in his health.
His ill-health was not noticeable as he was very sunburned,
looked strong and well, and in intercourse with others seemed
cheerful and full of his customary esprit. But in reality, he
was subject to the same ups and downs; as long as he did
not attempt to write, had everything read aloud to him, went
for long walks and had pleasant diversions, he felt comparatively well, but as soon as his creative powers gained
the upper hand and he plunged again into literary work,
the excruciating pains came back with redoubled force. Un-

fortunately no physician had the foresight and the energy to prescribe a year of total abstinence in the matter of reading and writing.

"If I were totally blind, I should be strong and healthy," my brother said of his own condition. At the time this sounded like a paradox, as none of his doctors, the oculist included, were by any means convinced that his trouble came entirely from the affection of the optic nerve. It makes me miserably unhappy to think of all the suffering my brother might have been spared had it been possible to locate the real seat of the trouble—a matter made all the more difficult by his extreme sensitiveness to the slightest change in the barometer.

But it would be a mistake to make his physical maladies responsible for all that he suffered at this time. Many things which robuster natures would have shaken off caused inexpressible torture to his extremely sensitive soul. As I have already said, one of the acutest causes of his mental distress was that of being obliged to appear other than he was, and during his entire stay in Sorrento he was endeavoring to bring his outer life into harmony with his innermost feelings, and thus this period served as a good preparation for the conditions surrounding him in later life.

When the sirocco began to blow in Italy, my brother returned to his beloved haunts in the mountains of Switzerland which he greeted as jubilantly as if he were again in his native land. He used to say: "The air of Southern Italy is too enervating for me."

We met in Lucerne and to my great joy, I found him looking remarkably well and full of courage for the beautiful plans he was making for the future. He spoke of Wagner in the warmest and friendliest tones, as he had now become reconciled to the thought that he must let Wagner go his own way and hoped to receive the same latitude on the part of Wagner in regard to his own activities. In this way, he would no longer be obliged to subscribe to anything antagonistic to his own feelings and judgment and in consequence of this, there would be no necessity for any deception or subterfuge on his part.

"All this came very near spoiling my amiable disposition," he said impatiently, in speaking of his last visit to Bayreuth and his repeated melancholy letters to Wagner. But impatience was not the predominating feeling in these reminiscences, for he realized full well what a degree of self-knowledge had been gained from these repeated efforts to bring his own views into harmony with those of Wagner, and from his endeavor to find in Wagner those qualities which he could admire and revere despite the discrepancies in their convictions.

Through these experiences, he was afforded an opportunity of studying at close range that most interesting of all subjects—a *genius*, which served as invaluable training in psychological matters. In realizing all this, he could look back upon this period with a feeling of genuine gratitude.

During the fortnight that we spent at the Pension Felsenegg in Lucerne, my brother was in a cheerful and optimistic mood in regard to the future, and this was reflected in his conversation and in the observations to be found in his notebooks of that period.

"I feel as if I were recovering from a long illness. I think

299

of the sweetness of Mozart's *Requiem* with inexpressible delight."

"The '*Ode to Joy*' (May 22, 1872) was one of the highest emotional moments of my life but it is only now that I am beginning to feel myself in this course—'*Frei wie seine Sonnene fliegen, wandelt, Brüder eure Bahn.*' * What a depressing and superficial festival was the one of 1876. . . . But later, it became the means of opening up to me a thousand springs in the desert. This period was of incalculable value to me as a cure for premature development."

"Now the significance of antiquity and of Goethe's judgment have dawned upon me. Now, *for the first time*, I have gained a clear view of the realities of human life. I luckily possessed the *antidote* with which to counteract the effects of a deadly pessimism."

Even though his health had not been completely restored by his sojourn in Sorrento, he had at least the satisfaction of knowing that he was on the right road to freedom and self-knowledge, and the result of this was a feeling of joyful self-confidence despite the chaotic and unstable character of his plans for the immediate future. Thoughts such as these undoubtedly occupied his mind at this time: "Were I already free, this struggle would not be necessary and I could turn my thoughts to some work or course of action upon which I could expend my full measure of strength. I can do no more than hope that, little by little, I shall become free; and I already feel that this is taking place. And so my day of *real work* is still to come and the *preparation for* the Olympian games may be considered as ended."

* From Schiller's "*Ode to Joy*" used by Beethoven in the Finale of his "*Ninth Symphony.*"

End of the Friendship

"I will restore to mankind that repose without which no culture can grow and exist, as well as the *simplicity, tranquility, purity* and *greatness*. And in the realm of style also I will give a faithful portrayal of this endeavor as the result of the concentrated powers of my nature."

Upon returning to Basle, we again established ourselves in our apartment although my brother had already recognized the categorical necessity of giving up his professorship, as under no circumstances could he impose upon his eyes the strain of his classical studies, particularly that of the Greek lettering. There were times when his resolution weakened, but his longing for complete freedom always returned. This meant not only freedom from his professional duties, and all the considerations belonging thereto, but also included freedom from the influence of friends and foes alike. Even in Sorrento, he had suffered greatly at times, from being in the society of his highly revered friend, Fräulein von Meysenburg, as his courtesy and consideration for her often led him to agree to plans far removed from his own inclinations.

"I must have absolute solitude," was the burden of all of his future plans, and for that reason he welcomed the change from Sorrento to Switzerland. His feelings in regard to this are beautifully expressed in a letter to Frau Baumgartner:

"There is a higher destiny for me to fulfill than that afforded me by my eminently respectable Basle position. I know it, I feel it! I am more than a mere philologian, in spite of the fact that I can make use of philology for my higher task. 'I thirst for myself'; that has been my constant theme for the last ten years. Now that I have lived alone with myself for a year, everything has become quite clear

301

and distinct to me. Notwithstanding all that I have suffered, I cannot tell you how inexpressibly rich I felt, and how full I was of the joy of creating as soon as I found myself quite alone. I can now say to you with conviction that I shall not return to Basle with the intention of *remaining* there. I do not know how things will develop, but I mean to capture this freedom, by force if needs be, however modest may be the external conditions of my life."

My brother had a veritable mountain of aphorisms when he returned to Basle. These were originally intended for a fifth *"Thoughts out of Season;"* in fact, there was more than sufficient material for six or seven new works. As the condition of his eyes would not permit him to bring these aphorisms together into a whole, as was the case in the previous *"Thoughts out of Season,"* he simply strung them together in a loose sequence but notwithstanding this, the conscientious reader will instinctively feel the inner relationship and be able to group these detached sentences. Above all, my brother's pure joy in the framing of aphorisms must be taken into account; his delight in not carrying one thought out to completion and binding it firmly to another, but rather allowing it to stand with its own beginning, development and end in a certain sense, and yet withal, contains a hint of continuation for the reader.

The observations which my brother noted down after his bitter disappointment in Bayreuth went to press under the title of *"Human, all-too-Human,"* and to Herr Heinrich Köselitz is due the credit of getting this manuscript ready for the printers. Köselitz had resumed his studies at the Basle university and dedicated all his leisure time to my brother, thus relieving him of the greater part of his writing.

End of the Friendship

While my brother was thus engaged in compiling his
"Human, all-too-Human" Wagner sent him a beautifully
bound copy of his *"Parsifal,"* with the following dedication:

> *"To my dear friend, Friedrich Nietzsche,*
> *with cordial greetings and wishes*
> from
> *Richard Wagner*
> (*Ecclesiastical Councillor:*
> Kindly inform Prof. Overbeck.)"

In his *"Ecce Homo,"* my brother relates that Wagner's
gift of *"Parsifal"* crossed his own of *"Human, all-too-
Human,"* but his memory played him false on this point.
He was, evidently, thinking of having sent off a part of the
copy to the printer about that time. On the whole, he had
a weak memory for unimportant details, which explains
many discrepancies, but it is not surprising that everyday
incidents should make but very little impression upon anyone
whose brain was as continually occupied with great problems
as was my brother's. We read the *"Parsifal"* with strangely
mixed emotions. In a letter to his friend, Baron von Gersdorff, dated January 4, 1878, my brother wrote " *'Parsifal'*
came into my house yesterday, sent by Wagner. Impressions after the first reading: more Liszt than Wagner, spirit
of the counter-revolution. The whole thing is much too
religious for me, bound as I am to the Greek and human.
Nothing but fantastic sort of psychology; no flesh, and
much too much blood (namely in the Communion Scene).
Moreover, I do not care for hysterical hussies! Much that
is tolerated by the inner eye, will be unendurable when trans-

formed into action; just imagine our actors praying,
trembling and going into paroxysms of ecstasy. Furthermore, it will be impossible to represent effectively the interior
of the temple of the *Holy Grail* and of the wounded swan.
All these beautiful pictures belong to an epic and no attempt
should be made to visualize them. Moreover, the language
of the drama sounds as if it were translated from a foreign
tongue. But the situations and their sequence—is that not
all poesy of the highest order? Do they not make a supreme
challenge to music?" The words "more Liszt than Wagner"
need a little explanation, and this my brother gives in one of
his notes: "Wagner's '*Parsifal*' was primarily a concession
to the Catholic instincts of his wife, the daughter of Liszt."
Whether this assumption of my brother was correct or not,
it is not my purpose to determine. It was based upon information received from the intimates of the family at
Bayreuth. But if there was any reason for doubting i.,
then we must also accept with a certain reservation the
theory that Wagner wrote "*Parsifal*" in order to cater to the
pious tastes of the Germany of that period. As a matter
of fact, all observations of my brother's referring to
Cosima's influence upon Wagner, date from a much later
period.

It is not my purpose here to publish notes and critical
comments indicating my brother's changed thoughts and
feelings, but I cannot refrain from quoting a passage from
a letter addressed to Peter Gast under the date of January
21, 1878, in which mention is made of the "*Parsifal*" music
independent of the dramatic content of the work. ". . . Recently I heard the Vorspiel of '*Parsifal*' for the first time (in
Monte Carlo!). When I see you again I should like to tell

you just what I *understood* by it. Quite apart from all irrelevant questions, (such as what purpose this music *can* and *shall* serve—) but purely from an æsthetic standpoint, has Wagner ever written anything *better?* The subtlest psychological explicitness and consciousness in regard to that which it is his intention to say, to express, to *impart*, through the medium of this music: the most concise and direct form of expression; every nuance of feeling worked out in epigrammatic form; music as a descriptive art as distinct as a design in relief emblazoned on a shield; and finally, sublime and extraordinary feelings, experiences and emotions of a soul submerged in music. All this does Wagner the greatest credit. Furthermore, a synthesis of circumstances, which will seem to a great many, even 'superior persons' to be unreconcilable, to be of judicial severity, in fact to be 'superior' in the most terrifying sense of the word; a degree of knowledge and perception that cuts through the soul like a knife, and of compassion, for *that* which is *here* viewed and judged. Only in *Dante* do we find anything comparable to it. Did ever a painter portray a glance of love as melancholy as Wagner has given us in the closing accents of his Vorspiel?" (The concert arrangement of the Vorspiel ends with the "Faith Motive" as given in line 3, page 9, of the piano arrangement of the score.

My brother was deeply impressed at receiving the *Parsifal* text just as he was finishing off his new book "*Human, all-too-Human.*" Realizing what a great shock the Wagnerian party would receive upon reading his book, he resolved to publish it anonymously. A pseudonym had already been decided upon and a *fable convenue* invented for the occasion, this deception being facilitated by the fact that this book was to come from the press of Schmeitzner. Wagner, however, was not to be left in ignorance of its authorship, and among my brother's papers was found a rough draft of a touching letter in which he endeavored to reconcile Wagner to the contents of the book without surrendering an iota of his own independence of thought.

Friedrich Nietzsche to Richard Wagner.

(Rough Draft.)

"In sending you this book, I place my secret in the hands of you and your noble wife with the greatest confidence and assume that is now your secret. I wrote this book; in it I have revealed my innermost views upon men and things and for the first time, have travelled around the entire periphery of my thoughts. This book was a great consolation to me at a period full of paroxysms and misery and it never disappointed me when all else failed to console me. I think it not improbable that I am still living just because I was able to write such a book.

"I was obliged to resort to a pseudonym for several reasons; in the first place, because I did not wish to counteract the effect of my earlier works, and secondly, because this was my only means of preventing a public and private befouling of my personal dignity (something I am *no longer* able to endure on account of the state of my health) and finally and chiefly, because I wish to make possible a *scientific* discussion in which all of my intelligent friends could take part, unrestrained by any feelings of delicacy, as has hitherto been the case whenever I have published anything. No one will speak or write *against my name!*

"I know of no one of them who entertains the ideas expressed in *this* book and must confess to a great curiosity as to the counter arguments which such a book will provoke.

"I feel very much like an officer who has stormed a breastwork despite his severe wounds; he has reached the *top* and unfurled his flag, and notwithstanding the terrifying spectacle by which he is surrounded, experiences much more joy than sorrow.

"Although I know of no one who shares my views, as I have already said, I am conceited enough to think that I have not thought individually but collectively. I have the most curious feeling of *solitude and multitude;* of being a herald who has hastened on in advance without knowing whether the band of knights is following or not—in fact, whether they are still living."

Unfortunately, the publisher would not agree to have the *"Human, all-too-Human"* appear anonymously, as he wished to profit by the advantages to be derived from my brother's name and if the truth must be told, he was not entirely adverse to creating a little scandal. My brother, therefore, went through the manuscript very carefully and eliminated everything that Wagner might think referred to him and at which he might take offense. He still hoped that Wagner would be willing to concede him the freedom of his convictions and that the whole thing would pass off without causing a complete break in their friendship. At all events he wished to make it as easy as possible for Wagner and therefore placed great emphasis on the fact that many things in the book must be regarded in the light of a joke. In the effort to recommend this attitude to the beloved friends, he wrote a very waggish dedication on the copy of the book and sent it to Bayreuth with his heart beating high and yet full of pleasurable anticipation.

I have often been asked what Nietzsche must have thought as to the manner in which Wagner would or should take the *"Human, all-too-Human."* My brother himself has answered this question in two aphorisms: "Humanity of friendship and humanity of mastership. 'Go thou toward the morning and I will go toward evening.' To be able to feel thus, is the highest test of humanity when brought into close intercourse. Without this feeling, every friendship, every discipleship, will become a form of hypocrisy at some time or other."

"Friend!—nothing binds us now. But we have taken pleasure in one another up to the point where one advanced the ideas of the other, even though these were diametrically opposed to his own."

But Wagner had no intention of interpreting the book after this fashion. He saw therein nothing but the apostasy of his former disciple—more than that of the *favorite* disciple and a *genius* to boot, (as Wagner had undoubtedly said to himself again and again) and therefore this occurrence had the effect of a blow and an insult. But I have resolved that this book shall contain nothing of all the ugly and hostile words written and said after this silent breach of friendship. No, let us rather cast one more "melancholy glance of love" upon those happy sun-lit paths upon which the two noble spirits once wandered, and thus bring this period to a close.

Once when modern literature was the subject of conversation, my brother (who it must be remembered had very

little use for erotic feelings) said to one of his pupils: "Why
is the tiresome theme of love between the sexes always taken
as the motive of all novels?"—"but what other feeling could
cause the same conflicts?" asked the student thoughtfully.
—"Why, friendship, for example!" answered my brother
vivaciously. "Friendship has quite similar conflicts, but
upon a much higher plane. First, there is the mutual at-
traction caused by sharing the same views of life, and then
the happiness of belonging to one another and forming
mutual plans for the future. Furthermore, there is the
mutual admiration and glorification. A sudden distrust is
awakened on one side, doubts arise as to the excellences of
the friend and his viewpoints on the other side, and finally,
the consciousness is borne in upon both that the parting
of the ways has been reached, although neither one feels
himself ready for this renunciation. Does all this not represent unceasing conflicts, carrying with them suffering of
the most intense character?"

The student looked dubious and it was evident that he had
never dreamed that friendship could be so passionate.

Step by step we have followed this romance of friendship
and the sympathies of the reader will have, consciously or
unconsciously, been enlisted on the side of one or the other
of the two friends. Naturally, my own are with the one
who suffered most, and that one was my brother. This
friendship unquestionably meant more to my brother than
to Wagner. When the master met my brother he was
already an aging man whose creative activity was nearing
its close, and consequently, a friendship with Nietzsche was
nothing more than an episode of his declining years, and one
having no appreciable effect upon his future. But my

brother's case was entirely different. When his orbit crossed that of Wagner, he was in the first flush of his youth and strength, and to this friendship he dedicated the most beautiful hopes and dreams of his life, as well as an enormous amount of time and intellectual strength. He placed Wagner upon a pedestal far transcending anything human and found his highest consolation in so doing; his thoughts had always been concentrated upon the perfection of the human type, and he believed to have found in Wagner the highest specimen of manhood. Now his idol lay in ruins at his feet—an idol who tyrannically wished to prohibit any intellectual tendency other than his own, now enfeebled by age and weakness. Looking back upon this painful experience, my brother cries out in very anguish of heart: "I shuddered as I went on my way alone; I was ill, or rather more than ill. I was weary—made so by the inevitable disappointment in all that remains to kindle enthusiasm in us modern men; weary at the thought of all the power, work, hope, love, youth flung to the winds; weary with disgust at the effeminacy and undisciplined rhapsody of this romanticism, at the whole tissue of idealistic lies and enervation of conscience, which here again had won a victory over one of the bravest souls; and not least of all, weary of the bitterness and harrowing suspicion that, from now on, I was doomed to distrust more deeply, to despise more deeply, and to be more *deeply alone* than ever before. For I had never had any one but Richard Wagner!"

Is it possible that Wagner suffered in like measure and only concealed his true feelings from a sense of pride? He, at least, could hope to replace my brother from the ranks of his gifted and enthusiastic disciples, whereas my brother was doomed to soul-solitude. Wagner's real feelings have never been divulged, but he gave me a glimpse of his innermost thoughts when I went to Bayreuth in the summer of 1882, to be present at the first performance of *Parsifal*. Wagner asked to see me alone, and after speaking of his "swan song," said softly: "Tell your brother that I am quite alone since he went away and left me." This was said six months before his death, at the period of his highest renown, with the entire world at his feet. Upon hearing this touching message of farewell, my brother wrote one of his loftiest aphorisms:

"We were friends and have become as strangers. But it is best so and we will neither conceal this nor draw a veil over it as if we had any cause to be ashamed. We are like two ships, each of which has its own course and its own goal; it may be that our paths may cross again and that we shall celebrate a feast-day together as we did in the past when the gallant ships lay in one harbor and under one sun, as if their common goal had already been reached. But then came a time when we were driven far apart by the inexorable power of our several missions into far distant seas and under strange skies, and perhaps we shall never meet again. Or it may be that we *shall* meet, and fail to recognize one another, so great will be the change that the various suns and seas have wrought in us! The law governing our lives has decreed that we should live, henceforth, as strangers; but just by reason of this, we shall become more sacred to one another! Just by reason of this will the memory of our friendship becomes more consecrated! The stars, apparently, follow some immense, invisible curve and orbit, in which our so widely varying courses and goals, may be comprehended as so many little stages along the way. Let us elevate ourselves to this thought! Our lives are too short, and our powers of vision too limited, to permit us to be friends other than in the sense of this lofty possibility.

"Therefore, let us *have faith* in our stellar friendship; * even though doomed to be enemies here on earth."

* This aphorism called "Stellar Friendship" is from *"Joyful Wisdom,"* Vol. X of the Complete English Edition of Nietzsche's works.